THE VICTORIAN HISTORICAL NOVEL 1840–1880

The Victorian Historical Novel 1840–1880

ANDREW SANDERS

First published 1978 by
THE MACMILLAN PRESS LTD
London and Basingstoke
Associated companies in Delhi
Dublin Hong Kong Johannesburg Lagos
Melbourne New York Singapore Tokyo

Printed in Great Britain by
Billing & Sons Limited, Guildford, London and Worcester

British Library Cataloguing in Publication Data

Sanders, Andrew
    The Victorian historical novel, 1840—1880
    1. Historical fiction, English — History and
    criticism   2. English fiction — 19th century
    — History and criticism
    I. Title
    823'.081   PR788.H5

ISBN 0-333-22093-5

To my mother and father

Contents

Preface

To all intents and purposes the historical novel sprang to life, fully accoutred and mature, with the appearance of *Waverley* in 1814, to be followed in fecund succession by the twenty-eight stories, not all of them historical, known collectively as the 'Waverley novels'. As any student of literature knows, Scott's impact on European culture was immense, for a time exceeding even Shakespeare's, and it proved to have an influence that was as popular as it was lasting. Scott alerted his readers to history and, by looking at politics, society, regionalism, or landscape in a new way, he made them aware of the vital links between the past and the present. If Scott's art now seems hard to appreciate as fervently as the Victorians appreciated it, if it now strikes us as stiff or impenetrable, it is still generally acknowledged that *Waverley* gave the European novel profitable new bearings. Nevertheless, as Scott's international reputation has declined this century, so, unfortunately, has the critical prestige of many of the historical novels written by his admiring, and often greater, successors.

Historical fiction remained in vogue throughout the European world for most of the nineteenth century; from Fenimore Cooper and Hawthorne in the far West, to Pushkin and Tolstoi in the East; from Galdos in Spain, to Sienkiewicz in Poland; from Manzoni in Italy, to Dumas, Hugo, Merimée, Balzac and Flaubert in France. 'Only historical novels are tolerable because they teach history', Flaubert wrote sardonically in the *Dictionnaire des idées reçues*, commenting on a common enough bourgeois prejudice. But, as an acquaintance with *Salammbô* might suggest, comparatively few historical novels of the period actually set out to teach history; most were directed by their authors at the same audience, with the same moral presuppositions, as stories dealing with contemporary life. They may have been more exotic in their subject matter, and they certainly required specialist research on the novelist's part, but their prestige and their steady popularity were founded on the same principles of good story-telling, 'high-seriousness', and social and psychological realism. To both readers and writers, history added a vital dimension to the proper concerns of the present.

This book does not set out to offer a survey of the variety and range of nineteenth-century historical fiction, nor does it attempt to be definitive. It confines itself to England, and to the fifty years following Scott's death. More precisely, it examines critically a select number of novels, written more or less under Scott's influence, between 1840 and 1880, and it places its main emphases on works by the great mid-century writers: Dickens and Thackeray, George Eliot and Mrs Gaskell. It omits reference to Trollope's early and inconsequential *La Vendée*, and it looks at one of Harrison Ainsworth's enduringly popular, and extravagant, stories rather than at one of the now forgotten G. P. R. James's. I have chosen to deal with one late novel by Scott's dourest Victorian successor, Bulwer-Lytton, but not with Frederick Marryat, any of Charles Lever's excursions into history, nor with R. D. Blackmore's *Lorna Doone*. I consider two novels by the now neglected Charles Kingsley in two separate chapters, though in the first I deal with *Hypatia* together with Catholic novels provoked by its unflattering picture of the early Church. In concluding with Hardy's *The Trumpet-Major* of 1880, I stop short of the best historical novels of R. L. Stevenson, and of both Pater's *Marius the Epicurean* and Shorthouse's *John Inglesant*. I have taken as my starting-point the sub-title to *Waverley* – 'Tis Sixty Years Since – and I have looked exclusively at novels which deal with a period anterior to a novelist's own lifetime. Thus, I have a chapter on *Romola* rather than one on *Middlemarch*, and I have not discussed Meredith's Italian stories, *Sandra Belloni* and *Vittoria*, which have sometimes been regarded as historical novels. My introductory chapter is meant purely as an introduction; my real argument is contained in the chapters which follow. The brief discussion of Charles Reade's *The Cloister and the Hearth* in the introductory chapter attempts to view the novel as representative of much of the once popular and acclaimed, but to us unfocused, historical fiction of the period.

Appropriately enough, this study was provoked by a past controversy on the relationship between literature and history. If, to E. H. Carr, history is the study of causes, I have become persuaded that historical novels consider historical effects.

Chapter 5 first appeared as an article in *English* in the Autumn of 1977.

My thanks are due to those friends and students who assisted, often unwittingly, in the formulation and development of ideas. Above all, I must thank Barbara Hardy for her kindness and constant stimulus. I also wish to thank Michael Slater, Jean Elliott, Rita Richards, and Edwina Porter for their remarks on individual chapters; Edwina Porter and Barbara Brunswick for typing the manuscript; Neil Berry for checking it, and for his assistance with proof-reading, and Della Couling for her thoughtful help in the latter stages.

Birkbeck College ANDREW SANDERS
October 1977

1 Introduction

History may be servitude,
History may be freedom. See, now they vanish,
The faces and places, with the self which, as it could, loved them,
To become renewed, transfigured, in another pattern.
                                        T. S. Eliot, *Little Gidding*

'Consider History', Carlyle told his readers in 1833, 'with the beginnings of it stretching dimly into the remote Time; emerging darkly out of the mysterious Eternity: the end of it enveloping *us* at this hour, whereof we at this hour, both as actors and relators, form part!'[1] The nineteenth century was an acutely historical age; it believed in the efficacy of the study of the past; it avidly collected the relics and the art of the past; and it rejoiced, just as Carlyle did, in the idea of being enveloped by Time, past, present, and future. If the century witnessed change on an unprecedented scale, in society and politics as much as in science and invention, a good deal of its art and its thought looked back, sometimes nostalgically, to traditions and to alternative forms. To confident European apologists for the age it was a century of progress, and the idea of progress was to be tested by a reconsideration and a resifting of all that had gone before to shape the attitudes and ideas of the present. To Carlyle history moved in cycles, each one moved into the next by the Hero, representative of the will of the times. In the labyrinthine sentences of an equally influential thinker, Hegel, history was the unfolding of Spirit (*Geist*):

The principle of *Development* involves also the existence of a latent germ of being – a capacity or potentiality striving to realise itself. This formal conception finds actual existence in Spirit; which has the History of the World for its theatre, its possession, and the sphere of its realization. It is not of such a nature as to be tossed to and fro amid the superficial play of accidents, but it is rather the absolute arbiter of things; entirely unmoved by contingencies, which, indeed, it applies and manages for its own pur-

poses. . . . The goal of attainment we determined at the outset:
it is Spirit in its *completeness*, in its essential nature, *i.e.*, Freedom.
This is development – that whereby it receives meaning and
importance. . . .[2]

Hegel's notion of a 'dialectic of transition' can be paralleled, less
complexly, by a wide range of European thinkers and popularisers of
other people's thought. Once it could be argued and accepted that the
present had grown by a reasonable and organic process out of the past,
the actual study of history became the necessary inheritance of every
good citizen, no longer just the preserve of Dr Jonas Dryasdust.
History was 'not only the fittest study, but the only study, and
includes all others whatsoever', it was 'the true Epic poem, and
universal Divine Scripture'.[3] Revolutions had been brought about
by revivals before, by Florentine humanists and Stuart lawyers
looking at the future through the spectacles of precedent, but men of
the nineteenth century saw themselves caught up in the forward
movement of time by the very fact of their being debtors to the acts
and monuments of their ancestors. Their present had an extra
significance because it had a lineage and because it appeared to
form part of an observable process. Hegel's idea of development
could be married to Darwinian evolutionary theory, or, more
crudely, to the outward and visible signs of change in any
industrialised nation. Regardless of the fact that the concept was
condemned by Pope Pius IX, and the very word 'progress' banned by
Tsar Nicholas I, rational observation seemed to prove the idea valid.
To Macaulay, writing in 1835, the history of England was 'emphatically the history of progress . . . the history of a constant movement
of the public mind, of a constant change in the institutions of a great
society'.[4] European man was on the move, industrially, colonially,
and intellectually, and the study of history was called upon to justify
his aggressive movement.

 Historical fiction had a particular appeal to a progressive age,
though its roots lay deep in the history of European literature and
civilisation. To the Jews, history had special meaning and importance
as the record of a divine mission in the past, and as a perpetual
reminder of the continuance of that mission into the future. Christian
Europe inherited the prejudice that history would prove it right,
despite temporary persecution or natural disaster; the Creator was the
Alpha and the Omega, the beginner and the finisher of Time, and
human history had a pivotal centre in the fact of the Incarnation, the

crossing of a divine with a human dimension. The New Testament ends with a plea for the speedy return of Christ as the Pantocrator at the end of Time. The Jewish sense of a past that cannot be abandoned was inherited by a Church looking to the new Jerusalem from the ruins of the old and, despite periodic rifts in the Christian tradition, the idea of a future worked out with reference to the past remained a constant in both conservative and radical interpretations of Scripture. If Byzantine and Holy Roman Emperors saw their rule as statically prefiguring a perfect and eternal order, sixteenth-century Reformers were to assert that they broke the mould of an erring Church only to restore a primitive model.

Of all the great Roman writers, Virgil had most appealed to Christian sensibilities, often so intolerant of the pagan past, largely because of his sense of the epic, progressive sweep of history and its movement towards fulfilment. Aeneas's vision of the future of Rome is awarded to him amongst the shades of his ancestors, but his role in Virgil's epic scheme also resembles the Judaeo-Christian concept of a predestined redeemer realising ancient prophecy. The Virgil of the *Eclogues* had been equally open to sympathetic Christian adoption. The Church had come to see its own role as that of the guardian of the relics of the old *Imperium*; the Empire had been sanctioned by God in order to allow for the easy spread of the Gospel. To St Augustine, if Rome fell to the Barbarians, its fall suggested that the new Rome, like the new Jerusalem, existed as the celestial city of God. The classical epic, therefore, became available − like the chronicles of the Jews − for new interpretation, while retaining its old authority.

With the Renaissance and the Reformation a growing sense of nationhood demanded a modern epic in the vernacular, expressive either of national or religious aspiration. The epic strain endured a metamorphosis into the novel, and especially into the historical novel, whether on the grand Russian scale, as in *War and Peace*, or as the focus of patriotic or spiritual hopes, as in the novels of Manzoni or Sienkiewicz, or even as George Eliot's *Romola* (where the heroine's name suggests her epic role). Virgil had glimpsed time moving forward, and he saw its direction sanctioned by the Roman hegemony; European novelists of the nineteenth century were less sure of their bearings, but they looked for meaning in realism, and in giving substance to the men of the past, by studying the forces moulding human society. They were no longer intent on clothing legend with flesh; they saw themselves instead as observers and recorders, or, in Carlyle's terms, as 'actors and relators' of history.

The past was no longer vaguely peopled with giants and heroes; it could be seen in the same terms as the present, with a hero's quest determined by knowable and reasonably familiar circumstances. James Joyce was later to see myth '*sub specie temporis nostri*'; Victorian historical novelists attempted to do the same with history, but they were also attempting to see the entire course of history '*sub specie aeternitatis*', ever present and eternal, and 'enveloping *us* at this hour'.

To many nineteenth-century critics the European novel had come of age with the work of Sir Walter Scott, the first major novelist to have transcended what were regarded as the limitations of a picaresque or a domestic tradition by seeing man as a diverse, noble, historic animal, more aware of himself by reference to the historic forces that had moulded him. As Scott himself had remarked in the postscript to *Waverley*, we are like those 'who drift down the stream of a deep and smooth river', unaware of the progress we have made 'until we fix our eye on the now distant point from which we have been drifted'. [5] To Hazlitt, on the defensive in 1825, Scott's novels seemed 'almost like a new edition of human nature', while to Heine in 1837, Scott 'effected a revolution, or rather a restoration, in novel-writing'. [6] To Balzac, prefacing his own *Comédie Humaine* in 1842, Scott seemed to have discovered the key to rendering 'the drama of three or four thousand people who make up society interesting'; the Waverley novels, he added, had raised fiction 'to the philosophical worth of history'. [7] Even Carlyle, not a determined admirer of fiction, felt obliged to admit that 'these Historical Novels have taught all men this truth . . . that the bygone ages of the world were actually filled by living men, not by protocols, state-papers, controversies and abstractions of men'. [8]

To Macaulay, however, Scott had changed not just the novel, but the very way in which history ought to be written. In its 'ideal state of perfection' history was a compound of poetry and philosophy, but with Scott the poetry of historical romance had triumphed to the detriment of the historian's philosophy:

> To make the past present, to bring the distant near, to place us in the society of a great man or on the eminence which overlooks the field of a mighty battle, to invest with the reality of human flesh and blood beings whom we are too much inclined to consider as personified qualities in an allegory, to call up our ancestors before us with all their peculiarities of language, manners, and garb, to

show us over their houses, to seat us at their tables, to rummage their old-fashioned wardrobes, to explain the uses of their ponderous furniture, these parts of the duty which properly belongs to the historian have been appropriated by the historical novelist. [9]

Scott had in fact made the novel not just morally serious, in Defoe's or Richardson's sense, but socially serious; not merely an entertainment, but an entertaining educator. He had not simply poached on the historian's demesne, however much the admiring but vexed Macaulay may have thought he did, he had broadened the scope of the novel by developing existing strains in eighteenth-century thought and literature, and by reconsidering precedents, above all the precedents of the epic tradition and the plays of Shakespeare. The power of the Waverley novels, as it struck Scott's admirers, lay not in what he had resurrected in history, but in how and why he had given it new life. Scott had learnt to shape his material according to the philosophical principles of the Scottish Enlightenment, but he learnt his craft as a writer from his inheritance from the Classics and, above all, from the plays of Shakespeare. [10]

Shakespeare's use — though to a conventional historian it might be seen as abuse — of history had been highly selective and had required both a telescoping of events and frequent inventive addition, but it had proved dramatically effective and supremely influential. If, to the Romantics, Shakespeare had emerged as an English equivalent to the Greek and Roman epic poets, his work had also served to mould English attitudes to national history and had shaped the prejudice that historical compromise had softened the impact of tragic circumstance. Henry IV's troubled reign stems from Bolingbroke's deposition of his predecessor, but his kingship counters the divisions dating back to Richard II's lack of control; the victories of Henry V redeem the old sin of usurpation, though the chaos made by his heirs requires a strong dynasty to bring about a new compromise and order. The closing speech of the consistently popular *Life and Death of King Richard III* had pointed the idea:

O, now, let Richmond and Elizabeth,
The true succeeders of each royal house,
By God's fair ordinance conjoin together;
And let their heirs (God, if thy will be so)

Enrich the time to come with smooth-fac'd peace,
With smiling plenty, and fair prosperous days.
Abate the edge of traitors, gracious Lord,
That would reduce these bloody days again,
And make poor England weep in streams of blood.
Let them not live to taste this land's increase,
That would with treason wound this fair land's peace.
Now civil wounds are stopp'd, peace lives again:
That she may long live here, God say amen.

History unfolds violently in Shakespeare's history plays, but a recognition of the need for order and the blessings of peace leads the kingdom towards a reconciling balance; Richmond's succession as Henry VII is viewed as a confirmation of the power of healing, not as a further usurpation, and England returns the Amen he directs to heaven at the end of the play. Like an Aeneas, blessed by the gods and his earthly father, Richmond, blessed by a Christian heaven and the saintly Henry VI, goes on to found a strong dynasty and to cast the kingdoms old into another mould.

Though the centre of the History Plays is held by the court characters, Shakespeare had increasingly shown the politics of the court affecting a broad spectrum of society beyond Westminster, even indicating that sound government was partly dependent upon popular assent to the throne. The themes of the Histories are to some extent echoed in the more political Comedies and in the Tragedies, where a decisive battle or a dynastic marriage can bring opposing forces to a point of rest or synthesis. Tudor and Stuart England, we sense, was to see a present lesson in the representation of its various and vexed past on the stage.

Scott shared with Shakespeare a dread of disorder and a *prédilection d'artiste* for describing the social perils of disorder. Like Shakespeare, he generally shows himself politically and morally conservative while being supremely able to evoke and understand the passions which divide nations, classes, families and friends. It was by no means casually that Scott chose as the motto to *Waverley* a quotation from *Henry IV, Part 2* – 'Under which king, Bezonian? Speak or die!' – a quotation which served his purpose in suggesting both his own debt to Shakespeare and in announcing the fact that his tale was to discuss the divisions caused by a disputed royal succession. The line is Pistol's, and it is addressed harmlessly enough to Justice Shallow in his Gloucestershire garden, but it indicates, with a whiff of violence and bravado, that court affairs *do* touch the ordinary citizen and his fortunes. It was Shakespeare's balance of public and private worlds, and his mixing of historical with invented, but representative, characters in the History Plays which taught Scott most, and which, through Scott, helped to determine much of the later development of the Victorian novel. Shakespeare's movement to peaceful compromise gave Scott a suggestion of his own dialectic shape for a story; Shakespeare's diversity of characterisation helped Scott to work out his own mix of classes and parties.

The often melancholy influence of Shakespeare on nineteenth-century drama is familiar enough from the failures it produced, like Tennyson's or Keats's attempts at poetical theatre, and from its partial successes like Schiller's *Don Carlos* or Pushkin's *Boris Godunov*, but Shakespeare's influence on the Victorian historical novel was both more consistent and more productive. The History Plays, and particularly the Henry IV plays, had depicted popular life; although the king remains the fount of justice and order, as well as the crowned national figurehead, he is by no means the chief centre of interest in the plays named after him. An audience might well find Prince Hal more immediate and complex, Hotspur more starkly a man of the times, or a Falstaff or a Shallow more rounded and actively appealing. The play as a whole, however, leads us to appreciate the nature of rule, and the responsibility shared by the ruler and the ruled. Hal, free of the deadening restriction of the court, is given an education which prepares him for the burden which has fallen so heavily on his father, and we see him as his father's successor, knowing both himself and those he governs. The England of the History Plays is glimpsed earning its living, or at leisure, even while it is troubled or galvanised by civil or foreign wars. In the generation before Scott's, Dr Johnson had been quite fulsome in his praise of Shakespeare's achievement:

None of Shakespeare's plays are more read than the *First and Second Parts of Henry the Fourth*. Perhaps no author has ever in two plays afforded so much delight. The great events are interesting, for the fate of the kingdoms depends upon them; the slighter occurrences are diverting, and, except one or two, sufficiently probable; the incidents are multiplied with wonderful fertility of invention, and the characters diversified with the utmost nicety of discernment, and the profoundest skill in the nature of man.[11]

It is interesting to contrast Johnson's appreciation of Shakespeare with Henry James's tribute to Sir Walter Scott:

> Before him no prose-writer had exhibited so vast and rich an
> imagination: it had not, indeed, been supposed that in prose the
> imaginative faculty was capable of such extended use. Since
> Shakespeare, no writer had created so immense a gallery of
> portraits, nor, on the whole, had any portraits been so lifelike. Men
> and women, for almost the first time out of poetry, were presented
> in their habits as they lived. The Waverley characters were all
> instinct with something of the poetic fire . . . Scott was a born
> story-teller: we can give him no higher praise.[12]

James, like so many of his contemporaries, saw nothing incongruous
in linking Scott's name to Shakespeare's. The Victorians over-rated
Scott's genius perhaps because they were too awed by its presence to
be able to place it in any less flattering perspective. Scott had
influenced them all too much, from childhood onwards, for them to
doubt his authority as the *fons et origo* of much of their art and
literature. They were nevertheless correct in the assumption that
Scott *was* Shakespearean in his balance of comic and tragic elements,
and in his mixing of love and resignation, of disaster and blessing, and
in his sense of history as immanent. His characters are moved not by
the fates or the stars, but by their psychological, social and historical
selves. Like Prince Hal, most of Scott's characters undergo an
educative process, moving among the very men and women
affecting, or affected by, the system of order in the state; they grow in
understanding, and they grasp and interpret the world around them.
Scott's most original and important innovation was his perception
that environment shapes the human consciousness, and his novels
brought it forcibly home to his readers that characters are the product
of the landscapes, townscapes and social groups which have formed
them. Ultimately, the Waverley novels lack the breadth of
Shakespeare's invention, his poetry, and the variety of his response to
a subject from play to play, but, as James argued, Scott had given the
prose fiction of the nineteenth century a new seriousness and purpose.
The impact of Scott's understanding of the nature of man and society
was to point the Victorian novel towards social realism, and Victorian
thinkers to a greater awareness of social responsibility.

Despite the sharp decline in Scott's critical reputation in this century,
the Waverley novels have not lacked powerful friends and com-

mitted advocates, notable amongst them being Georg Lukács, a critic himself moulded by his study of Hegel and Marx. To Lukács, Scott's art is both progressive and in a true sense revolutionary, structured on the economic and ideological basis of the European reaction to the Revolution in France. Scott's inherent conservatism, which Lukács readily acknowledges, is seen as giving him a special kind of objectivity as a social critic, for by studying conflict, and by seeking to balance political opposites, Scott emerges as a dialectical thinker looking forward to Hegel and Marx. To Lukács, the 'classical form of the historical novel' evolved by Scott shows a real understanding of the 'progressive' nature of a compromise which leads to evolution, Hegel's 'dialectic of transition':

> He attempts by fathoming historically the whole of English development to find a 'middle way' for himself between warring extremes. He finds in English history the consolation that the most violent vicissitudes of class struggle have always finally calmed down into a glorious 'middle way'. Thus, out of the struggle of the Saxons and Normans there arose the English nation, neither Saxon nor Norman; in the same way the bloody Wars of the Roses gave rise to the illustrious reign of the House of Tudor, especially that of Queen Elizabeth; and those class struggles which manifested themselves in the Cromwellian Revolution were finally evened out in the England of today, after a long period of uncertainty and civil war, by the 'Glorious Revolution' and its aftermath.[13]

Scott's conservative 'middle way' allows for a broad view which stretches panoramically from Scotland, through England, to Europe beyond. But the essence of his compromise lies in his use of what Lukács styles a 'neutral' hero, a figure caught up, like Edward Waverley, in a political crisis, and coming into immediate contact with men and causes which represent the extremes of political division. The neutral hero stands as the representative of society as a whole, and is able to learn from the extremes he sees and from the humanised historical figures he meets, not as heroes but as men among men.

Lukács is a forceful apologist, despite the fact that his analysis tends to distort or under-rate the work of Scott's major successors in the English tradition. He sees the historical novel as the recorder of social evolution and of 'the life of the people' and he is led to trace a line running through Stendhal, Balzac and Tolstoi rather than one which can readily accommodate a Dickensian or Thackerayan dissent or even the determined 'provinciality' of much nineteenth-century English fiction. This bias towards 'social realism' in Lukács's work properly excludes the escapism of a novelist like Harrison Ainsworth, but it also manages to avoid mention of George Eliot's concern with individual spiritual evolution. His philosophical bias insists on seeing history as progressive and that the relevance of a given historical period is dependent upon its meaning to the present, but it blinds him to the real diversity of Victorian historical fiction, and, moreover, to the advances of the twentieth-century novel, breaking away from the well-explored confines of social realism.

Lukács fails to appreciate that the very distinctiveness of English history, and of the inherited tradition in fiction, made for an equally distinctive and varied response to Scott, one which can necessarily be paralleled by developments on the Continent. The prejudices moulded by a bourgeois democracy in a nation which had not experienced invasion since the eleventh century and which had produced a typical compromise in its reaction to the Reformation, made in turn for 'provincial' fictional treatment of subjects derived from incidents in the French Revolution, or the Norman Conquest, or in the religious conflicts of the sixteenth and seventeenth centuries. Victorian historical novelists chose individual solutions to problems they found suggested in the Waverley novels, and they felt free either to take what they wanted from Scott's example or to adapt Scott's formulae to their particular ends.

To Nassau Senior, writing in 1821, Scott's novels 'from their number, their merit, their originality, and their diffusion, have more influence than is exercised by any others within the whole scope of our literature'.[14] That influence helped to shift Victorian fiction as a whole away from experiment and away from the diversity of eighteenth-century narrative forms, into a determined realism which saw man as a social animal with pre-eminent social responsibilities. Although they have most often been seen as both symptoms and causes of Romanticism, the Waverley novels examined man in an essentially un-Romantic sense, as gregarious rather than solitary, detached but involved in mankind, viewing society as determining rather than wrecking the individual's destiny, and the individual himself as commonsensical instead of possessed. Scott's central characters may admire the flamboyant gestures of rebels or questors, but they come to acknowledge the need for conformity in the interests of the majority. Although the organisers of the Eglinton

Tournament, and later, Mark Twain, considered *Ivanhoe* to be a call for the revival of chivalry, Scott himself made it plain that his novel was a critique of an absent crusading king and of the divisions perpetuated by a false sense of honour.[15] If we can now see the Victorian novel as, in some degree, a reaction against the wilder excesses of Romanticism, Scott had played an important part in making it so, though he can also be accused of giving it a narrower purpose within the boundaries of realism. The new wave of English fiction in the late 1830s and early 1840s showed itself to be freshly alert to social problems, concerned with local colour, and actively determined to prove that, through the novel, history had a place in modern life. *Waverley* and its successors had quickened a creative impulse while giving the novel a new prestige and popularity.

Although its influence can be felt through the entire range of Victorian fiction, *Waverley*'s importance for the historical novel lies in what it demonstrated of a means of examining the life of a period separated from the present by at least a full generation, or, in terms of its sub-title, by some sixty years. Scott's later work dealt with far earlier periods, but *Waverley* had established a pattern of accounting for social change, and explaining even comparatively recent changes to a world that was beginning to lose touch with its past. 'To elder persons', Scott told his readers in 1814, 'it will recall scenes and characters familiar to their youth; and to the rising generation the tale may present some idea of the manners of their forefathers.'[16] Certainly, for the novelist himself, details of his story had to be researched rather than remembered or simply invented. Beyond *Waverley* Scott stretched further into the dark backward of Scottish, then English, then European time, adapting his heroes and their social environment accordingly. Just as he had made the past present and the distant near to historians like Macaulay and Carlyle, so, to a new generation of novelists, Scott seemed a precedent, a challenge, and an example. Themes of revolution, dissent, war, violence, transition and decay which had been constants in the Waverley novels were consequently to find a readier place in the historical novels of the later nineteenth century than they were to do in stories concerned with contemporary life. The past could be seen to reflect the present, and, as a consequence, modern problems could be judged more detachedly for being considered within an historical perspective. Victorian historical novels are not, as a rule, escapes into a romantic past, but an attempt to prove that man and his society develop as part of a process which includes and envelops the present. At their best, the historical novels of the period deserve to stand beside the major triumphs of Victorian fiction, a place that was certainly granted to them in their own time but which has been often denied them since by changing critical and literary fashions.

Among critics of the first half of the nineteenth century there is evidence of a widespread optimism as to the potential of the historical novel and to the challenge it presented to the aspiring novelist. 'All who choose to take the trouble can possess themselves of the antiquarian facts,' wrote J. A. Heraud in the *Quarterly Review* in 1827, 'but the novelist undertakes something more than merely to transcribe from the old documents. . . . He is to go beyond the letter that kills, and to give us the spirit that makes alive.'[17] Such *dicta* were to be regularly echoed. Writing eleven years later in the *Monthly Chronicle*, Edward Bulwer-Lytton urged that prose fiction now formed 'so wide and essential a part of the popular literature of Europe' that it was appropriate to set out laws as a guide to future progress. Of the historical novelist in particular, he demanded 'a perfect acquaintance' with the characteristics and spirit of the past, and affirmed that the novelist's art 'will be evinced in the illustrations he selects, and the skill with which they are managed'. Perverse as it might seem to any reader familiar with the drudgery of Bulwer's own historical fiction, he goes on to insist that the novelist should 'avoid all antiquarian dissertations not essentially necessary to the conduct of his tale', simply because 'minuteness is not accuracy'. Bulwer ends by hinting at his own ambitions for, he tells us, an historical novelist who continues from where Scott had left off would have to 'deeply consider all the features of the time, and select those neglected by his predecessor; – would carefully note all the deficiencies of the author of *Kenilworth*, and seize at once upon the ground which that versatile genius omitted to consecrate to himself.'[18]

It was, with others', Bulwer-Lytton's youthful work as the recorder of the vices, crimes, and whims of his own times, both from a 'silver fork' and a 'Newgate' angle, which appears to have most offended the superior-minded Archibald Allison, taking 'The Historical Romance' as the subject of an article in *Blackwood's Magazine* in 1845. The Victorian novelist, Allison objected, had a vocation beyond that of an illustrator of low-life subjects:

We protest against the doctrine, that the lofty art of romance is to be lowered to the delineating the manners of cheesemongers and grocers, of crop-head charity boys, and smart haberdashers' and milliners' apprentices of doubtful reputation. If we wish to see the manners of such classes, we have only to get into a railway or steamboat; the sight of them at breakfast or dinner will probably be enough for any person accustomed to the habits of good society.[19]

Such disdain is worthy of Lord Melbourne, reacting in a similar manner to *Oliver Twist*, but for Allison the real strength of modern fiction lay in its power of evoking history, for as such the novel could take its place 'beside the plays of Shakespeare'. The effect of the publication of *Waverley* thirty years previously, he notes, with an appropriately Shakespearean simile, was 'like the invention of gunpowder or steam (sic)' and worked a similar change in the 'moral world'. He proceeds, waxing yet more effusively pompous:

From that moment the historical romance was born for mankind. One of the most delightful and instructive species of composition was created; which unites the learning of the historian with the fancy of the poet; which discards from human annals their years of tedium and brings prominently forward their eras of interest; which teaches morality by example, and conveys information by giving pleasure; and which, combining the charms of imagination with the treasures of research, founds the ideal upon its only solid and durable base — the real.

Having thus announced his reasons for considering the historical novel to be intellectually serious, he goes on to stress its moral seriousness: 'Considered in its highest aspect, no art was ever attempted by man more elevated and ennobling than the historical romance. It may be doubted whether it is inferior even to the lofty flights of the epic, or the heart-rending pathos of the dramatic muse.' He seeks to cap his claim by arguing, somewhat more spuriously, from the evidence of popularity — 'Homer and Tasso never, in an equal time, had nearly so many readers as Scott' — and he notes that it will probably prove to be impossible to estimate the influence of 'the fascinating art' of the historical novelist over future ages. He does, however, remark on one happy influence already evident, one that would doubtless have delighted Sir Walter, for we are told that the Waverley novels have 'gone far to neutralize the dangers of the Reform Bill'.

Like Bulwer, Allison was also anxious to define rules for the future writer, and to extract 'principles', in truly Aristotelian manner, from extant examples and evidence. The romance should be above all things 'elevating and yet interesting in subject', and ideally its subject should be drawn from national history, or at least based 'on incidents cousin-german . . . to those of its own national existence'. As a consequence he prefers *Ivanhoe* to *Anne of Geierstein*, and *The Last of the Barons* to *The Last Days of Pompeii*, and ends by praising Fenimore Cooper's *The Last of the Mohicans* and the 'admirable delineation of the manners, ideas, hopes and fears, joys and sorrows, of humble life' which he found in Manzoni's *I Promessi Sposi*. To Allison, as to Bulwer or to Charles Reade, 'the real' and 'truth to nature' find their highest and most accurate expression in historical fiction, with history giving a vital and epic dimension to social realism.

This confidence about the future was not necessarily justified by the evidence of the present, for in the following year, 1846, G. H. Lewes was to complain bitterly of the 'mediocrity' of most of the numerous progeny of the Waverley novels. Lewes excepts Scott – 'that wonderful writer' – from his strictures, but he finds most of the historical fiction of the 1840s to be served up according to a cheap commercial recipe, the secret of which he divulges: 'Sprinkle largely with love and heroism, keep up the mystery overhanging the hero's birth till the last chapter; and have a good stage villain, scheming and scowling through two volumes and a half, to be utterly exposed and defeated at last – and the historical novel is complete.'[20]

But the repetitiveness, ignorance and incompetence of Scott's imitators disturbed an unknown reviewer of 1847 in *Fraser's Magazine* less than the prospect of further fictional challenges to the authority of the conventional historian. Posing the question 'Walter Scott – Has History gained by his writings?', he argued that the historical novel had wrecked a reader's proper detachment:

It is very difficult to take up a volume of Scott in anything like a spirit of critical examination. One cannot read him in cold blood. He sets all one's tastes and sympathies working at once to the dire distraction of the reason. Flooded by his humour, and exhilarated by his heartiness and freshness, one lingers in the company of his gloriously life-like creations about as much disposed to question their title to the name they bear, as the opium-smoker to doubt the existence of his imaginary Houries.[21]

It is an indirect compliment to the power of the Waverley novels, but it is hard to imagine such ideals standing up in the face of the emotive force of the prejudices and style of a Gibbon, a Carlyle or a Macaulay. Nevertheless, the critic does not go further in his censure of Scott's method, though he voices a suspicion of imaginative literature which sets him in an honourably Platonic tradition; instead he transfers his venom to the work of Scott's shabbier successors, and especially to G. P. R. James. It would be vain to attempt to shield James from the attack, but it is interesting to note that this antipathy to the 'dandy littérateurs' was shared by serious historical novelists as disparate as Bulwer, Kingsley and Thackeray, all of whom were offended that Scott's image should have been so recklessly defaced, and his reputation so tarnished. For all three, however, the answer to the impertinent question as to whether or not history had gained from Scott's novels was an emphatic 'Yes'.

By the late 1850s there was good evidence of fresh invention and renewed energy in English historical fiction, and it was understandable that a critic should proclaim that the novel was by now the 'essential' complement to the study of history. Academic history on its own, readers were told, was insufficient to bring out 'the nature and power of a people's genius – what they thought, hated, loved'. The attraction of historical fiction lay 'not in any facility which it affords for the construction of a better story, nor any superior interest that attaches to the known and prominent characters with which it deals, or to the events it describes: but rather the occasion it gives for making us familiar with the every-day life of the age and country in which the scene is laid.'[22]

By suggesting that the strength of any novel lay in its power to evoke 'every-day life', we sense that the reviewer acknowledges both the importance of realism and the consequent variety of response to a variety of situations. Indeed, by the time of the review, Thackeray had brilliantly dispensed with Scott's historic detachment in his *Esmond*, Kingsley had looked intently at the puckered face of a long-dead Alexandria in his *Hypatia*, and Dickens was already serialising his very personal response to the French Revolution in *A Tale of Two Cities*. All of them had first established their literary bearings in novels dealing with the world of their contemporaries, but history had given each a new dimension. The 1860s were to be marked by the acclaim accorded to George Eliot's *Romola* and to Reade's *The Cloister and the Hearth*, and by the comparatively muted response to Mrs Gaskell's *Sylvia's Lovers*. The very fact that so many of the major artists of the period had turned to history for subjects, and that novelists in particular chose to attempt stories set in the past, can be seen to stem from Scott's continuing authority over an age so acutely aware of the value and relevance of an historical sense.

Lukács's definition of a 'classical form' based on the novels of Scott, with a neutral hero and a movement towards a balance of opposites, is, generally speaking, a useful one, even though it is restrictive in terms of an appreciation of the variety of character and structure in the Waverley novels themselves. If *Waverley* is taken as the type case, its pattern can hardly be said to have been followed in some of its most admired successors — *Old Mortality* or *The Antiquary*, for example. *Rob Roy*, it is true, only slightly varies its shape, moving Francis Osbaldistone into Edward Waverley's role as the Englishman caught up in an especially Scottish aspect of the political conflict which affects the combined fortunes of Scotland and England. A second, but more significant variation on the idea is that of the Scotsman in England, Nigel Olifaunt in *The Fortunes of Nigel* for example, or the Scotsman abroad in *Quentin Durward*, or even the Englishman abroad, as in Scott's last, floundering novel, *Count Robert of Paris*. A further important adaptation is to see a Briton mixed up in an alien political struggle within his homeland, as happens in *Ivanhoe, The Betrothed, Woodstock* and *Redgauntlet*, and which is a device borrowed later by Stevenson in his most Scott-like novels. Finally, there is the epic, exploratory experience of Jeanie Deans, journeying out into a wider world in *The Heart of Midlothian*, and symbolically reconciling Scotland to the Union and to a Hanoverian dynasty in London. In all the novels a comparatively innocent, but intelligent, central character learns, matures, and independently works out a kind of resolution of the opposed forces that he or she encounters, either through an acceptance of the *status quo* or through a commitment to a progressive new order. In some prominent cases, notably *Ivanhoe* and *Woodstock*, a concluding marriage brings personal fulfilment to the hero while also standing as a public sign of social reconciliation. In the great majority of Scott's novels — though *The Talisman* is a possible exception — the hero is neutral because he is also fictional and therefore a free agent, able to form decisions which are not necessarily tied by the restrictive need to follow the events of recorded history. The neutral heroes meet, admire, dislike, follow or reject the 'great men' of history by first seeing them as fallible and human. His heroes can be drawn emotionally, like Scott himself, to Jacobitism and Popery, or to Royalist, Saxon or Highland resistance to change, but like their creator, they are also likely to come to acknowledge the historic inevitability of change. They see rights and wrongs on both sides, and they become involved as rounded human beings, aware of conflicting loyalties, and of family or romantic obligations, while still moving towards a recognition of the creativity and practicality of commitment.

Scott's successors and imitators were able to vary this flexible enough 'classical form' as it best suited their tastes and fictional ends, though they did so at times conscious that they were aiming at a broader and more ambitious kind of historical novel. Tolstoi's variation on the Scott pattern, for example, might at first seem complex, though it is really only an exceptionally subtle and expressive duplication of the *Waverley*-type, giving *War and Peace* a shape based on parallel heroes and families, caught up severally, then together, in the Napoleonic disruption of Russian life. In England the fifty years following Scott's death witnessed a considerable amount of experimental activity, rarely the tired, scholarly imitation which has been all too often assumed. Harrison Ainsworth's novels have much to answer for in having given historical fiction a bad name, but they in fact tend to ignore Scott's precedent in an attempt to restore and re-embellish the Gothic fiction of the early century. Despite his considerable initial success, Ainsworth proved to be incapable of development or of sustaining his achievement; he ransacked English history for likely plots, and often he ended up with unlikely ones; he looked to sensationalism to sell his novels, and he pleased neither his early critics nor a later and more critical audience. By the 1850s Ainsworth had already outwritten the fashion for the kind of romance he had hoped to rejuvenate. Bulwer-Lytton's drab, learned, and aristocratic historical novels form a surprising contemporary contrast to Ainsworth's and to those of G. P. R. James. Bulwer aimed high, and meditated long and publicly about what he should be doing; he saw Scott as deficient in accuracy and guilty of distortions of chronology and character, and he attempted instead to restore the academic prestige of the novel, making it worthy of serious study. He had a real enough respect for Scott's achievement, however, as the shape of his enduringly popular *The Last Days of Pompeii* suggests, with its forward looking conclusion and its range of characters invented from miscellaneous archaeological details. Bulwer's later novels took Scott's pattern to an extreme by attempting to function as imaginative, and only partly fictional, biographies of the great men of history. Despite the fecundity of his ideas, he had little talent as a story-teller, and scarcely any at all as a writer of English, and as a consequence his novels remain cramped by their musty artificiality.

Of the abler novelists of the first half of the nineteenth century only Charles Kingsley followed Bulwer in experimenting with the biography of a known historical figure presented as a kind of *Heldenleben*, though in the case of *Hereward the Wake* he was lucky to have chosen a hero who was far more shadowy than Bulwer's King Harold. Kingsley's development as a novelist reveals a movement away from the use of a central character who is not so much neutral as opaque (Philammon in *Hypatia*), towards a muscular Christian type (Amyas Leigh) and finally to a primitive nordic ideal. Like Carlyle, Kingsley believed in heroes and in the virtues of modern hero-worship, and his novels expound ideas which he considered to be vital to the troubled world of his own times. If he now strikes us as a clumsy Jingoist or a blood-curdler it is perhaps because Kingsley reflects precisely those Victorian attitudes which have proved to be least accessible to the post-Victorians.

The thinning of the neutral *Waverley* hero to a state of semi-opacity had already been attempted by Dickens in his *Barnaby Rudge* of 1841. In his novel Dickens had set out to show states of mental disturbance, not simply in his rabble-rousing villain, but also on a wider, public level in the excesses of the mob and in a general intolerance and lack of social will. With an imbecile prominent amongst his characters, and the one from whom the book is named, the novelist added a new dimension to his theme, for Barnaby is at once exploitable, and capable, because vulnerable, of accentuating both innocence and guilt. With Barnaby's imbecility compensated for by the growing awareness of the commonsensical Gabriel Varden (who was originally to have been the title character), the novel is a far more masterly and intelligent historical study than it has often been credited with being. It is nevertheless remarkable that when Dickens returned to historical fiction, and to the problem of popular unrest and revolution in *A Tale of Two Cities*, he chose a more individual form to express his by now more developed ideas. Like *Quentin Durward*, *A Tale of Two Cities* moves Britons abroad to France and observes their reactions to a foreign political crisis; unlike Scott's novel, however, it includes no well-known historical figures amongst its characters, and, as its title suggests, it considers phenomena which are common to both London and Paris, even though it shows that the Parisian inheritance of hatred and disorder is the more disastrous. Dickens's knot of fictional characters are only partly detached from the Revolution which overtakes them, but the novel takes family connections, private histories, and the ties of responsibility, and uses them as a means of explaining, and then privately resolving, the public divisions between philosophies, classes, and nations. Dickens uses his plot as a kind of myth which can contain and fulfil the historical problem examined in his novel. Whatever *A Tale of Two Cities* may be said to lack in comparison to its author's other mature novels, it compensates by transferring a Dickensian formula, a private resolution of a public challenge, into an emotionally charged historical context.

Dickens's posing of a private answer to a general question resembles the solutions evolved intellectually in two very different novels, George Eliot's *Romola* and J. H. Newman's *Callista*. In *Romola* George Eliot explored the central theme of her work, the individual's moral choice between egotism and altruism, within an historical perspective provided by the diversity of Renaissance Florence. Newman's *Callista*, set in third-century North Africa, is a far less impressive achievement but it too looks at moral choice, and considers the struggle of an intelligent woman for belief in an alien world. Both novels are shaped around the progress of the heroine, and, as many contemporary commentators recognised, the struggles of both Romola and Callista project a very Victorian *Ahnung* backwards into history. The yearning of the individual for purpose is seen as a constant human aspiration rather than as the product of specific historical circumstances, but the growth of the heroine's awareness is taken as a token of the parallel between the progress of the soul and the forward movement of humanity.

The shift away from the 'classical form' is yet more pronounced in two novels centred in provincial communities rather than in a political vortex. Thackeray had dispensed with the heroic in *Henry Esmond*, but both Mrs Gaskell in *Sylvia's Lovers* and Hardy in *The Trumpet-Major* looked at societies in which the possibility of heroism is restricted by the milieu of the province. Both novels consider the historical process as it touches the lives of ordinary men and women, troubled by war and the rumour of war, but rarely probing the meaning of their experience or able to see the long-term consequence of it. For Mrs Gaskell and Hardy, village or small-town society has changed only in outward circumstances in the sixty years which separate the writer from his subject, but both take as a central idea the real edge of violence added to maritime life in the Napoleonic Wars by the presence of the press-gang. 'Great men' only marginally involve themselves, but their decisions interfere indirectly with the patterns of life otherwise determined by the seasons or by landscape. *Sylvia's Lovers* and *The Trumpet-Major* are primarily love-stories in which private malice, the pains of unrequited love or simply jealousy, find a new dimension in the violence of war. Both writers, from their very different points of view, offer a new stress on the private worlds of their characters, minutely recording the overlappings of private and communal pasts, or recorded and unrecorded history, or of tradition and 'unhistoric' action. Simple men and women are seen to contribute as fully to the slow progress of humanity as the kings and the generals.

Nevertheless, the most radical departure from the *Waverley* form in the fifty years following Scott's death remains Thackeray's *Henry Esmond* of 1852. Thackeray saw history not as a charted stream but as a series of currents and eddies moving slackly forwards. But his real challenge to the Scott norm lies in his choice of an autobiographical narrator, a moody, sensitive, and involved character who can only describe what has happened to him from the point of view of his own 'uniscience'. The 'history' witnessed by Henry Esmond is vivid and significant enough, ranging from the 'Glorious Revolution' and the Seven Years War to the succession of the Hanoverians, but because Esmond is telling his own story as well, he can never have the detachment of Scott's omniscient narrator. As a further consequence of his chosen form Thackeray rejects the tidy resolutions of the Waverley novels, leaving us instead with his hero's withdrawal from the political arena, still, it seems, divided in his loyalties but married to the woman he never suspected he loved. There is a chance of private happiness, but, as with most human observers, many other aspects of experience are left unresolved, avoided, forgotten or abandoned by the wayside. In the end the 'hero' of an 'unheroic' but virtuous life leaves for a traditionless new world in Virginia. For Esmond history is an act of memory, and as an alert, but frequently biassed, narrator he views the heroic and the tragic through the quotidian, acknowledging the equal importance for the individual of the petty and inconsequential decision as well as of political or social resolve. History emerges in Thackeray's disconcerting scheme as a series of arbitrary acts, not as a determined progress, and, for the novelist, art alone gives shape and meaning because it tells a human truth.

To many Victorian critics, however, the most successful and innovatory historical novel of the century was Charles Reade's *The*

Cloister and the Hearth. To modern readers it might well seem to have
a claim to have been the most overrated English novel of the age, and
even George Orwell, a rare twentieth-century admirer of Reade's,
considered it the novelist's bad luck 'to be remembered by this
particular book, rather as Mark Twain, thanks to the films, is chiefly
remembered by *A Connecticut Yankee at King Arthur's Court'.*[23]
Nonetheless, when *The Cloister and the Hearth* first appeared in 1861,
the *Saturday Review* proclaimed that Reade had achieved what
scarcely any other Englishman of his generation had shown himself
able to do. He had written an historical novel 'that is pleasant and
touching to read'. The story was declared to be not unworthy of
comparison to one of Scott's, but, the reviewer went on to note, time
had begun to expose Scott's shortcomings:

> There is a certain thinness – not a poverty, but a scantiness – in the
> *Waverley Novels*, which modern readers, turning back to them
> after the interest of the first reading has long passed away, can
> scarcely fail to feel. There are heroes in Scott's historical novels,
> there are attempts to paint and analyse character, there are many
> passages introduced in order to bring before us the historical era as
> the author conceives it. But there is much that is left sketchy and in
> outline in all this. The heroes are amiable dummies, and so are the
> heroines. Their feelings, and the feelings of their friends and
> enemies, are mostly on the surface. It is astonishing in how very
> few pages we come to the end of even the best scenes of Scott.

It is a rare Victorian response, though a valid enough one, but the
reviewer continues by remarking on the rapid development of new
literary styles and attitudes; 'modern romances of the highest class', he
told his readers, 'are more thorough and elaborate':

> Sir Edward Lytton has shown us what industry and a power of
> combination can do in this way, although the great inferiority of
> his conception of character will not permit us to rank him as an
> historical novelist with Mr. Reade. What we have gained, so far as
> it is a gain, since Scott wrote, has been gained by the greater
> minuteness of reflection, analysis, and knowledge which we have
> cultivated during the last thirty years.[24]

Reade is seen, then, as reflecting advances in fictional and historical
investigation. Some months later the *Westminster Review* added its

own acclaim. 'There are some novels', it remarked, 'of which the general excellence is so conspicuous, that judges need not hesitate about stamping them with the seal of their approbation.' Reade's characters merited like praise: 'No creation of modern fiction is more true to nature and, at the same time, a more loveable character' than Margaret Brandt; Catherine, Gerard's mother, bore 'a certain resemblance to Mrs Poyser', while Denys was nothing short of a French Falstaff.[25] To Swinburne, in an essay still republished as a Preface to the Everyman edition of the novel, it was difficult to find 'a story better conceived or better composed, better constructed or better related.'[26]

Such adulation was not unmitigated, even some admiring critics complained of the novel's excessive length, but *The Cloister and the Hearth* continued to be thought of by many readers as the greatest English historical novel until well into the twentieth century. Since its decline in popularity it has, like the rest of Reade's output, been, not always unjustly, neglected. It is certainly now a hard book to appreciate as heartily as its original audience appreciated it, impeded as it is by melodramatic twists, digressive excursions into aspects of mediaeval life, and by a painfully artificial dialogue. But *The Cloister and the Hearth* remains typical of its period as a serious and ambitious historical novel of the second rank, one which neither broke new ground nor consolidated familiar fictional territory. Its interest lies in its Englishness, for despite its Continental setting and Reade's cosmopolitan reading, it is quirky, untidy, provincial, and lacking in real philosophical or intellectual direction. Reade's contemporaries mistook its bittiness for a varied and accurate account of life in the period before the Reformation, but it is more likely to strike a modern audience as ragged and uneven, learned and lyrical by turns, but as often frenetic and more than a little vulgar.

The novel's loose structure gave Reade's encyclopaedic mind full play, and its central wandering movement from the Netherlands to Italy and back again allowed for an episodic treatment of jarring characters, ideas, and cultures. Its structure, so strangely admired by Swinburne, depends upon discord, and Reade attempts to balance the settled, domestic life of his Dutch family against the southward wanderings of their alienated son. It is a balance which Reade's digressive and woolly mind finds it hard to maintain. *The Cloister and the Hearth* has a variety and freedom which might well have appalled Scott, but it sadly lacks the order and developed resolution of the best of the Waverley novels, and it falls short of the looser control over the elements of an historical plot evolved after Scott by Thackeray, Dickens or George Eliot.

Reade proclaimed his purpose at the outset:

> Not a day passes over earth, but men and women of no note do great deeds, speak great words, and suffer noble sorrows. Of these obscure heroes, philosophers, and martyrs, the greater part will never be known till that hour, when many that are great shall be small, and the small great; but of others the world's knowledge may be said to sleep: their lives and characters lie hidden from nations in the annals that record them. The general reader cannot feel them, they are presented so curtly and coldly: they are not like breathing stories appealing to his heart, but little historic hail-stones striking him but to glance off his bosom: nor can he understand them; for epitomes are not narratives, as skeletons are not human figures.
>
> Thus records of prime truths remain a dead letter to plain folk: the writers have left so much to the imagination, and imagination is so rare a gift. Here, then, the writer of fiction may be of use to the public — as an interpreter. [27]

Reade is not mourning the silence of village Hampdens, for, like Thackeray, he is aspiring to a history which is 'familiar rather than heroic', or like George Eliot in the Finale to *Middlemarch* he is proclaiming his faith in 'unhistoric acts'. Like his greater contemporaries he is doubting the Carlylean historical thesis and looking to the novel as an amplifier of conventional history. But *The Cloister and the Hearth* only partly justifies this opening statement of intent, for Reade undermines his stated intention by giving us, if not the history of a great man, at least the history of a great man's parents. Gerard's and Margaret's experience is given a fresh relevance at the end of the story by the revelation of the future destiny of their son. Like Tolstoi in *War and Peace*, though with hardly any of Tolstoi's deftness, Reade suggests that the future will develop dramatically in the period after the close of the narrative. Erasmus looms over the novel's last pages, and a sudden flash illuminates our understanding of what has gone before, but the 'little historic hail-stones' cease simply to glance off our bosoms once we are bidden to look up to the Reformation storm-cloud.

The musty chronicle, 'written in intolerable Latin', which the novelist mentions as his source for the story in his third paragraph proves to be Erasmus's by no means ill-written or obscure autobiographical fragment published posthumously as the *Compendium Vitae* at Leiden in 1615. Indeed, at the end of the narrative Reade himself admits to having derived some of his best scenes from Erasmus's 'mediaeval pen', having borrowed both ideas and details directly from the *Colloquies* and the *Encomium Moriae*.[28] It is an excusable enough sleight of hand and even the initial dismissal of the 'musty chronicle' helps to maintain the secret of the real future identity of young Gerard. Otherwise Reade emerges from all of his novels, and not just *The Cloister and the Hearth*, as much a determined 'truth-teller' in fiction as Bulwer-Lytton. While he was working on his historical novel, Reade remarked on the relationship between fact, fiction, and history, citing Erasmus's *Colloquies* as supporting evidence: 'They are a mine of erudition and observation; but so are most of his works; but in the 'colloquies' there is fiction, and its charm, superadded to his learning, language, method, and philosophy – as in the immortal Macaulay.' It is a clumsy and somewhat illogical sentence, but it is one which is attempting to link the philosopher to the historian and to the writer of fiction – the interpreter of dead letters to plain folk: 'Where things so rare and solid as long and profound research, lucid arrangement, and empire over language, meet in an historian, there he has a good chance of immortality; but, where he blends with these rare virtues the seductive colours of fiction, he turns that good chance into a certainty.'[29] Reade balances uneasily, and probably unwittingly, between two distinct schools of thought; on the one hand, he sides with 'the immortal Macaulay' as an historian first and an inventor of history second; on the other, he feels himself one with Thackeray as an accurate story-teller, incorporating facts into fiction. Reade does not go on to explain himself further, nor does his historical novel suggest what he believed the real distinction between an historian and an historical novelist to be. He does not even appear to recognise any distinct philosophy of history. Like Bulwer, he claims equality and respect for the novelist's contribution to the study of the past, but he blurs definitions and claims to sovereignty to leave his readers instead with the impression of a vacillating and unsteady mind.

Like most of Scott's successors, however, Reade devoutly trusted in the virtues of 'realism' and in the developing æsthetic doctrine of 'truth to nature'. With George Eliot and Sir David Wilkie, though not with Ruskin, he admired the popular domesticity of the seventeenth-century Dutch genre painters; his artist-figure in the earlier *Christie Johnstone*, having expressed solidarity with 'Gerard Dow and Cuyp and Pierre de Hoogh', goes on to proclaim loudly in italics:

The resources of our art are still unfathomed! Pictures are yet to be painted that shall refresh men's inner souls, and help their hearts against the artificial world; and charm the fiend away, like David's harp!! The world, after centuries of lies, will give nature and truth a trial. What a paradise art will be, when truths, instead of lies, shall be told on paper, on marble, on canvas, and on the boards!!![30]

As some early critics of Reade suggested, it is the mediaeval Dutch school which most touches *The Cloister and the Hearth*, and the novelist even goes to the length of introducing artists and paintings into his tale.[31] But Reade's doctrine of accuracy went deeper than a desire to describe interiors or the circumstances of fifteenth-century scullery-maids; he believed in the radiance of the commonplace, and in the intensity of ordinary experience. Like Jan van Eyck, who appears briefly in the novel, he crowds his canvas with people and things, but each part is intended to capture and express the wholeness and wonder of creation. The novel takes the details of a lost world, from its faith to its fleas, and makes a picture of them. Reade assumes that his picture will have a natural unity simply because it is true to life. The pains he took to compose *A Good Fight*, the fragmentary original of *The Cloister and the Hearth*, were stressed by the tired but proud novelist in a letter to James Fields:

You may well be surprised that I am so long over 'Good Fight', but the fact is, it is not the writing but the reading which makes me slow. It may perhaps give you an idea of the system in which I write fiction, if I get down the list of books I have read, skimmed, or studied to write this little misery.

He then lists the titles of some seventy-nine volumes, adding 'etc., etc.,' when he had done. 'Surely this *must* be the right method,' he commented with a hint of desperation.[32] There was, in fact, nothing unique about his method; *Romola* left George Eliot 'an old woman', and even Dickens claimed to have consulted a 'cartload' of reference books in the preparation of *A Tale of Two Cities*, but like a literary

Pre-Raphaelite Brother, Reade seemed to trust solely to the efficacy of detail, and to the idea that accuracy imparted life to his art.

Each episode in the novel is arranged by another, not purely for dramatic effect, or for contrast, or as a means of moving his plot forward, but because each 'tells the truth' about the particular aspect of mediaeval life he wants to describe. *The Cloister and the Hearth* is really little more than an assemblage of not always harmonious parts; plot, for Reade, comes second to cumulative experience, and, rather than let his characters shape his narrative, or find their destiny in themselves, he lets them wander until he sees fit to nudge them back into the loose arching pattern provided by his love-story. Reade never keeps an idea or a theme steadily before us and, as a consequence, his story neither holds us while we read it, nor brings us to a point of rest when we have finished it.

If Reade had models in mind for *The Cloister and the Hearth* they were probably the comic novels of Fielding and, before him, of Cervantes. Unlike most Victorian historical novels, Reade's remains in an eighteenth-century picaresque tradition. Nonetheless, Fielding's notion of a comic epic in prose in *Tom Jones* had derived as much from the Homeric and Virgilian epic shape as it had from Cervantes, providing his novel with its twelve books and its tripartite structure. Tom's journey to London merely forms the second third of the narrative account of his developing fortunes and moral awareness, sandwiched as it is between sections which establish him first as Squire Allworthy's ward, then as an independent man in Town. As Coleridge was to acknowledge, Fielding's complex and neat plot gives the novel much of its distinction. Reade possessed neither Fielding's ordering imagination, nor a hero to match Cervantes's. If he can be said to have aimed at 'unity by inclusion', he really has so vague a sense of architectural design, that his details habitually impede our appreciation of his whole. Gerard discovers little during his lengthy journey away from Holland, but if, like Thackeray in *Henry Esmond*, Reade had wished to persuade us of the arbitrary nature of experience, it would have greatly assisted his scheme if, like Thackeray, he had first determined the balance of art to learning, and fiction to fact. *The Cloister and the Hearth* attempts too much, and tries to be too many kinds of novel, without ever managing to persuade us of its own consistency and its own conviction.

In common with Thackeray, however, and later, with Mrs Gaskell and Hardy, Reade was proposing a view of history in his novel which ran counter to Carlyle's. His anti-Carlyleanism is most blatantly stated in *Christie Johnstone*, where the novelist's mouth-piece, Lord Ipsden, loudly but somewhat clumsily attacks a mediaeval enthusiast's opinion of past and present, suggesting that

'Five hundred years added to a world's life made it just five hundred years older, not younger, — and if older, greyer, — and if greyer, wiser.

'Of Abbot Sampson,' said he, 'whom I confess both a great and good man, his author, who with all his talent belongs to the class muddle-head, tells us, that when he had been two years in authority his red hair had turned grey, fighting against the spirit of his age; how the deuce, then, could he be a sample of the spirit of his age? . . .

'The earnest men of former ages are not extinct in this. . . . There still exist in parts of America, rivers on whose banks are earnest men, who shall take your scalp, the wife's of your bosom, and the innocent child's of her bosom. . . .

'Moreover, he who has the sense to see that questions have three sides is no longer so intellectually as well as morally degraded as to be able to cut every throat that utters an opinion contrary to his own.'[33]

However much Reade may be distorting, or simply misunderstanding the thread of the argument of *Past and Present*, Lord Ipsden's words do manage to suggest why the novelist came to treat mediaeval history as he did in *The Cloister and the Hearth*. He saw the 'spirit of the age' expressed in common life, not in the thoughts and actions of the world-historical hero, and he saw earnestness as responsible for intolerance, bigotry, and cruelty. Trust as he might in progress, Reade believes in Erasmus's satiric darts rather than Luther's or Knox's cudgels. Firm convictions make heroes and martyrs, but they also contribute to antagonism and oppression. Modern man should be open to the three sides of any given question. Reade's historic heroes are limited by the narrowness of their own times and, in their passivity, represent the true spirit of the world he is describing.

Nevertheless, as its title suggests, *The Cloister and the Hearth* deals with the tension that Reade saw as symptomatic of the end of the Middle Ages, that between the Church and the family, between celibacy and marriage, and between the contemplative and the active life. The novel's comment on mediaeval religion and, by extension, on a romanticised view of the pre-Reformation Church, is as deliberate and critical as its opposition to the 'heroic' view of history. The central tragedy of the story derives from the Church's imposition of celibacy on its clergy, and this Reade sees both as a restriction of personal freedom and as a perversion of human sexuality. Celibacy distorts relationships and infects public morality. To the novelist himself, his enforced bachelorhood as the Fellow of an unreformed Oxford College was a vexing survival of a defunct prejudice. At the end of his novel his anger breaks through the otherwise tolerant surface:

> Thus, after life's fitful fever these true lovers were at peace. The grave, kinder to them than the Church, united them for ever; and now a man of another age and nation, touched with their fate, has laboured to built their tombstone, and rescue them from long and unmerited oblivion.
> He asks for them your sympathy, but not your pity.
> No, put this story to a wholesome use. . . .
> I ask your sympathy, then, for their rare constancy and pure affection, and their cruel separation by a vile heresy in the bosom of the Church; but not your pity for their early but happy end.

The vile heresy is celibacy — 'an invention truly fiendish' — and the story is intended to stand as a warning to a freer and maturer age, one that has outgrown the restrictions accepted by its benighted ancestors. Like Kingsley in his *Hypatia*, Reade finds a relevant modern message in a study of pre-Reformation Christianity; he assents to progress which moves men away from superstition, and he hints at the dangers to the nineteenth century of a revival of monasticism.[34] Unlike the yet more rabid and unbalanced Kingsley, however, Reade might strike us elsewhere as being surprisingly tolerant of the abuses he attacks; he implies criticism rather than attempting frontal assaults on moral patterns that his characters take for granted. Gerard and Margaret accept the state of society in which they find themselves, they see its shortcomings and argue over them; they suffer, but they submit only to love each other at a distance.

The novel moves forward to its key, the revelation that the house in the Brede Kirk Straet will eventually bear the inscription: '*Haec est parva domus natus qua magnus Erasmus*' and we know that Erasmus will herald the changes of the sixteenth century. But, in the course of his narrative, Reade has suggested that change is already in the wind. In Rome, Gerard's semi-pagan friend and patron, Fra Colonna, seems determined to prove that the Church's order and its ceremonies derive from only partly suppressed heathen mysteries. As a man of the Renaissance, Colonna is convinced that he lives in a fallen world, and that ancient virtues are to be preferred to modern ones; at times he is little more than yet another of the novelist's mouthpieces – 'Thou seest, the heathen were not *all* fools. No more are we. Not *all*.' Although Gerard's journey to Rome does not prove to be a quest, it at least seems to give him sufficient strength and resource to emerge from the temporary atheism, occasioned by the news of Margaret's death, into a quieter, empirical faith. Gerard's rational religion, though we never determine its source and inspiration, looks forward to his son's. In Chapter XCVI he urges the dying Margaret not to invoke a saint as an intercessor, but to turn to Him 'to whom the saints themselves do pray'. She expires with the name Jesu on her lips, to be echoed some time later, at the same hour, by her pining, faithful lover. For Reade the pair have worked out a simple, practical, rational faith which gives some kind of meaning to their muddled, cruel and credulous world. 'To their early death', readers are warned, 'apply your Reason and your Faith, by way of exercise and preparation.' We are also, it seems, being asked to look forward to a temperate Protestantism and to the nineteenth century which is reaping the benefits of the Reformation.

In its time *The Cloister and the Hearth* was often compared favourably to *Romola*; both novels are set in the late fifteenth century, and consider a society which is seeking new directions; both Reade and George Eliot look to some kind of spiritual progress to provide meaning to the hurly-burly of history. Swinburne's essay on Reade attempted, not very successfully, to chart a *via media* between an excessive admiration of *Romola* and, as it now seems, the extraordinary view that George Eliot had been inspired and influenced by the earlier novel. Swinburne affirmed that no rational admirer would dispute the assertion that the author of *The Cloister and the Hearth* 'could not have completed – could not have conceived – so delicate a study in scientific psychology as the idlest or least sympathetic reader of *Romola* must recognise and admire in the figure of Tito', but he urged that there was a 'well-nigh puerile insufficiency of some of the resources by which the story has to be pushed forward or warped round before it can be got into harbour'. Even if he were posing as a strict realist, Swinburne is unnecessarily harsh, but one could hardly expect him to sympathise with the reasons *why* George Eliot manhandles her heroine's boat into the harbour of the plague-stricken village. Romola is capable of growing, maturing, breaking and growing again; for all the vividness of their setting, Reade's characters are comparatively static and bland. To George Eliot the human psyche contains an infinite complexity and potential for choice; to Reade the details of a confused, irrational, and various external world present the only reality that an artist can paint. George Eliot is sure of her moral bearings, and she makes sense of history because of it; Reade looks at fragmentary experience, and takes the design of the whole for granted without caring to explain what the design means. Arthur Conan Doyle is said to have paid tribute to *The Cloister and the Hearth* by describing it as like 'going through the Dark Ages with a dark lantern'.[35] The dimness of Reade's kindly guiding light now only allows us the odd glimpse of the faded brightness of his historical vision.

'It has been said', Samuel Butler remarked in an aside in *Erewhon Revisited*, 'that though God cannot alter the past, historians can; it is perhaps because they can be useful to Him in this respect that He tolerates their existence.'[36] Butler's theological premises might now strike us as soundly based, but to most nineteenth-century readers an historian was not simply tolerated by Heaven, he was an inspired unfolder and explainer of the ways of God to man. To an age of progress and ringing grooves of change, the study of history offered proof that men were moving efficiently and inexorably onwards, drawn towards the climax of Creation by a divine force. If God, for a growing number, did not exist, it proved intellectually convenient to replace Him with a new faith in an evolving, progressing, creative humanity. The two propositions were not mutually exclusive, even though a religious man might be tempted to settle for social passivity, while the atheist opted for revolution; both were interpreting and expressing the *ens realissimum*, and both were proving useful to their God.

In literature a more significant moral and cultural gulf now divided those who continued to believe in an unchanging human condition, from those who held, with Sir Walter Scott, that man was conditioned by his environment. It was an argument that had ancient roots in the Pelagian controversy of the fourth and fifth centuries, and it is still shaping branching opinions in our own. Henry Fielding's eighteenth-century lawyer in *Joseph Andrews* is 'not only alive, but hath been so these four thousand years'. In the Dedicatory Epistle to *Ivanhoe*, however, Scott suggested that for the majority of his readers it was easier to accept the foreignness of a backward and distant country than that of another age. A modern gentleman reader 'surrounded by all the comforts of an Englishman's fireside' was

> not half so much disposed to believe that his own ancestors led a very different life from himself; that the shattered tower, which now forms a vista from his window, once held a baron who would have hung up at his own door without any form of trial; that the hinds, by whom his little pet-farm is managed, a few centuries ago would have been his slaves; and that the complete influence of feudal tyranny once extended over the neighbouring village, where the attorney is now a man of more importance than the lord of the manor.[37]

Fielding's English lawyer might, but for his buckle-shoes, have been recognised on the Athenian stage; Scott's attorney has a social function that changes with time and with shifts in power. The past is another country and as circumstances alter so does the individual's world-view; the novelist's role is not simply to describe mankind in general, but to show how specific men have been moulded by specific historical manners. Fielding spoke with and to the moral prejudices of a neo-classical age; Scott and his successors expressed the confident moralising spirit of their own age.

To the Victorian historical novelists the past was not frozen by eternity, nor was it, unlike the scenes of Keats's Grecian Urn, rendered eternal, silent, and unravished by art. To Scott's successors history was contemporary, synchronic and enveloping; it was living and vibrating in the present, and the artist represented its reality as if it were an act of personal memory. The past reinforced rather than undermined the present. Though to many Victorians the past, like the sea lapping Tennyson's Ithaca, moaned with many voices, those voices seemed to call for continued advance into the future.

2 A Gothic Revival: William Harrison Ainsworth's *The Tower of London*

> The clothes were strewn on the grass. Cardboard crowns, swords made of silver paper, turbans that were sixpenny dish cloths, lay on the grass or were flung on the bushes. There were pools of red and purple in the shade; flashes of silver in the sun. The dresses attracted the butterflies. Red and silver, blue and yellow gave off warmth and sweetness. Red Admirals gluttonously absorbed richness from dish cloths, cabbage whites drank icy coolness from silver paper. Flitting, tasting, returning, they sampled the colours.
>
> Miss La Trobe stopped her pacing and surveyed the scene. 'It has the makings . . . ' she murmured. For another play always lay behind the play she had just written. Shading her eyes, she looked. The butterflies circling; the light changing; the children leaping; the mothers laughing – 'No, I don't get it,' she muttered and resumed her pacing.
>
> Virginia Woolf, *Between the Acts*

William Harrison Ainsworth had a deep and romantic attraction to the England of the Tudors and Stuarts, and he wrote popular books about the period for an audience which shared his passion. Ainsworth wrote quickly and spiritedly, and, for the first decade of his literary career at least, he maintained a phenomenal and often inexplicable success. He was a best-seller in an age which enjoyed the benefits of industrialism for the production and distribution of literature, but which nevertheless affected a sentimental attachment to a time and place without machines. His novels catered for a taste for easily assimilated historical romance, even though, like his audience, Ainsworth held an equivocal view of the relevance of the study of history. On the one hand, he was content to be a Victorian Englishman and to have escaped the plagues, racks and bigotry of the past; on the other, he was drawn to history in search of an imaginative release from the drabness and relative stability of life in the nineteenth century. Ainsworth was a product of the declining era of Romanticism, and of the Romantic tendency to long for an escape from modern reality; paradoxically, he happily accepted a concept of social progress and was both amused and shocked by the narrowness of his ancestors' world. He had, in fact, no real idea about history, simply a delight in being surrounded by its trappings. The relatively scholarly taste for history, for Gothic architecture and for tradition which marks the 1840s, was a product of intellectual advance, as well as a reaction against it; the study of the past revealed the advantages of living in the present, but it also suggested that society had fallen away from a more vivid pattern of conduct. To an alert mind the culture of the early Gothic Revival presented a dilemma. At its best the age produced Carlyle's *Past and Present*, Ruskin's *Seven Lamps of Architecture*, and the designs and polemics of Pugin; its shabbier, escapist side is represented by Ainsworth's novels. It is revealing to remember that Ainsworth, who was so proud of his Mancunian origins and education, should habitually have described his home town not as Cottonopolis, but in its placid, pre-industrial aspect.

The expansion of popular antiquarianism in the first quarter of the nineteenth century influenced both Ainsworth's choice of subjects and the very form of his novels. It seems to have encouraged his tendency to see his novels as, in part, archæological hand-books. Five of his stories published between 1840 and 1854 were given titles drawn from important national monuments, and, in the cases of *The Tower of London*, *Old Saint Paul's* and *Windsor Castle*, he selected settings with very complex historical and architectural associations. When he builds a novel around a castle, a cathedral or a palace, he regards it as a novelist's duty to tell the story of the building as much as that of his characters. In the Preface to *The Tower of London*, for instance, he stressed his 'cherished wish' to make a novel out of this 'proudest monument of antiquity', and then proceeded to complain to his readers of the poor state of the fortifications and to refer them to a short reading list.

It would be unfair to suggest that Ainsworth was simply pinning stories to guide-books, for he was genuinely committed to the idea of a novel which would resurrect the style and technique of Gothic fiction, injected with a revivifying dose of instruction. His didacticism is of a peculiarly unimaginative kind, however, for he was not so much concerned with moral teaching as with the value of facts and dates. Above all, his novels reveal that, unlike most other Victorian writers, he had learnt very little indeed from Sir Walter Scott. As a young man, fresh from the North, he had actually submitted an early fictional experiment for Scott's approval. Although Scott made the effort to read the book, and was kind enough to the aspirant when he met him, his journal reveals how widely Ainsworth had missed the mark. Scott was generally depressed by the poor quality of the work of those who attempted to imitate him: 'They have to read old books and consult antiquarian collections for their information; I write because I have long since read such works, and possess, thanks to a strong memory, the information they have to seek for. This leads to a dragging-in of historical details by head and shoulders, so that the interest of the main piece is lost in minute descriptions of events which do not affect its main progress.'[1]

Scott was perhaps fortunate not to have lived to witness Ainsworth's later popular success and esteem. The Waverley novels had proved that history could be the proper, and profitable, matter of fiction, but they had also shown that successful historical fiction was best rooted in a detailed investigation of character and environment. Ainsworth signally failed to grasp the full impact of Scott's achievement and, though his literary career outstretches those of Dickens, Thackeray and George Eliot (his last novel appeared in 1881), he seems to have remained unconscious of, and oblivious to, most contemporary developments in the novel. Scott's view of his early experiment would be equally justified as a criticism of most of what came later. Even his steadily popular *The Lancashire Witches* (1848), with its attempt to reproduce the dialect and customs of a province, shows little evidence of his having learnt, as George Eliot or Hardy certainly had, from the example of Scott's regional novels. To its detriment, Ainsworth's work only barely relates the meaning and impact of an historical crisis to the experience of the individual, and the novelist seems happy with simply telling an involved, and often incredible story about people who happen to be historical.

Ainsworth's first independent novel, *Rookwood*, was published in 1834, eight years after he had submitted the collaborative *Sir John Chiverton* to Sir Walter Scott. The novel deals with the exploits of Dick Turpin, culminating in his celebrated ride to York, but it opens 'within a sepulchral vault, and at midnight'. In a later Preface the novelist acknowledged what many readers must readily have recognised, that the 'inexpressible charms' of Mrs Radcliffe had been the chief stylistic influence on the narrative. In this same Preface, he asserted that his main aim had been to transfer the predominantly Continental characters and settings of Gothic fiction to English ground. He was attempting a true revival: 'The chief object I had in view . . . was to see how far the infusion of a warmer and more genial current into the veins of the old Romance would succeed in reviving her fluttering and feeble pulses'. When *Melmoth the Wanderer* appeared in 1820, it had struck the critic of the *Edinburgh Review* as an ill-judged attempt to resurrect 'the defunct horrors of Mrs Radcliffe's school', but some thirty years later[2] Ainsworth appears to be serenely confident that *Rookwood* was heralding a new phase in the advance of the English novel.[3] England, he believed, was lagging behind the Continent: 'Modified by the German and French writers – by Hoffman, Tieck, Victor Hugo, Alexandre Dumas, Balzac, Paul Lacroix – the structure commenced in our own land by Horace Walpole, Monk Lewis, Mrs Radcliffe, and Maturin, but left imperfect and inharmonious, requires now that the rubbish which choked up its approach is removed, and only the hand of the skilful architect to its entire renovation and perfection.' He may not be claiming the role of the skilful architect for himself, but he does appear to be seeking comparison with established writers of the calibre of Hugo, Dumas Père and Balzac, novelists whose best work has a complexity and scope in dealing with history which is quite lacking in his own. Perhaps more extraordinarily, Scott's name does not appear in Ainsworth's catalogue of models. His own novels somehow bypass Scott's achievement, and return to the less investigatory, less fluid modes of his predecessors; they reject social and psychological analysis in favour of a revived stress on fantastic action, on the supernatural, and on the superficial glamour of costume drama.[4]

This determined preference for the 'Mrs Radcliffe school' perhaps explains the somewhat cavalier approach to historical fact and interpretation in Ainsworth's work. Most of his books have a vigorous and straightforward plot, but characters, both fictional and factual, tend to conform to stereotypes, and to be repeated from novel to novel. Plots are moulded around historical crises which oblige the novelist to follow a line of development faithful to his sources, but his sub-plots, which are often more involved, show more of a desire for variety than for a complement to the main story. Against a background of historical intrigue, he habitually plays groups of comic, low characters, and a melodramatic story of the wooing of a beautiful young heroine by a virtuous and generally aristocratic hero. The hero is pitched against a clearly defined villain, but it seems a matter of chance whether or not he will actually involve himself in the historical events on which the novel ostensibly turns. In most of the novels plots are tripartite, and Ainsworth seems to be more concerned to balance his historical, comic and amatory interest than he is to maintain a focus on a single, influential group of characters. Rarely are we led to feel that history impinges upon any but the statesmen playing an aristocratic game.

Any serious attempt to investigate the social impact of historical events is further diffused by Ainsworth's re-introduction of the clichés of Gothic fiction into his novels. Characters gesture or orate, and speeches tend to be little more than declamations revealing intentions, not motives. He avoids psychological development in character as though he regards it as an impediment to the movement of his story. At their best, however, the novels have fast-moving and visually effective plots which chiefly lack the advantages which tighter structuring might have given. They are rarely sufficiently tense, for Ainsworth contorts action in order to provide for the unexpected *frisson*, the hair-breadth escape, or the supernatural manifestation, and thereby detracts from any sustained interest in a situation. Walls are threaded with secret passages; panels and trapdoors fly open; the living are confused with the dead, the dead with the unearthly. Characters appear or disappear to suit the novelist's convenience in delivering them into or from difficulties. Where it is appropriate, and often where it is inappropriate, rituals are performed, or unspecified horrors suggested. Unlike Monk Lewis or Maturin, Ainsworth prefers not to go into details. At the ends of the novels, the virtuous are rewarded by benign monarchs, the villains have their villainy proved, or, if unpunished, we are assured by the narrator that history, as well as the novel, shows them to have been in the wrong. At their worst, but by no means uncommonly, the novels end as arbitrarily as they began. Ainsworth does not lack gusto; he is simply deficient in a controlling artistic intelligence.

Despite his pretensions to scholarship and to didacticism, Ainsworth takes considerable liberties with the facts of history in his novels, and in this he reveals the gulf that separates him from the more serious of Scott's successors, from Bulwer to Hardy. In *Guy Fawkes*, for instance, Fawkes himself is rivalled in his affection for the heroine by the young hero. Somewhat disturbingly, Fawkes wins the struggle, and marries before his attempt to blow up Parliament, while his disgruntled rival retires to respectable bachelorhood in Manchester as the future founder of Chetham's Hospital. In *Windsor Castle*, the novelist invents a rivalry between the Duke of Richmond and the Earl of Surrey for the hand of the fair Geraldine, and Anne Boleyn schemes her way to the crown, despite the fact that Henry VIII seems to be more interested in a peasant girl he has observed in Windsor Forest. In *Old Saint Paul's* the fictional heroine is pursued by an unprincipled, and unpoetic, Earl of Rochester. History is moulded to suit the requirements of sensationalism, despite the damage done to credibility. Often Ainsworth forgets to tie up all the ends of his plots, leaving elements unresolved, or unbalanced after a concluding marriage or a disaster. He will attempt to bring his fictional story to a happy end, while offering no solution to the vaster historical problem which he purports to be describing at the centre of the novel.

Many of his important historical characters are presented with a destructive ambiguity simply because he has not thought out the implications of his plots with sufficient thoroughness. In some cases, like those of Guy Fawkes or Mary Tudor, he attempts to challenge a conventional view of the character, but instead of offering a re-interpretation of action and motive, he develops one line of approach before abruptly switching to another. In *Old Saint Paul's*, Charles II and the Earl of Rochester appear at first as reckless and immoral; by the end of the story they have inexplicably assumed both dignity and decisiveness through their behaviour during the Great Fire of London. In *Guy Fawkes*, Ainsworth ambitiously set out to make a case for the Jacobean recusants, but he succeeds only in confusing the political issue still further. Fawkes emerges as an enigma, with a tormented conscience, moral scruples and a wife, while Frs Oldcorne and Garnet put the novelist in the equivocal position of exploiting a case against persecution *and* justifying a traditional English suspicion of Jesuits. In all his novels, Ainsworth's kings are fickle, arrogant, and ill-advised but, he tells us, unfailingly regal and nearly always justifiable.

This ambiguity is equally evident in his treatment of ordinary citizens. In his stories, unlike Scott's, the common people are allowed to express the novelist's prejudices without appearing to have evolved any kind of understanding of what is happening to them. They are rarely more than spectators observing events which they have no power to influence. Voices emerge from a crowd, or a yokel is engaged in comic dialogue. The crowd, especially in the novels about the Tudor period, is unthinkingly legitimist and monarchist in its sentiments; it admires bluff King Hal for his bluffness, and Good Queen Bess for her goodness; it accepts Mary Tudor's claim to the throne and suspects Lady Jane Grey's; it distrusts Anne Boleyn, but respects Henry VIII's marital whims as evidence of his capacity to rule. 'I love my king,' proclaims the host of the Garter Inn in *Windsor*

Castle, 'and if he wishes to have a divorce, I hope his holiness the Pope will grant him one, that's all.' When a butcher in the Inn declares that the king is tyrannical, he is denounced as a traitor and is arrested without a murmur of protest from the other guests. In *The Tower of London*, the 'low' characters swim with the religious current of the Court; there is little room for subtlety, and no sense at all of a society which is corporately involved in, and affected by, the complex political and religious situation. The intrigues of the great are played against a background of common assent and acceptance. When Ainsworth does attempt to describe popular uprisings, as he does at the beginning of *The Lancashire Witches*, he prefers to concentrate upon figures of popular authority. Readers, like the crowd, are generally required to assent to the *status quo*, and however much Ainsworth attempts to challenge conventional judgements of events or characters, he always balances his challenge against an equally telling restatement of the convention. History is observed as a series of rights and wrongs, and all that the novelist does is to suggest that, on occasions, certainties can contain areas of doubt within them without actually ceasing to be certainties.

The Tower of London appeared in 1840 in illustrated monthly parts; its author was still engaged in the composition and publication of *Guy Fawkes*, and before he had finished his new novel he was to have started *Old Saint Paul's*. The *Tower* is his fourth historical novel, and it marked a peak in Ainsworth's popular and commercial success. By 1841 only Dickens could rival his fame and income as a writer, and even Dickens could not quite maintain the same pace in producing novels for an established market. The two men were friends, and it is possible that Dickens was encouraged to continue his own scheme for an historical novel by the evident popularity of Ainsworth's work. From the 1840s the careers of the two men diverge; while Ainsworth was content merely to repeat the formulae of *The Tower of London* in its successors, Dickens discovered a new range in his art in *Barnaby Rudge*. The two novels are roughly contemporary, but they could not be more different in what they reveal of the respective abilities of their authors.

Ainsworth had first seen the Tower in 1824, and even at the age of nineteen he had sensed, according to his biographer, its likely potential as the subject of an historical novel.[5] The Tower had been for centuries an object of national veneration, and its decline in importance as a fortress was countered by its rise in popularity as a tourist attraction. 'What its Capitol was to ancient Rome,' wrote a topographer of the early 1840s, 'what its Kremlin is to Moscow, such is its TOWER . . . to London.'[6] In spite of the complex history of the building he describes, Ainsworth sensibly determined to select only a short but involved period around which to build his story. The novel, he told his readers in his Preface, would exhibit the Tower in 'its triple light of a palace, a prison and a fortress'. His choice of the short reign of Lady Jane Grey therefore, enabled him to incorporate, without excessive fabrication, two coronations, two executions, a royal marriage and a siege into his plot. The story, he announced, would be so contrived as to 'naturally introduce every relic of the whole pile – its towers, chapels, halls, chambers, gateways, arches and drawbridges'. Nevertheless, the final effect is of a nervous indigestion resultant from an overindulgent desire to prove that facts are palatable if they are dressed and served to the author's taste.

The determination to instruct as much as to divert is accentuated by the original illustrations by George Cruikshank, illustrations which have perhaps rescued the novel from critical oblivion through their peculiar individuality. Artist and author visited the building before each monthly part of the novel was due, and both made notes of the details necessary for the forthcoming issue. Large steel plates show scenes from the novel, while small woodcuts, embedded in the text, show the Tower as it would appear to the Victorian visitor, with the building given over to the domestic needs of its garrison. The two types of illustration are often juxtaposed to show how modern excrescences have altered the appearance and function of the fortress. Ainsworth and Cruikshank even incorporated a plan of the Tower in Tudor times so that the reader can follow characters into parts of the building which have since vanished.

Although the novel is freer of the discursive descriptions of the fabric which intrude into the central parts of *Windsor Castle*, *The Tower of London* never escapes having to function partly as a guide-book. The author's didactic voice interferes and interrupts the flow of the story; we are told what happened in the reign of Edward III, or what will happen in the reign of James I, rather than simply the significance of events in the period of the novel's setting. At best, Ainsworth is inconsistent, at worst, he seems quite unconscious of being anachronistic. In Book II, for example, the complicated developments of the plot are suspended when the villain of the piece, Simon Renard, looks out from the roof of the White Tower accompanied by a yeoman warder:

'There you behold the Tower of London,' said Winwike, pointing downwards.

'And there I read the history of England,' replied Renard.

'If it is written in those towers it is a dark and bloody history,' replied the warder. . . . 'I can recount to your worship their foundation, and the chief events that have happened within them, if you are disposed to listen to me.'

(Book II, Chapter III)

Renard accepts the offer of instruction, and Ainsworth gives us some twelve pages of dark, bloody, and largely irrelevant past history.

In seeking to make his novel comprehensive, Ainsworth brings together as many elements as he can, regardless of their effect on the unity of his work. *The Tower of London* is various and elaborate, but it is clumsily put together and disorganised where it most needs artistic control. The novel is built around abrupt contrasts. The fortunes of characters rise and fall, and, despite the probable accuracy of this as an impression of Tudor politics, readers are left with what seems to be an arbitrary succession of events, fictional as well as historical. When, for example, Sir Thomas Wyat's rebellion against Queen Mary fails, and the defeated rebels are imprisoned, Ainsworth shifts suddenly from a sombre mood to a comic one and describes the advancement of Xit, the royal dwarf. As he does so, he lamely remarks on the effect he hopes to achieve:

Life is full of the saddest and the strongest contrasts. The laugh of derision succeeds the groan of despair – the revel follows the funeral – the moment that ushers the new-born babe into existence is the last, perchance, of its parent – without the prison-walls, all is sunshine and happiness – within, gloom and despair. But throughout the great city which it commanded, search where you might, no stronger contrasts of rejoicing and despair could be found than were now to be met with in the Tower of London.

(Book II, Chapter XXXV)

The point being made is valid enough, but the novel is too overcrowded with characters and incidents to allow an effective balance of moods to succeed. The contrasts jar because they do not form a part of an organic whole. All Ainsworth achieves at this point is to remind us that he is switching from one group of characters to another in order to develop their individual plots equally. Although he contrasts Queen Mary's victory with Wyat's defeat, and he tells us that we should rejoice with one and mourn with the other, he never really allows us to feel for either side. Above all he does not tell us in the novel why the rebellion has taken place and what its significance is for the Queen and for the country. Here, as so often elsewhere, we are unable to take the play of emotions seriously because there is no firm basis for the emotions.

The confusion at the core of *The Tower of London* derives not simply from Ainsworth's failure to work out his plot with sufficient care, but also from the fact that he cannot sustain interest in the broad spectrum of his characters. He mixes the fictional and the historical indiscriminately, but, unlike the best Victorian historical novelists, he derives no strength from what he does, nor any fresh insight into the development of the events he describes. The antics of the comic characters — Xit, the dwarf, and the giant yeoman warders — are intended to be amusing parallels to the intrigues of the Court, and to be foils to the black comedy of the jailors, Nightgall and Wolfytt, and the headsman, Mauger, but they merely work as a digression. The novel's chief defect in characterisation is found not in the low characters, but in the neutral and fictional hero and heroine, Cuthbert and Angela, and, more significantly, in the historical characters involved in the struggle for the royal succession.

Lady Jane Grey is more than just the centre of a political plot, she is the moral centre of the novel. In his attempt to be fair, and it is little more than an attempt, Ainsworth also insists that Queen Mary, her rival and successor, is both justifiable and righteous. Around the two women the confusion doubles and redoubles, with the French and Imperial ambassadors scheming to outmanoeuvre each other and the English nobles, and with the Earl of Devonshire flirting first with Mary, then with Elizabeth, her sister, then with Mary again. Elizabeth herself would be only a shadowy, and irrelevant figure, were it not for Ainsworth's portentous reminders of the future glories of her reign. Because the novel concentrates so many characters and events into one place at one time, Ainsworth seems to find it impossible to vary the pace and speed of events, and to concentrate on one important group of characters more than the rest. The history is muddled in the interests of the romance, but the romance is never able, as it does in Scott or Dickens for example, to unmuddle the history.

The Tower of London is pre-eminently about Lady Jane Grey, but Lady Jane is so confused in a jumble of other interests that we never have a sufficiently clear view of her or her problem. The novel opens with her entry to the Tower as claimant to the throne, and it ends with her execution as a threat to the legitimate sovereign. Jane is the only important historical figure whose story is followed to a conclusion or a resolution. All the other major figures, Ainsworth reminds us during the novel, to the detriment of his fiction, have destinies which expand beyond the scope of his chosen framework. The invented characters are given their appropriate marital partners, but they will have little chance of influencing the future history of England if their careers in the story are anything to go by. Mary and Elizabeth Tudor have their reigns before them, the bishops have persecution or martyrdom, the ambassadors and courtiers new schemes, but they are left in suspension as the novel closes with Lady Jane's death. The novel may have set out to investigate a national crisis, and the Tower's part in it, but leaves the problem only partially solved, and the small solution it offers is ambiguous. Throughout the story we are required to assent to the justice of Mary Tudor's claim to the throne, and to acknowledge the folly of Jane's usurpation; Mary is a worthy woman and a just ruler, despite the narrowness of her religious opinions. At the same time, however, we are asked to sympathise with Jane's hope of replacing an illiberal Catholic regime with a progressive Protestant one. Ainsworth relies on the fact that his reader will accept the premiss that Protestantism will rightly succeed in the end, despite the evidence of the events of the novel, and that Jane's cause will be vindicated by history. In matters of politics Mary is right and Jane wrong; in matters of religion the reverse position holds. Ainsworth plays the one against the other, without appearing to sense that, for a Tudor monarch as much as for a Tudor citizen, the two positions might have been one. He also seems oblivious to the fact that his own extended view of Tudor England, and its effect on periods which succeeded it, is not shared by any of his characters. He sees them merely as puppets with predetermined roles, rather than as men and women working out their destinies with horizons limited by their ignorance of the future.

Throughout his novel Ainsworth portrays Lady Jane Grey as noble, self-assured, pious and guileless, but trapped by the schemes of politicians. Her loyalty to her family and her faith, and the pressures exerted by them, lead to her ultimate destruction. Unfortunately the novelist never manages to persuade us that Jane's dilemma is tragic. Any attempt at establishing a personality for her is inevitably hampered by the clutter of plot in which she is embedded, and by

Ainsworth's own imaginative limitations. He has not planned an ambitious psychological study of an historical figure on Bulwer's model, but in choosing so conspicuous and morally justified a heroine, he leads us to expect a more investigatory novel than he gives us. The status of the central figure is diminished by a general lack of precision in understanding either Jane's private world or her public one. In the middle sections of the novel she even seems to fade from view while the novelist concentrates on other strands in his plot. At the end of his novel, her imprisonment, trial and execution are really little more than a pendant to a story which has effectively concluded elsewhere in the marriages of Mary Tudor, Cuthbert Cholmondeley and Xit.

Jane is presented as the champion of Protestant rectitude and consequently in the mainstream of the development of English culture. Even though he gives no details of the nature of her theological arguments (one should be grateful that Ainsworth does not make the attempt), the novelist shows her Catholic opponents to be retrogressive, unscrupulous, and bigoted. When Jane is offered pardon for herself and her husband in exchange for her submission to Rome, the offer is presented as blackmail, and she predictably rejects it. Ainsworth adds weight to Jane's moral stand by making all the virtuous characters in the novel sympathetic to it, and leaving no room for spiritual, political, or psychological subtlety. In their last interview the Queen offers Lady Jane a final chance of saving her life by accepting conversion:

> 'Your highness will not impose these fatal conditions upon me?' cried Jane, distractedly.
> 'On no other will I accede,' replied Mary, peremptorily. 'Nay, I have gone too far already. But my strong sympathy for you as a wife, and my zeal for my religion, are my inducements. Embrace our faith, and I pardon your husband.'
> 'I cannot,' replied Jane, in accents of despair; 'I will die for him, but I cannot destroy my soul alive.'
> 'Then you shall perish together,' replied Mary, fiercely.
> (Book II, Chapter XXXI)

It is a typical enough piece of dialogue from the novel, with the adverbs pointing the melodrama rather than suggesting emotion or conviction. The language deflates the passion which Ainsworth wants us to read into the scene, and the characters seem to be doing little more than assuming poses in a *tableau* representing defined rights and wrongs.

All the important conflicts are presented as clumsily. If Jane Grey's tragedy is never given a sufficiently forceful expression, the study of Mary Tudor is too deeply ambiguous for it ever to persuade us that the Queen may have been wronged by generations of Protestant historians. In his Preface, however, Ainsworth leads us to expect that he truly wishes to challenge the conventions:

> To those, who conceive that the Author has treated the character of Queen Mary with too great leniency, he can only affirm that he has written according to his conviction of the truth. Mary's worst fault as a woman – her sole fault as a sovereign – was bigotry: and it is time that the cloud, which prejudice has cast over her, should be dispersed.

The very use of the term 'bigotry' here suggests that the pretence of open-mindedness cannot long withstand the pressure of a traditional view of Mary, who, as Dickens reminded his readers in *Barnaby Rudge*, did more harm in her grave than she ever did on the throne. Religious and historical prejudices are predetermined. Jane, though no persecutrix, is every bit as 'bigoted' in her opinions as Mary; both are unmovable, but Jane is admirable for her stand, while Mary is open to the strongest criticism. In nearly all her actions in the novel Mary is seen to justify the antagonistic attitudes of historians, while the book as a whole, with its asides and assumptions as to the virtues of Jane and Elizabeth, serves to reaffirm the convention.

Ainsworth's portrait of Mary as Queen closely follows the pattern, to be found elsewhere in his novels, of what he believes to be proper in a sovereign. Arbitrary decisions are approved of as evidence of a monarchic will to rule, but royal immovability is relieved by the sort of bluff sense of humour which the novelist takes to be indicative of superior understanding. Mary is most honoured, and best obeyed, by the novel's apolitical yeomen-of-the-guard, servants, and faithful citizens, and from them we gather that open criticism of a monarch is tantamount to treason. The limits to Mary's humanity may be contrasted to Jane's learned simplicity, and to Elizabeth's dignity and political acumen, but she is never explicitly criticised for her actions. Ainsworth lets us see very little of the persecution prophesied by Bishop Ridley in the first chapter, though, of course, readers know what the Bishop means. The only Protestant 'martyr' to die in the story is the fanatical Edward Underhill who virtually courts prosecution, and whose death at the stake allows both the novelist and the illustrator an excuse for horripilation. Mary's unpopular Spanish match is viewed as being the outcome of sound diplomacy, though close adherents of the Queen, like Bishop Gardiner, are uneasy at her decision. Ainsworth undermines his apologia in his clear suggestion that Mary turns to Philip of Spain because she has been slighted by an English suitor (Devonshire), and because she is jealous of her sister. We see nothing of Mary's married life, although we are told that beyond the scope of the novel she will be 'coldly treated by a haughty and neglectful husband', and that she will die childless (Chapter XXXVIII). The ambiguity works against Ainsworth's attempt to offer an historical judgement; within the novel Mary is respected for her decisions, outside it we are told that posterity has proved her wrong. The two options are allowed to co-exist without any resolution or balance being offered through the narrative.

In spite of, or perhaps because of, their intellectual slightness, a few of Ainsworth's early novels have remained popular well into the twentieth century.[7] A taste for them may well have been restimulated by their closest parallels as entertainments, the simplified images of European history projected by Hollywood in the 1930s. To many of his contemporaries, however, Ainsworth reflected the taste of a decade for an escape into the past; he then receded into literary obscurity. He continued to produce historical novels until shortly before his death in 1882, but he had outlasted his public and thin sequels to established successes failed to win it back. Even his admiring biographer records how unfashionable Ainsworth had become by the 1860s, when Browning told a literary party that he had just met, but only barely remembered, the 'forlorn-looking' figure of Ainsworth in the street. 'Good Heavens!' exclaimed John Forster. 'Is he still alive?'[8] The anecdote testifies not only to a loss of prestige, but to the fact that the literary friends of Ainsworth's youth had fallen away with it. The development of English fiction in the 1840s and 1850s had left him stranded, while he had little sympathy with the new advances of former friends and contemporaries. He disliked *Dombey and Son*, speculated that *Jane Eyre* might be the work of his rival G. P. R. James, and was actively annoyed by Thackeray's characterisation of Marlborough in *Henry Esmond*.[9]

In Ainsworth's work the common complaint that the English historical novel is outside the mainstream of fiction might seem to be justified. In *The Tower of London*, he had dealt with a period which contained within it a conflict of ideas which was to influence the subsequent history of Britain, but he had taken historical events and trivialised them as a source for a sensational plot. In discussing Ainsworth's novels in 1844, the critic R. H. Horne outlined his idea of the true significance of an historical novel which was able to

> throw the soul back into the vitality of the past, to make the imagination dwell with its scenes and walk hand in hand with knowledge; to live with its most eminent men and women, and enter into their feelings and thoughts as well as their abodes, and be sensitive with them of the striking events and ruling influences of the time; to do all this, and to give it a vivid form in words, so as to bring it before the eye, and project it into the sympathies of the modern world, this is to write the truest history no less than the finest historical fiction; this is to be a great historical romancist – something very different from a reviver of old clothes.[10]

In Horne's terms, Ainsworth was little more than a reviver of old clothes, and his novels were destructive of the real potential of historical fiction. In considering whether or not that potential was ever realised in the Victorian novel, it is essential to look beyond the model that Ainsworth left.

3 The New Seriousness: Edward Bulwer-Lytton's *Harold*

> The Historian, wanting the precept, is so tyed, not to what should bee, but to what is, to the particuler truth of things, and not to the general reason of things, that hys example draweth no necessary consequence and therefor a lesse frutfull doctrine.
>
> Sir Philip Sidney, *An Apologie for Poetrie*

When Byron passed away, the feeling he had represented craved utterance no more. With a sigh we turned to the actual and practical career of life: we awoke from the morbid, the passionate, the dreaming, 'the moonlight and the dimness of the mind', and by a natural reaction addressed ourselves to the active and daily objects which lay before us. . . . We were in the situation of a man who, having run a certain career of dreams and extravagance, begins to be prudent and saving, to calculate his conduct, and look to his estate. Politics thus gradually and commonly absorbed our attention, and we grew to identify ourselves, our feelings and our cause, with statesmen and economists instead of poets and refiners.[1]

Edward Bulwer-Lytton's address to England and the English of 1833 suggests the extent to which a post-Romantic and post-Revolutionary generation took stock of itself and of the prodigal age which had preceded it. A new seriousness was abroad which channelled Romantic fervour in deliberate, and frequently dour, new directions; there was an awareness that society now mattered more than the isolated individual, the concrete more than the abstract, the visible more than the invisible, resolve more than impulse. Revolution, either in the state or in the arts, was by no means a dead letter, but it required a combination of thought and action, no longer an elevation of the heart over the head. Man for Bulwer, as much as for Disraeli or Comte or Marx, was a political animal, responsible to the society around him, and responsive to historical, economic and social pressures. A new generation of artists saw the need, like Tennyson, to withdraw from the Palace of Art and to shatter the mirror of Astolat; an earnest, nationalistic consciousness inspired the music of Weber and Schumann; historicism informed the theorising of the Nazarenes, the Pre-Raphaelites, and the Gothic revivalists; a sense of the vitality of human community made for much of the vigour of the early novels of Balzac and Dickens. Such a mood, shaped in part by the benign influence of the Waverley novels, was to prove especially favourable to the continued esteem and popularity of historical fiction, and perhaps no English novelist of the 1830s and 1840s more pointedly reflects the intellectual mood of the times than Edward Bulwer-Lytton.

Bulwer's first, and widely acclaimed, historical novel, *The Last Days of Pompeii* was published in 1834; his last, *Harold, the Last of the Saxon Kings* in 1848, the year of manifest civil unrest at home and of spectacular political and social upheaval abroad. 1848 was also the year of *Dombey and Son*, of *Vanity Fair*, *Mary Barton* and *Yeast*, and though it might now seem justly overshadowed by them, *Harold* is like its contemporaries in being a response to a general concern with the problems of a changing society. Bulwer was no longer primarily interested in an immediate social problem for which the novel provided propaganda, nor was he willing to dramatise a solution in the guise of a love-story, but he was a novelist who was centrally concerned with the complex, and to him frequently tragic, development of society, its institutions and customs. In *Harold* the question of social progress and its human consequences is considered within an historical perspective and the novel is an attempt to suggest that an analysis of an historical crisis can throw light on a modern dilemma. If the stories of Harrison Ainsworth and G. P. R. James are escapes into a wildly imagined and nightmarish past, Bulwer's discussion of historical problems aims, by contrast, to be relevant to the modern 'condition of England' and to an urgent debate on the value and meaning of progress. Scott had helped to change attitudes to history; Bulwer aimed to carry his torch into a new era.

Bulwer's novels, and especially his historical romances, merit serious consideration because their author took both himself and the art of the novel seriously at an important juncture in literary and intellectual history. He was Scott's most immediate, if not his most talented, successor, and Bulwer can be said to have re-established the

English historical novel on a newly respectable, scholarly and distinctly Victorian base. He dispensed with the Brummagem Gothic of the Ainsworth school in favour of high-seriousness and high principles. Throughout his career he professed the greatest confidence in the future of his art. 'We may despair of the novelist', he wrote later, 'who does not look upon the novel as a consummate work of art, who does not apply to it . . . the rules which belong to the highest order of imagination.'[2] Elsewhere in the same collection of essays he asserted of the novel in general that it in substance belongs to poetry, obeys the same conditions, and necessitates the same indulgence.[3] To Bulwer the nineteenth century demanded a truly national art which blended æsthetic, political, social and patriotic considerations, and the novel lay at the core of his hopes and ambitions.

If Bulwer seems to us a prominent, but by no means unique, example of an artist whose aspirations were not matched by his talent, it should at least be acknowledged that since his death he has not been so much underestimated as ignored. He had a surfeit of ideas and a dedication to his literary mission, but he failed to acknowledge and to exploit his very real limitations. He shared with Scott a belief that a theory of historical development was properly expounded within a fictional framework, but he habitually sought to out-do Scott by adding what he considered to be Shakespearean resonance to a detailed analysis of an historical period. To Bulwer the pattern of *Waverley* was both unnecessarily fanciful and confined, and he aspired instead to poetry without poetic licence. As he prepared his readers for the crisis in his Italian political novel, *Rienzi* (1835), he suggested that 'whoever seeks to place before the world the true representation of a man's life and times, and enlarging the Dramatic into the Epic . . . will find himself unconsciously . . . the imitator of Shakespeare'.[4] Romantic critics had come to see Shakespeare's plays as an English equivalent to the *Epos* of the ancients, but to the self-confident Bulwer, the Victorian novelist's task was to 'enlarge the Dramatic into the Epic' in order to give the novel the serene and encyclopædic aspect of heroic poetry. Homer or Virgil or Shakespeare had drawn on national myth, and had retold and embellished old stories; the modern novelist could turn to history in the knowledge that he stood in an august tradition, though he had an advantage over his predecessors in being free to exploit a vast new range of historical investigation. Myth must now be founded on fact, and legend related to all that was known about the likely period of its setting. Calliope,

Erato and Melpomene could join hands with Clio, acknowledging their new debt to her. Though Scott had shown the way, a new generation, alert to the 'actual and practical career of life', could go on where he had left off and could redeem his faults of learning and understanding. If most earlier novelists had seen prose fiction primarily as a vehicle for comedy or for domestic tragedy, Bulwer was determined that his own work should express moral truth, complex ideas, and sound national resolve.

Bulwer's praise of Scott can at times seem only grudging, but there is ample evidence in his Prefaces and in his Essays of his real appreciation of the achievement of the Waverley novels. In particular he stresses Scott's Shakespearean quality of 'impartiality', an impartiality derived from what he calls 'knowledge of the world':

> History, in its highest ideal, requires an immense knowledge of the world; it requires also something of the genius and heart of a poet, though it avoids poetical form — that is, the difference between an accurate chronicler and a great historian is to be found partly in knowledge, not only of dry facts, but of the motives and practical conduct of mankind, and partly in the seasonable eloquence, not of mere diction, but of thought and sentiment, which is never to be found in a man who has nothing in him of the poet's nature.[5]

Bulwer might almost be echoing Macaulay were he not taking the novelist's rather than the historian's part, for he sees the true historian as a poetic imaginer and an accurate recorder. Like Carlyle rather than Macaulay he sees history as biography and as the study of the private and public worlds of the heroes on whom events had turned. But it is this determination to represent the inner complexity of an historical hero which marks the area in which he diverges from Scott's precedent to approach what he deemed to be a Shakespearean ideal. In Bulwer's conception of the historical novel, the major figures of a given era become the central characters in a story which is only partly fictional, and the artist's creative imagination needs to balance invention against recorded fact. Thus a Rienzi, a Warwick or a Harold are made the subjects of heroic biographies. Impartiality and knowledge of the world serve to adjust the techniques of psychological examination, as evolved by the novelists of the previous century, to the study of the character and motives of distinguished historical figures. To Bulwer this was a new challenge for the Victorian novelist, breaking new ground for fiction, and demonstrating the real superiority of the realist novelist over the conventional historian.

In thus concentrating on the fortunes of prominent men of the past, rather than, as Scott had done, on imaginary characters, Bulwer can never really allow his heroes to be defined, in James's sense, by the plot of the novel in which they appear. Both plot and character are dependent upon external sources and reference books, and the novelist's role is reduced to offering a redefinition or a reinterpretation of what happened in history. Bulwer always feels a need to look over his shoulder to a chronicler or to an alternative interpretation of his story. Furthermore, he rarely seems to distrust history, either as a science or as simply another form of fiction, for he believes that he is pursuing the same truth by way of an alternative but parallel path. Ultimately, it seems that the only imaginative freedom he desires is that of a theatrical director, interpreting another man's plot, or a designer clothing another man's characters. The historical novelist, he appears to accept, was only at liberty to speculate in limited areas of the consciousness of an historical figure, and he acknowledges that his account can only offer a parallel to that presented, rather less fluidly, by a conventional historian. Unlike Sydney Carton or Henry Esmond, Harold Godwinson is imprisoned by the historic 'last of the Saxon Kings' and he cannot move out of a pattern of thought and action established by generations of chroniclers. All Bulwer attempts is to provide justification after suggesting motive. It is small wonder that very few other historical novelists have followed his example.

Although he came to the historical novel in the mid-1830s as an experienced writer, anxious to try new subjects, Bulwer lacked the artistic resources, rather than the intellectual ones, which might have best fitted him for his chosen task. He was incapable of extended and interesting psychological analysis, and he never managed to evolve an easy, fluent and expressive narrative style, both of which were essential to the potential success of his stories. His historical novels tend to leave us with enigmatic figures who have existed sporadically, not consistently. *Harold* never strikes us as psychologically consistent, though it purports to be a fresh reading of the character of an outstanding and noble man, one whose political failure was due to circumstances beyond his control and not to a deep moral flaw. Much of Bulwer's trouble stems from his unfortunate assumption that his historical characters share a moral view in accordance with his own; they are noble, rational and liberal in a nineteenth-century manner and in line with a nineteenth-century view of the role and function of a hero. Harold's failure results from his being born in advance of his times, and from the lack of a proper response to a voice crying in a wilderness of superstition and barbarism. If history seems to emerge as a tragic process throughout Bulwer's work, it is often because we see it destroying prophets dishonoured by the countries and centuries which produced them.

Despite this moral anachronism, and the defects which limit the reality of his characters, Bulwer went to great lengths to be accurate. More than any of his successors he shows off his research, trusting that it will be efficacious in persuading readers of the truthfulness of his narratives. We are constantly referred in footnotes to works of further reference for details of clothes, armour, food or manners, for explanations of unusual terminology, or, worst of all, for alternative opinions on what is happening in the story. Bulwer seems to have been incapable of taking facts for granted, or at least of letting his characters move in a world which they at least take for granted. When Henry Esmond walks into a room there is no need for the narrator to give us details of its furnishings and period decoration because it is part of an environment which he accepts and knows; Harold's world is, by contrast, labelled and catalogued like a period room in a museum, and one feels that he ought to be stumbling over the clutter of antiques rather than finding it ordinary and familiar. When Bulwer annotates Harold's environment he merely adds to its artificiality and awkwardness, and he intrudes extraneous material which would be more appropriate to social history than historical fiction. It is ironic that Bulwer should have complained of 'inaccuracies' and 'erroneous notions' in Scott, for he succeeds in accentuating one of Scott's most irritating traits.[6]

There is reason behind the habit, however, for Bulwer believed, just as Charles Reade did, that he was adding to the credibility of his fiction by tying it to detail. It is part of his ideal of 'truth to Nature', just as his understanding of the processes of history reflect a universal truth imprinted in creation. With Wordsworthian conviction he later declares: 'Art, in fact, is the effort of man to express the ideas which Nature suggests to him of a power above Nature, whether the power be within the recesses of his own being, or in the Great First Cause of which Nature, like himself, is but the effect.'[7] Spots of local colour, like a detailed psychological portrait of an historical character, or an account of the movement of historical time, express a true picture of the world in obedience to the fullest human perception of Nature, both as it is and as it was. In the Preface he added to *Rienzi* in 1848 he looked back, with evident satisfaction, on his achievement:

> The success of this experiment confirms me in my belief that the mode of employing history in the service of romance is to study diligently the materials *as* history . . . and obtain that warm interest which fiction bestows by tracing the courses of the facts in the characters and emotions of the personages of the time.

His novels were to be what he terms 'chronicles of the human heart' which would see man whole by seeing him moving through time, though caught in an historical period. Bulwer seeks to give us a view of man and environment which is integral, and to show us man and his environment developing and being reconstituted as part of a single process. He wants to show us that history is a progressive force, moving towards the present, but he more often seems trapped in the past and by a view of the past which appreciates losses more than gains.

It was perhaps because of its elevated moral and intellectual tone that Bulwer's fiction was so overrated by many equally earnest Victorians.[8] His mind ranged widely and interestingly, but he was at the same time a reflector and populariser of significant trends in contemporary thought. Though history seems to be a forward movement in his historical novels, it is equally a process which involves considerable suffering and which destroys the ancient and honourable with the defunct and the decadent. His notion of evolution, and his nostalgia for the past, can be paralleled in Tennyson or Chateaubriand, but the strange determination to let a diachronic view of history co-exist with a synchronic one is peculiarly and damagingly Bulwer's own. The titles of his historical novels emphasise his preoccupation with last things, and with the passing of old orders, but the narratives show only a very muted confidence in the rightness of advance. In common with many of his politically minded contemporaries, however, he was persuaded that progress was beneficial, and that social reform was justified, both by the experience of the past and by the inevitability of Nature herself, a force which not only abhorred vacuums but also fostered evolution. In his novels, Bulwer seems to respond more to the heroism demanded by suffering than to the knowledge that all life is transient, and he mourns the instability of human institutions more than he welcomes changes which usher in new forms. His prejudices lead him to see history as tragic, but his reason prompts him to acknowledge that progress means enlightenment. It would be a mistake to conclude that Bulwer was a pessimist, but there is comparatively little in his novels to match the confident assertions of the benefits of progress which are to be found in his Essays.

In his 'On the Spirit in which new theories should be received', Bulwer draws an analogy between the progress of human society and that of the natural world; all communities, he argues, which advance 'durably and safely' contain, like Nature, 'two antagonistic powers — the one inert and resisting, the other active and encroaching'.[9] It is a succinct re-statement of the themes developed so laboriously in *The Last of the Barons* and *Harold*. Bulwer's Essay explores the idea in terms of his Disraelian Toryism; the novels in terms of passing orders. The Essay argues that if society is observed to develop according to natural principles, and change in Nature is inevitable, then society and its rulers must welcome reform; the novels suggest that Nature is cruel and unsympathetic to man's aspirations. The idea of development, he indicates in another essay, is best understood by means of an appreciation of the forces at work in history and in the distinctions between one society and another: 'Progress does not mean transformation: it means advance towards the fullest development of forces of which any human organisation, whether it be man's or society's, is capable. What is progress in one state may be paralysis in another.'[10] Societies have died and been reborn in the past, and the England of Harold and of Warwick the Kingmaker has given way to the England of Victoria and the Reform Bill. But though the historical novels set out to awaken a similar awareness, and a consciousness of the meaning of history, they effectively leave us with a vision of failure rather than with an insight into the nature of an 'advance towards the fullest development of forces of which any human organisation . . . is capable'.

In spite of his liberal convictions, and his public assertion of them, Bulwer's fiction tends to redirect the radical suggestion in Scott that conflict is the product of a central human struggle for liberation. To the author of *Harold*, conflict is simply a destructive element in the natural order of things, an element which will eventually be worked out by a slow and gradual process of social evolution. The novel ends with the spectacular defeat of the progressive last of the Saxon kings, but its conclusion mutedly implies that the victorious Normans will regenerate a decayed political system and that, given time, the Saxons will rise again. If he regrets the passing of a hero and of the principles which inspired him, Bulwer is also attempting to suggest that the nineteenth century should learn a lesson from history, and feel confident in the prospect of peaceful and non-violent advance before it. His view of the Conquest is hardly free of patriotic bias, but he accepts its inevitability and its usefulness as a warning to the present. *Harold* appeared while the thrones of Europe were tottering and falling, but it set out to suggest that an active and encroaching power was capable of breaking any institution once it became ossified. If England had survived the threat of revolution, it was partly due to historical advantage, and partly to racial characteristics, but she must still heed the novel's implied message as to the dangers of decadence. It is only on the level of a national reveille that *Harold* could be called hopeful, and it is only by seeing it in the context of its time that it can be seen to contain a political message.

With Kingsley, Bulwer shared the common Victorian conviction that the Norman Conquest was the crux of English history. Like *The Last of the Barons*, *Harold* is a scholarly study of a subject from national history which had an epic potential. These two novels are distinct from the rest of Bulwer's fiction in that they move away from the foreign settings of his earlier historical fiction (*Rienzi*, *The Last Days of Pompeii* and *Zanoni*), but they introduce the kind of historical analysis which had not been attempted in the stories which had merely been *set* in the English past (*Eugene Aram* for example). The English historical novels show the involvement of great men in the processes of dynamic change, and they both attempt to trace the formation and social impact of momentous political decisions. *The Last of the Barons* had been conceived as an illustration of

> the actual history of the period; and to bring into fuller display than general history itself has done, the characters of the principle personages of the time, – the motives by which they were probably actuated, – the state of the parties, – the condition of the people, – the great social interests which were involved in what, regarded imperfectly, appear but the feuds of rival factions.
>
> (Preface)

It is an impressive enough programme, but neither novel manages to realise it by endowing so complex a range of material with sufficient human interest. *The Last of the Barons* in particular leaves us with the 'imperfect' picture that the Middle Ages *did* only consist of 'the feuds of rival factions', for Bulwer's account of the England of Edward IV is both over-schematised *and* confusing. It is also amongst the most drably written of all of his books.

The subject of *Harold* was, despite its historical importance, yet more remote and unpromising than that of *The Last of the Barons*. Bulwer nevertheless appears to have considered it something of a patriotic duty to deal with the Norman Conquest in a work of fiction, divided into twelve books in the epic manner. He introduced his new novel to his public by explaining:

> The main consideration which long withheld me from the task, was my sense of the unfamiliarity of the ordinary reader with the characters, events, and, so to speak, with the very physiognomy of a period *ante Agamemnona*; before the brilliant age of matured chivalry, which has given to song and romance the deeds of later knighthood, and the glorious frenzy of the Crusades. The Norman Conquest was our Trojan War; an epoch beyond which our learning seldom induces our imagination to ascend.
>
> (Dedicatory Epistle)

Bulwer is stressing not simply that his novel will be different from *Ivanhoe* or *The Tales of the Crusaders* or *The Last of the Barons*, but also that he is thinking of a modern counterpart to the Homeric epic. Like Sharon Turner whose monumental *History of the Anglo-Saxons* had appeared between 1799 and 1805, or the French historian Augustin Thierry whose *Conquête de l'Angleterre par les Normands* had been published in Paris in 1825, Bulwer was convinced that the 'British Trojan War' touched on issues of fundamental importance which had directly influenced the growth of modern attitudes and systems of government. But if Homer had been free to invent, or at least to amplify, a national myth, Bulwer was attempting to resurrect the real men of history who had fought unknowingly to make the subsequent fortunes of the British race.

Given the already established style of Bulwer's historical fiction, *Harold* is overburdened with abstruse information and involved explanations of the social and political background to the story. The novelist himself was aware of the dangers of what he was attempting, and offered some kind of justification of his method in his Dedicatory Epistle:

> My main object has been one that compelled me to admit graver matter than is common in romance, but which I would fain hope

may be saved from the charge of dulness by some national sympathy between author and reader; my object is attained, and attained only, if, in closing the last page of this work, the reader shall find, that in spite of the fictitious materials admitted, he has formed a clearer and more intimate acquaintance with a time, heroic though remote, and characters which ought to have a household interest to Englishmen.

He almost seems to be apologising for mixing fiction with hard 'fact', though the novel itself is deeply indebted to the very history books which he had tried to better in his own account. The 'graver matter than is common in romance', however, proves to be a solid diet of pasty and unappetising fact, relieved here and there by interpretation. The major flaw of Bulwer's method is not its dullness, but the manner in which it dispels rather than explores the remoteness of Saxon England. He takes away any sense of wonder or strangeness by explaining too much away, or by stressing how alien Harold's world seems to a modern reader. Bulwer never seems to sense that in de-mythologising his characters, by emphasising the validity of his own historical credentials, he diminishes both their heroism and their humanity.

Harold opens, incongruously as it must have seemed even to Victorian readers, in the Old Kent Road. Its first scene is set amidst the ruins of a Roman villa, and Bulwer attempts, by mixing cultures and attitudes, to introduce us to major characters and themes. Its general effect, however, is strained and somewhat melodramatic. The ruins have become the residence of a Norse *vala*, Hilda, and her ward, Edith, the future mistress of the hero of the novel. Hilda has the role of the necromancer which seems obligatory in Bulwer's historical novels, deriving as it does from the novelist's own deep fascination with the occult. In *Harold*, Hilda represents an older and pagan faith which has successfully resisted the inroads of Saxon Christianity, and her magical mumbo-jumbo is contrasted, not to the enlightened religion of the Christians of *The Last Days of Pompeii*, but to the sentimental piety and superstition of Edward the Confessor. As he rides towards London, Bulwer's Edward seems to be more interested in the relics of the saints by whom he perpetually swears than he is in governing his decaying kingdom. The Confessor is in turn contrasted to William of Normandy, riding by his side, and evidently willing to please his host in the interests of becoming his heir. The first chapter contains some of Bulwer's lamest mock Saxon dialogue, ('Now, by

my halidame, I honour and love thee Edward . . . and were I thy
subject, woe to man or woman that wagged tongue to wound thee by
a breath.'), but it is really intended to outline the future political
development of the story. England, Bulwer implies, is debilitated like
its king, and the king, like a bored shepherd, does not heed the wolf.
By the time Harold enters, in the second chapter of the third Book,
we are meant to conclude that England truly has need of him.

   More so than most other historical novels of its type, the novel is
dominated by the fortunes and actions of a hero who is also a well-
recorded historical figure. Other characters are subordinate to him in
terms of the novel's viewpoint and often they seem to be incidental to
his heroic progress. Only rarely are the threads of the destinies of
other characters drawn out beyond the frame of Harold's story,
despite the fact that Bulwer claims that he is offering us a picture of an
entire nation undergoing violent and decisive change. *Harold* does not
have an especially complex structure, but it is far from easy to read,
impeded as it is by a surfeit of information. The complications of the
plot come through the involvement of the hero in personal and
political intrigue, not really through a carefully considered pattern of
human relationships or through any psychological development. But
in choosing to concentrate on the decisions and motives of a
dominant protagonist we often tend to lose sight of a central
argument or theme, unifying features which the novel badly needs.
At times it seems that one of the story's many cul-de-sacs may
suddenly emerge as the main road of its development, though none
does until after the Confessor's death. Bulwer gives us a view of
events which is intended to confirm Harold as a Carlylean hero, but
by so doing he directs us away from a broad view of the many forces
which are determining the fate of Saxon England. *Harold* must be
seen in the final judgement to be a more cramped study of an
historical period than any of the best of the Waverley novels.

   Bulwer's attitude to his hero had also been outlined in the
Dedicatory Epistle:

   While I have carefully examined and weighed the scanty evidences
   of its distinguishing attributes . . . I have attempted . . . to shadow
   out the ideal of the pure Saxon character . . . marked already by
   patient endurance, love of justice, and freedom – the manly sense
   of duty rather than the chivalric sentiment of honour – and that
   indestructible element of practical purpose and courageous
   will, which, defying all conquest, and steadfast in all peril, was

ordained to achieve so vast an influence over the destinies of the world.

Harold is an ideal of whom much is required. He is the embodiment of English virtue, past and present, though he must, at the same time, be seen as the final flower of dying Saxondom. He must seem to be free of the shortcomings of his contemporaries, yet he must also draw on the glories of a shared Saxon past for inspiration. Bulwer does not show him to be flawless, but the deficiencies of his character are extravagantly excused. He appears as both the prototype and the archetype of the coming race of Englishmen, but there are many moments in the story when Harold seems to have no definable character at all. Though the novel reveals that the king devastatingly fails to save his kingdom, it also implies that readers should grasp the extended moral that men of Harold's stamp will rise up again to make a future Britain great and imperial.

Harold is no thinker, and his own moral perceptions seem vague, but his valour and his unflinching patriotism carry all before them. When we are given an impression of the hero's intellect at the beginning of Book IV, the novelist tells us that in Harold 'what we call common-sense was carried to genius', and that his unspeculative Saxon brain is 'singularly practical and sagacious'. His virtues are stolid, but they are by and large uninteresting and they fail to persuade us of his actuality. He is devout, but rational; wondering, but never superstitious; politic, but incapable of political deviousness himself or of understanding it in others. When we see him surrounded by his fellow thegns he is as distinct from them as Virgil's Aeneas is from his Trojans, but like Aeneas he has the right qualities for his mission and they render him a smug paragon.

So strong is Bulwer's partiality, however, that his hero is justified as far as it is possible to justify a character whose recorded history suggests more than a degree of selfish ambition. When Harold swears his famous oath to help William of Normandy to the English crown, for example, Bulwer buttresses his action with excuses; Harold has been outwitted by cunning and perfidious enemies; he is the ingenuous Englishman abroad; his forthright nature has been tricked; his real and selfless motives have been vulgarly misunderstood. In the preceding chapters which recount his capture and imprisonment in Normandy, Bulwer shows us a Harold working from motives of disinterested patriotism, but once we reach the climactic and, it must be admitted, dramatic, scene in which he swears on the bones of the

Norman saints we have yet another run of provisos and excuses:

> All of this was so sudden — all flashed so rapidly upon the Earl,
> whose natural intellect, however great, was, as we have often seen,
> more deliberate than prompt — so thoroughly was the bold heart,
> which no siege could have sapped, taken by surprise and guile — so
> paramount through all the whirl and tumult of his mind, rose the
> thought of England irrevocably lost, if he who alone could save her
> was in the Norman dungeons . . . mechanically, dizzily, dream-
> ily, he laid his hand on the reliquaire, and repeated, with
> automaton lips:
> 'If I live, and if God aid me to it!'
>
> (Book IX, Chapter VII)

The novelist's elaborate intervention on behalf of his hero suggests
that Harold's action, as recorded by contemporary historians, does
not speak clearly for itself. Bulwer only lets us glimpse Harold's
thought process; there is no real inner debate, no weighing of issues,
no interior monologue. He is, we are told, 'taken by surprise', but
we never see how he is surprised, how he reacts, or how he loses
control of the difficult situation. The words 'sudden', 'surprise',
'guile', 'tumult', 'whirl', 'mechanically', 'dizzily', 'dreamily' and
'automaton' only provide us with one-sided information; Harold is
tricked and in his confusion he acts like a machine not like a soldier
used to making quick decisions at moments of difficulty. Bulwer
hopes that we will find Harold excusable, not because he is weak or
morally unaware, but because he is guileless and sees only one,
mildly dishonourable, way forward. Bulwer has told us that he is
'more deliberate than prompt', but we are in fact seeing the reverse in
operation; there is no deliberation, but a prompt solution to his
problem lies in taking an oath which he does not intend to keep. The
scene works because it is tense and fast-moving, but Bulwer does not
want to pause to consider the private drama inside his hero; on the
face of it Harold appears stupid, mechanical, culpable, while the
novelist attempts to persuade us that his hero is acting with patriotic
bluntness and with a soldier's practicality. It is a crucial moment in the
story for it touches the issue on which both Harold's heroism and his
ambition must be judged, but it is squandered by the novelist's not
appearing to sense how damaging his ambiguity and special-pleading
are. There is no hint of perjury later in the novel when Harold makes
no further effort to help William to the throne. He is presented

instead as the honest upholder of the dignity and independence of his race. Later events settle into a convenient and justified sequence, with William as the aggressor and Harold as the slandered defender of ancient rights. Only the novel's villains, it seems, keep promises, and Albion appears to have a long tradition of unacknowledged perfidy.

This same bias is evident in Bulwer's treatment of Harold's timely desertion of his mistress, Edith, for a politically advantageous match. Marriage to Aldyth leads directly to his accession to the throne for it wins him powerful friends and silences ecclesiastical scruples over his former illicit relationship. Given what we have been told of Edith's passionate nature, her meek acceptance of her rejection, and her placing of the interests of her country over those of her own heart, do not ring true. Her reaction comes as a surprise, but it is a convenient one for the novel's plot, for their separation comes at a point in the story at which it would have been embarrassing to Bulwer to have suggested any culpability on Harold's part. Nor does Edith seem to feel herself dreadfully wronged:

> 'O Harold!' she exclaimed, 'dost thou remember that in the old time I said, "Edith had loved thee less, if thou hadst not loved England more than Edith?" Recall, recall those words. And deemest thou now that I, who have gazed for years into thy clear soul, and learned there to sun my woman's heart in the light of all glories native to noblest man, – deemest thou, O Harold, that I am weaker now than then, when I scarce knew what England and glory were?'
>
> 'Edith, Edith, what wouldst thou say? – What knowest thou? – Who hath told thee?, – What led thee hither, to take part against thyself?'
>
> 'It matters not who told me; I know all. What led me? Mine own soul, and mine own love!' Springing to her feet and clasping his hand in both hers, while she looked into his face, she resumed: 'I do not say to thee, "Grieve not to part;" for I know too well thy faith, thy tenderness – thy heart, so grand and so soft. But I do say, "Soar above thy grief, and be more than man for the sake of men!" Yes, Harold, for this last time I behold thee. I clasp thy hand, I lean on thy heart, I hear its beating, and I shall go hence without a tear.'
>
> (Book X, Chapter X)

Bulwer's experience in the Victorian theatre is clearly standing him in good stead here, but the rhetoric is too thin for a novel which purports to be offering us a psychological insight into historical characters and developing complex private lives beside public ones. It is not just that Bulwer's language is stilted, though it is damaging enough to the effect he had aimed at, for the entire dialogue in the scene consists of speechifying, or when emotion breaks into the eloquence, of extravagant phrases ('Hush! hush! — This is a dream — wait till we wake! True heart! noble soul! — I will not part from thee!'). The high sentiments about honour, or duty, or country, are meant to carry the scene and to cover the private agonies, but Bulwer's melodramatic heroics are no substitute for a picture of the real sufferings of real lovers. At the end of the story Edith is given token justice, for it is she and not Aldyth who claims her lover's body after Hastings and finds her own name tattooed, with that of his country, over his heart. Yet even here Bulwer cannot escape from thinking in terms of a theatrical tableau; Edith dies heartbroken on Harold's cold breast without ever having seemed to come alive as a faltering, trusting, loving woman.

Once Harold has been proclaimed king of England in succession to Edward the Confessor, no doubt is allowed to remain as to his worthiness for his role. The election is seen as the fulfilment of his native promise as a true-born Saxon, and patriotic ends are justified by white-washed means. Even his fellow thegns in the Witan, once carping and divided, seem suddenly to have woken up to his qualities and prepared to forget the past sins of the House of Godwin. As the Saxon nation unites behind him in the struggle to maintain national independence, Harold is said to embody the free, democratic spirit of his race; he is the

> first Saxon king, since England had been one monarchy, selected not from the single House of Cerdic — first Saxon king, not led to the throne by the pale shades of fabled ancestors tracing their descent from the Father-God of the Teuton, but by the spirits that never know a grave — the arch-eternal givers of crowns, and founders of dynasties — Valour and Fame.
>
> (Book XI, Chapter II)

Even though Harold is not of the blood-royal, and though his election might be viewed as strictly irregular, Bulwer implies that his kingship is prophetic of future decisions by a free Parliament and People, and that it stands in line with the Bill of Rights and the Glorious Revolution. It is an untypically radical gesture on the novelist's part, for by seeking to apologise in full for his hero, he puts himself in the position of asserting the right of a nation to choose its leader, regardless of historical precedent. If Harold's reign had proved more successful perhaps Bulwer's appreciation might have been qualified. The last of the Saxon kings founds no new dynasty, nor does he manage to retain the crown awarded to him by Valour and Fame, for he seems to be checked by Destiny for his presumption. To Bulwer, Harold's spirit and his ideal of kingship are ahead of their times and they jar against the slow movement of mediaeval history. His cause can only be vindicated by the future that he distantly foreshadows.

Nevertheless, Bulwer does not let a suspicion of usurpation or anticipatory prophecy disturb his, or Harold's, temporary confidence. Harold is to be identified with the very soul of the nation in the latter stages of the novel. Just before his authority is challenged by the Norman invasion, Bulwer insists that man and nation are one:

> From this time, Harold's private life ceased. Love and its charms were no more. The glow of romance had vanished. He was not one man; he was the state, the representative, the incarnation of Saxon England: his sway and the Saxon freedom, to live or fall together!
> (Book XI, Chapter VII)

Not only is his hero elevated to a position where he should not be questioned, but Bulwer tells us that there is no longer any valid reason *why* he should be questioned. Harold is as free of self-doubt now as he is of any other thought than of England and his creator suggests that to scruple with the king is to doubt the very concept of nationhood. So completely is Harold England that he ceases to have private passions or wandering thoughts. Partiality so narrows the novelist's understanding that it appears to release him from the need to represent the inner man, though it wrecks his aim of offering a detailed, but detached, view of the demise of Harold and his cause.

Throughout the story the hero's uprightness had been played against the debility of his predecessor and the craft of his successor. But William of Normandy is not utterly blackened, nor is his train of Norman barons portrayed as a pack of bullies. Bulwer suggests that moral, cultural and social differences divide Saxons and Normans but he never examines these differences closely, despite his play with the chivalry of Mallet de Graville and with the cruelty of Odo of Bayeux. Unlike Harold, however, William is an astute politician, perhaps even an unscrupulous one; he is violent and easily provoked, but he can show himself to be an honourable man and a generous victor. As in Kingsley's *Hereward the Wake* we see the strength of the Norman will, and the valour of the Norman army, but Bulwer manages to avoid the compromise and imbalance which disturb Kingsley's argument by not admitting too strong an admiration for the coming man. Bulwer's William is no Carlylean hero, he is simply the representative of a new order which is inevitable, efficient and harsh.

As its title properly implies, this is Harold's novel, and he, not William, signals the future. England will evolve towards Saxon and not Norman virtues once the Conquest has been accepted and the conquerors assimilated. But the focus on an ideal Saxon king undermines any attempt at imitating the impartiality which Bulwer so admired in Scott and Shakespeare. There is little feeling of an organic society around the hero, and little real sympathy with the culture of a dead world. Above all, the novel fails to examine the effects of the Conquest on the people of England. The story ends with the essentially private mourning of Edith for her dead lover, and it is Edith's, and not England's, desolation which is most marked. The sense of reconciliation or compromise which is so crucial to Scott's method, and which is reflected in so many greater Victorian historical novels, is merely hinted at in *Harold*'s last paragraph:

> Eight centuries have rolled away, and where is the Norman now? or where is not the Saxon? The little urn that sufficed for the mighty lord [William] is despoiled of his very dust; but the tombless shade of the kingly freeman [Harold] still guards the coasts, and rests upon the seas. In many a noiseless field, with Thoughts for Armies, your relics, O Saxon Heroes, have won back the victory from the bones of the Norman saints; and whenever, with fairer fates, Freedom opposes Force, and Justice, redeeming the old defeat, smites down the armed Frauds that would consecrate the wrong, – smile, O soul of our Saxon Harold, smile, appeased, on the Saxon's land!

Defeat at Hastings, we are led to understand through Bulwer's wordiness, is merely a temporary eclipse of the real England, for the spirit of the old Saxons will eventually show itself again in the struggle for freedom and empire. This last stress on a dying, redeeming hero implies the distant promise which is to be realised through future social and moral progress. With Harold, but not because of him, dies an old and worn-out England. The novel ends with a vision which is denied to Bulwer's epic hero, but through which the novelist intends to re-establish an epic dimension by relating the example of the last of the Saxon kings to a panoramic view of the coming fortunes of his kingdom.

Harold brought Bulwer considerable personal satisfaction, especially as it won him the respect of those he had been most anxious to impress – the conventional historians and antiquarians. Macaulay, for example, told the novelist that he had read *Harold* 'too eagerly for criticism', and he added that he would eventually prefer to criticise the book as history rather than as fiction. The eminent constitutionalist, Francis Palgrave, to whose research Bulwer had admitted his debt, was delighted that his own 'dull prose' should have contributed to the 'admirable poetry' that he had somehow managed to find in the novel. Thomas Wright, the antiquary, thanked the novelist for the complementary copy he had been sent, regretting only that Bulwer was alone amongst historical novelists; the others, he complained, had 'never really studied history' and had consequently 'perpetuated prejudices of the most vulgar kind'.[11] A final flattering compliment to the novel was paid too late for Bulwer to appreciate it. In 1877, four years after the novelist's death, and after a long period of antipathy to Bulwer's work, Alfred Tennyson effusively acknowledged his own debt to the form and ideas of *Harold* when he came to compose his historical verse drama of the same name.[12]

Critics in the major contemporary journals were far less impressed, and far more stinting of their praise. *Fraser's Magazine*, for example, appreciated the delineation of history in the novel but it deplored Bulwer's literary style as 'incoherent and unbecoming'. Some two years later it is somewhat surprising to find Charles Kingsley complaining of Bulwer's dyspepsia, an 'indigestion of facts' which has resulted from 'overgorging himself with Anglo-Saxon at some hospitable country house'.[13] In a general criticism of the author's novels in 1865 the *Westminster Review* argued that they were the product of a mind that was 'in the fullest sense of the word, commonplace', and the advice was tendered, 'If Sir Edward Bulwer-Lytton would be content to be taken for what he is, a respectable place might be assigned to him in the ranks of modern novelists.' The reviewer went on to point an important comparison: 'In describing the growth of character and the influence of varying circumstance upon it – the branch of art on which he most plumes himself – he never comes within distance of George Eliot.'[14] However partisan one might expect the *Westminster* to have been, placing Bulwer's work beside George Eliot's continues to expose his severe limitations. *Romola* too deals with the mediaeval past, and it has an ideal as its central character, but George Eliot is fluent, analytical, compassionate where Bulwer strains or miscalculates or steps sideways in order to avoid problems. Even the research behind *Romola* is artfully used compared with the stuffy pedantry which determines the tone of *Harold*. In spite of their occasional originality, their daring or their drama, Bulwer's historical novels are really only a prelude to the greater achievements of Victorian fiction.

Bulwer's once impressive European reputation is nevertheless witnessed by the fact that his *Rienzi* inspired both an opera by the revolutionary young Wagner, and a revolutionary painting by the young Holman Hunt.[15] But a closer artistic parallel to his novels can be found in the work of a painter of the calibre of Daniel Maclise. Like the novelist, Maclise was a member of the Dickens circle; he illustrated the work of both writers, and his pictures were as much in vogue at Gad's Hill as they were at Knebworth. With Bulwer, Maclise was instinctively drawn to the melancholy aspects of historical change, and like him he found battles, cataclysms and disasters congenial subjects. His masterpiece, the great frescoes for the new Houses of Parliament, like the series of illustrations of the Norman Conquest that he later produced, are carefully designed, crowded compositions which moved and impressed his contemporaries. To another age, however, their grey splendour seems cold and inanimate, expressive of dead conventions and an icy and unyielding view of heroism.

Another side of Bulwer's personality was expressed in the setting he created for himself at his country house at Knebworth. The house was cluttered with the paraphernalia of one of Maclise's battle pictures, and it prompted Matthew Arnold to comment sourly on the building and its owner after a visit in 1869: 'The house is a mass of old oak, men in armour, tapestry and curiosities of every description. But like Lord Lytton himself, the place is a strange mixture of what is really romantic and interesting with what is tawdry and gimcracky.'[16] There is much in Bulwer's novels that is able or original, and much that suggests an active thinker, a scholar, and a serious absorber of post-Romantic impulses, but there is more of what Arnold calls the 'tawdry and gimcracky'. Bulwer tried hard to make his impact on the English literary tradition, but as the relevance of his research and many of his ideas has receded with the passing of time, so has most of the interest and vigour of his novels.

4 The Track of a Storm: Charles Dickens's Historical Novels

Whether the gate of my prison be opened with an oyld key (by a gentle and preparing sicknes), or the gate be hewen downe by a violent death, or the gate be burnt downe by a raging and frantique feaver, a gate into heaven I shall have.

John Donne, *Death's Duell*

It was the best of times, it was the worst of times, it was the age of wisdom, it was the age of foolishness, it was the epoch of belief, it was the epoch of incredulity, it was the season of Light, it was the season of Darkness, it was the spring of hope, it was the winter of despair, we had everything before us, we had nothing before us, we were all going direct to Heaven, we were all going direct the other way — in short, the period was so far like the present period, that some of its noisiest authorities insisted on its being received, for good or for evil, in the superlative degree of comparison only.

Thus, with a series of juxtaposed propositions and a balance of contraries, Dickens opens *A Tale of Two Cities*. His opening attempts, in its second and third paragraphs, to place the story in an historical period, some eighty years since, but it also places it in a time 'so far like the present period' that we are always to find it like our own. Dickens is stating his apprehension of a truth concerning the past, and he is introducing a theme which will be developed in the course of his novel. We are drawn together to look at history in much the same way as we would consider our present, and to find in it the same certainties and doubts, the same contradictions and conflicts of opinion, which mark a familiar and contemporary world.

Although Humphry House was not the first to argue the case, it has often been accepted since the publication of *The Dickens World* that

Dickens had scant understanding of, and even less affection for, history. House remarked in his opening chapter: 'It is curious that he, who was so scornful of the moral abuses of the times in which he lived, should have almost universally condemned the times before him. There is no trace of idealizing the past. When he writes of the Middle Ages, or even of the late eighteenth century, he does so with an amused contempt for their standards of life, which shows him as a proud Victorian conscious of living in a progressive age.'[1] House develops this assertion by arguing that in most of his fiction Dickens is both vague about dates and preoccupied with the England of his childhood and adolescence. While the novelist is hazy with respect to period detail, his nonchalance shifts into a horrified contempt for all previous ages. House gives the impression of clinching his argument by referring to the sequence of false book-backs in the study at Gad's Hill, the titles of which purported to describe the 'Wisdom of our Ancestors' under the headings 'Ignorance', 'Superstition', 'The Block', 'The Stake', 'The Rack', 'Dirt' and 'Disease'.

Though the substance of House's criticism is sound enough, he nevertheless under-rates Dickens's grasp of history, both as an abstract idea and as an expression of the collective experience, rather than simply the 'wisdom', of our ancestors. The 'amused contempt' proves to be far less of a feature of *Barnaby Rudge* and *A Tale of Two Cities* than we might otherwise be persuaded to believe. As the opening of the later novel suggests, Dickens's idea of history to some degree resembles Thackeray's; outward traits, fashions, laws or *mores* change, but mankind remains fallible, recognisable, and familiar beneath the fancy-dress. Unlike Thackeray, however, Dickens holds steadily to his faith in social and moral progress. In both his historical novels he treats periods of social disruption close enough to his own time, but rendered distinct from it by the nature and determining historical circumstances of that disruption. The study of history for Dickens implied a warning for the present, and it illuminated the way forward.

As the garbled and opinionated *A Child's History of England* amply suggests, Dickens believed in progress both as a concept and as an observable fact and throughout his writing career he lambasted those who opposed reform, or who resisted change by professing an attachment to the good old days. In *The Chimes* of 1844, for example, he undercut a recitation of the myth of Merry England by putting it into the mouth of a befuddled associate of the contemptible Alderman Cute:

'The good old times, the grand old times, the great old times!
Those were the times for a bold peasantry, and all that sort of thing.
Those were the times for every sort of thing, in fact. There is
nothing now-a-days. Ah!' sighed the red-faced gentleman, 'The
good old times, the good old times!'

The gentleman didn't specify what particular times he alluded
to; nor did he say whether he objected to the present times, from a
distinguished consciousness that they had done nothing very
remarkable in producing himself.

(First Quarter)

The red-faced gentleman appears to be able neither to discriminate
nor to express an intelligible notion of history. Dickens is as pointed in
his attack here as he is sure of his own faith in progress later in the same
story:

'The voice of Time', said the Phantom, 'cries to man, Advance!
Time IS his for advancement and improvement; for his greater
worth, his greater happiness, his better life; his progress onward to
that great goal within its knowledge and its view, and set there, in
the period when Time and He began. Ages of darkness, wickedness, and violence, have come and gone: millions unaccountable
have suffered, lived and died: to point the way before him. Who
seeks to turn him back, or stay him in his course, arrests a mighty
engine which will strike the meddler dead; and be the fiercer and
the wilder, ever, for its momentary check!'

(Third Quarter)

The forward movement of Time is inevitable and beneficial, and
men, or societies, stand in its way at their peril. In *A Tale of Two
Cities*, as Carlyle had already suggested, Monseigneur and his order
are as much the victims of retributive Time as they are of Saint
Antoine. The warning in *The Chimes* was timely enough, but it was
one which had already shaped *Barnaby Rudge* with its reiterated idea
of the absurdity of turning the clock back. Sir John Chester postures
and sneers, much as the Marquis St Evrémonde was later to do,
selfishly enjoying the advantages of privilege; on another level,
Dennis, the hangman, also regards *his* social role as 'the glory of
England', and bemoans the threat of a future reduction of the death
penalty. An age without the gallows, Dennis tells us, will look back
nostalgically and say of the eighteenth century 'those were days

indeed, and we've been going down ever since'. Sim Tappertit's 'Prentice Knights have their own empty chivalric code, based on non-existent ancient rights, but like the red-faced gentleman, they never quite manage to form a 'distinguished consciousness' of what their code and their rights are:

> . . . they united therefore to resist all change, except such change as would restore those good old English customs, by which they would stand or fall. After illustrating the wisdom of going backward, by reference to that sagacious fish, the crab, and the not unfrequent practice of the mule and donkey, he described their general objects; . . .
>
> (*Barnaby Rudge*, Chapter 8)

Sim's objects are to seek vengeance on the Tyrant Masters and to press for 'ancient rights and holidays', but, as we learn from the story, all that the 'Prentice Knights manage to achieve in their quest is an addition to the anarchy which lies at the heart of the picture of England in *Barnaby Rudge*. Like Lord George Gordon and his 'No Popery' campaign, Sim is indeed crab-like in his attempt to move back to old battles and to revive dead customs, and like Gordon's, his campaign leads to a disorder worse than the supposed problems he had set out to redress. For Dickens, progress required a mind open to 'advancement and improvement', not one closed by an historical illusion to the pressing needs of modern man.

In spite of Dickens's real enough distaste for an illusory and sentimental view of the past, his antipathy does not extend to an incomprehension of the workings of an historical society or to a distorted view of the role of the historical novel. As the opening of *A Tale of Two Cities* indicates, the novels set in the past are of much the same order as those set in the nineteenth century, for both kinds of novel observe the shortcomings of society and criticise inhumane or irrational ideas and institutions; though they rely on historical circumstance, both the historical novels look at the violent consequences of the failure of proper reform. History, to Dickens, is not an escape, or a release, or a relaxation, or even an object of amusement; it is as much of a nightmare as the present can be, even though the present has succeeded in alleviating some of the abuses and prejudices which once made for disorder. Both *Barnaby Rudge* and *A Tale of Two Cities* present a picture of 'ages of darkness, wickedness and violence', but they also show that a similar pattern of desuetude, repression, and revolt are capable of threatening the relative calm of modern life if modern men shut their eyes to progress. Much as it was for Dickens's friend, Bulwer-Lytton, the past was a process of growth and decay; but for Dickens, the parallel with nature suggested that the individual citizen could also experience death and resurrection. For Bulwer history regenerates itself; for Dickens it is man who can be reborn amid his inheritance of confusion, sin and death.

It has been urged by several commentators on the novel that *Barnaby Rudge* in particular reflects the restlessness of England and the Continent in the 1830s and 1840s.[2] Although it is likely that Dickens was indeed aware of the analogy between the Gordon Riots and modern Chartist agitation, it is surely equally true that he is observing a social problem which he regards as undesirable but perennial. As the subjects of both his historical novels suggest, he was, again like Bulwer, fascinated by social upheaval. He is clearly shocked both by the retrospect he offers and by the prospect of history repeating itself, but in his stories the line of the plot leads us out of communal disorder into private order and resolve. Like the Victorian stories, the historical novels offer a resolution of social ill in a hope of regeneration which extends from the individual outwards. Though he was emotionally drawn to revolution, as George Orwell, amongst others, noted, Dickens could not see revolutionary violence as creative itself, however much he was creatively involved as a writer in describing it.[3] Like Scott, he lets the pattern of a novel resolve an historical conflict, but Dickens will look to the human heart, and to private commitment, before he will attempt to draw broader conclusions.

Those disappointed critics who have complained of the narrowness of Dickens's treatment of revolutionary ideas in his historical fiction have tended to forget that, to most Victorians, revolution and war were foreign, or at least unfamiliar. Sporadic organised revolt in Britain never got near to toppling a government, let alone a throne, and it was only after Dickens's death that the prospect of deep social change became a serious political consideration. Only in the historical novels of the mid-century is the subject of civil war, dissent, or revolution considered as a matter of social significance, but even there, as for Scott, there proved to be a soothing distance separating the novelist from his subject. Though Scott was prepared to establish a fictional dialectic in his stories, Dickens was not concerned with an analysis of a revolutionary situation; he cites causes, and he observes those who are unwittingly and innocently caught up in the conflict, but he sees only one effect: disorder. He has no other political point to make. As elsewhere in his books, the historical novels show injustice crippling human freedom and stifling natural goodness, but riot and revolution are seen to bring worse injustice and new varieties of restriction. The novels call for an alleviation of the causes of social division simply because Dickens believes that society should be one in its steady movement forward.

In those of his novels which consider the decay of the old order, a resolution, or at least a point of rest, is achieved through the change of heart in a central character, or in a hopeful marriage, or in a fresh commitment to social benevolence. Systems which destroy the human spirit, we are led to appreciate, should be reformed by those who have already discovered their own pattern of redemption. The novel offers us a kind of myth which can be related out from the imaginative world of the book into our own world. Real human charity, devoutly believed in, may produce, like George Eliot's 'growing good of the world', circumstances in which universal goodness may flow more freely. The education, or the discipline of the heart, leads to individual freedom and to resolved and responsive independence. On a relatively uncomplicated level this is Scrooge's progress; on a denser, subtler level it is David Copperfield's or Pip's advance to self-knowledge. As in the Waverley novels, however, marriage can signal a wider reconciliation; the once divided interests of Edward Chester and Emma Haredale are conjoined, as, more significantly, are those of Charles Darnay and Lucie Manette. But, for Dickens, the unions are more than symbolic, they are affirmations, and for Lucie and Charles a happy end is only made possible through the equally affirmative and self-realising sacrifice of Sydney Carton. Such resolutions are not the result of an historical analysis, of philosophical enquiry, or even of an allegorical schematisation, but of Dickens's firm, even religious, belief in what Keats called 'the holiness of the heart's affections'.

Nevertheless, one major contemporary thinker, Carlyle, does stand behind Dickens's historical novels. For Carlyle, as for Dickens, the French Revolution moves inevitably towards the institutionalised violence of the Reign of Terror, but its retribution is the result and realisation of a long and almost unavoidable process:

The harvest of long centuries was ripening and whitening so rapidly of late; and now it is grown *white*, and is reaped rapidly, as it were, in one day. Reaped, in this Reign of Terror; and carried home, to Hades and the Pit! — Unhappy sons of Adam: it is ever so; and never do they know it, nor will they know it. With cheerfully smoothed countenances, day after day, and generation after generation, they, calling cheerfully to one another, Well-speed ye, are at work, *sowing the wind*. And yet, as God lives, *they shall reap the whirlwind*: no other thing, we say, is possible, — since God is a Truth and His World is a Truth.[4]

To Carlyle the Revolution comes as a purgation, a destructive, inevitable, but refining fire, prepared for as part of a providential pattern; it tests souls as well as tempts them to perdition; it sweeps away sham and imposture. As *The French Revolution* shows, however, the end of the new popular anarchy is the rise of a determining hero, and with Bonapartism the Revolution is 'blown into space'. History is cyclic, but each phase awaits the world-historical hero who will mould the successive phase, his actions being justified by the 'spirit of the age'. If Dickens accepted Carlyle's analysis of the causes and progress of the French Revolution, he did not follow him in drawing the same conclusions. But in his eschewal of the elemental and determining hero he departs not just from Carlyle's example, but also, to some degree, from Scott's. Although all three consider the implications of a given historical moment, at no point does Dickens go on to contemplate the formation of a superman, or even of a man of public action. In his novels, partly in opposition to Scott, and certainly to Carlyle, it is in private, and not public life, that he beds his solution to a social problem. Private reactions to historical events are determined by an inner response rather than by any new political or historical awareness. It is a Christian emphasis which is decidedly Dickens's own, even though it is one that led a critic like Georg Lukács to dismiss the faith proclaimed in Dickens's historical novels as 'petty bourgeois humanism and idealism'.[5]

Dickens's literary and philosophical debt to Carlyle has definable limits, but he still seems to have approached the problem of historical fiction with an uncommon seriousness. Neither of the novels set in the past is notable for its humour or for the sparkle of its dialogue, but both have a variety of characterisation which does suggest a debt to the stolider amongst the Waverley novels. In terms of Dickens's career, *Barnaby Rudge* is the more experimental of the two, and it intermixes the historical and the fictional, the high-born and the low, the public and the private, very much in Scott's manner. But if one looks back to its immediate predecessor, *The Old Curiosity Shop*, it is evident that much of the vigour that went into a Quilp, a Mrs Nubbles, or a Mrs Jarley, has been diminished amidst an apparent self-consciousness. The process has gone even further in *A Tale of Two Cities*. A comparative lack of animation, and the long gestation period which preceded work on *Barnaby Rudge*, have suggested to some commentators that Dickens was ill at ease with historical subjects. It could be asserted, with greater justice, that, as with George Eliot's *Romola*, an historical novel marked a turning-point in the novelist's career, showing a deepening awareness of structure and of the use of thematic material as a unifying feature. Despite its tendency to *tirer les choses en longueur*, *Barnaby Rudge* marks the end of Dickens's first phase; despite its heavy-handedness, *A Tale of Two Cities* begins the last.

Dickens's debt to Sir Walter Scott in both novels is plain enough.[6] It is surely not coincidental, for instance, that both *A Tale of Two Cities* and *The Heart of Midlothian* begin with unkind observations on the state of eighteenth-century roads and with a stage-coach halted in mid-course. With the entry of *Barnaby Rudge*'s major historical figure, Lord George Gordon, after a five-year gap in the novel's time scheme the scope of the story broadens dramatically, much as *Waverley* or *Rob Roy* open up from domestic scenes into a discussion of the conflicts of the Jacobite rebellions. But, rather than adopt Scott's traditional formula of involving his central character in an historical crisis, Dickens only gradually expands his private themes into a public realm, and it is to the private themes that he emphatically returns at the end. In *Barnaby Rudge* he adds emphasis to the transition by introducing his vital new character, Gordon, and by slowly involving his fictional characters in the consequences of Gordon's campaign; in the later novel he moves his group of fictional characters to the centre of the Revolution in Paris, where, despite their innocence or foreignness, each in turn becomes involved. Scott's balance is not ignored, it is remoulded to suit a different and less analytical kind of novel, not necessarily more flexible in form, but imaginatively more open and capable of moving to a different kind of synthesis.

Both of Dickens's historical novels place a fictional emphasis above an historical one, showing us public disruption through its effects on an already established private world. Even in the case of Gordon in *Barnaby Rudge*, the novelist adjusts history to suit his scheme, transferring much of the blame away from the 'poor mad lord' onto his *éminence grise*, Gashford, a figure with only a slender basis in fact.

By considering the impact of civil disorder on the private and apolitical citizen, and by giving us the reactions of both the possessors and the dispossessed to riot, Dickens explored an idea which was to determine the treatment of an interdependent society in his later fiction. *Barnaby Rudge* shows us characters uprooted and confused by the events that overtake them, but like the later, yet darker novels, we glimpse a world in which every citizen has a responsibility for his neighbour and for the social group, albeit a responsibility which is so often abused or ignored. The fictional, private world thus becomes a norm by which we judge the public and historical affairs treated in the novel as a whole.

The shape of *Barnaby Rudge* has been extravagantly praised and equally extravagantly disparaged. Edgar Johnson regards its plot as 'clumsy and broken-backed', while George Gissing glowingly described the novel as 'Dickens's best constructed story; and, in one sense of the word, the best written'.[7] In a review of 1842, Thomas Hood adopted a musical analogy to account for the effect of Gordon's arrival in the thirty-fifth chapter: 'This circumstances, instead of being a defect, is to the advantage of the story. . . . The famous overture to *Der Freyschütz*, with its infernal music, certainly forestalls, and therefore, in some degree, impairs the horrors it precedes. . . . The novel, on the contrary, opens with peaceful and pastoral scenery – greenly and serenely, like the calm before a storm.'[8] Though Hood's suggestion of a green and serene opening to the novel misses Dickens's point, he at least puts his finger on the key dramatic feature in its total structure. The shape of *Barnaby Rudge*, like that of *A Tale of Two Cities*, points to its meaning. The first movement is into a private world which is divided against itself, but which, in its divisions, foreshadows the public conflicts of later on; the different groups of characters that we encounter at the beginning seem placid enough, but they are already subject to sporadic violence, or they oppress or are oppressed. Miggs is intolerant of men, Sim of masters, Mrs Varden of Popery, John Willet of his son, Sir John Chester, it seems, of everybody who disagrees with him. The mystery of the Haredale murder haunts the Warren (a significant name), and its consequences harrow the Rudge family, with Barnaby the living victim of the 'one horror, in which before his birth, his darkened intellect began'. The same mystery provides the novel's opening topic of conversation at the Maypole. As the story develops, however, private faction, dissent, and murder, become swept up in the public upheaval of London in 'The Riots of 'Eighty'.

Just as the murder at the Warren continues to haunt the habitués at the Maypole, it provides the novel with a core of suspicion and violence. Solomon Daisy reminds us at the end of the first chapter:

> The crime was committed this day two-and-twenty years — on the nineteenth of March, one thousand seven hundred and fifty three. On the nineteenth of March in some year — no matter when — I know it, I am sure of it, for we have always, in some strange way or other, been brought back to the subject on that day ever since — on the nineteenth of March in some year, sooner or later, that man will be discovered.

Although our interest in the unravelling of the Haredale mystery is likely to become lost in the spectacular account of the Gordon Riots, the thread of guilt which was spun in March 1753 gradually serves to draw all the characters together, and gives the story an underlying strand of horror which surfaces in the public violence. The hidden circumstances of Oliver Twist's ancestry, or of Smike's birth, give an equivalent mystery to their respective novels, but they have none of the force of the steady undercurrent of guilt and death in *Barnaby Rudge*, an element which Gordon Spence rightly calls Gothic.[9] The unsolved murder links this novel forward to *Bleak House* or *Our Mutual Friend*, though here Dickens relates the impact of an event in the private past of the characters to the fact that he has set his story in the historical and public past. As later in *Bleak House*, the intimacy of the seemingly diverse sections of a stratified society is slowly revealed, linking man to man, class to class, and the innocent to the guilty, but in *Barnaby Rudge* the growth of characters into understanding is paralleled by the progress of history. We are separated from them just as they are separated from their own pasts. The passage of time moves us out of darkness into relative light, just as a general movement forward untangles past imponderables and offers solutions.

The comparative stasis of the early part of the novel does nevertheless contrast dramatically, and sometimes damagingly, with the fast and involved movement of its second half. It is a deliberate choice of rhythm on Dickens's part, but it is one that can leave us with an impression of having been jerked from one kind of story into another. The novelist does not shift his centre of interest, but he changes the speed and the nature of events, and the novel tends consequently to be made up of juxtaposed sections. Such is the impact of the treatment of the Riots that they are likely to dominate our total view and eclipse the established patterns of the first thirty-two chapters. Even the movement back to order and placidity at the end does not really succeed in giving it a satisfyingly rounded shape, or help in forging the two moods into a unity. *Barnaby Rudge* stops and starts again without the artistry of *The Winter's Tale*, but with some of the need for rewinding that we sense after the death of Little Paul in *Dombey and Son*.

Despite this bipartite tendency, Dickens does attempt to keep groups of characters before our eyes in order to show us the changing impact of developing events. At the real centre of his novel is the Varden family. Gabriel was, in the early stages of planning, to have been the title character, but Barnaby's usurpation does not affect the locksmith's crucial importance to Dickens's point of view in his novel.[10] The Varden family come to be a representative image of the ills and potential hopes of society.[11] Our first glimpse of Gabriel's wife in the seventh chapter is telling:

> Mrs. Varden was a lady of what is commonly called an uncertain temper – a phrase which being interpreted signifies a temper tolerably certain to make everybody more or less uncomfortable. Thus it generally happened, that when other people were merry, Mrs. Varden was dull; and that when other people were dull, Mrs. Varden was disposed to be amazingly cheerful. Indeed the worthy housewife was of such a capricious nature, that she not only attained a higher pitch of genius than Macbeth, in respect of her ability to be wise, amazed, temperate and furious, loyal and neutral in an instant, but would sometimes ring the changes backwards and forwards on all possible moods and flights in one short quarter of an hour; performing, as it were, a kind of triple bob major on the peal of instruments in the female belfry, with a skilfulness and rapidity of execution that astonished all who heard her.

Mrs Varden's 'uncertain temper' and 'capriciousness' are like those of the aimless citizens who as suddenly and as uncertainly form themselves into a mob, and, like the crowd, Mrs Varden is uncontrolled. Her devotion to the 'Protestant Manual', and her constant empressment of the sour Miggs to her cause, indicate the real divisions within the Varden household, divisions which we later see enlarged in the city and nation. If Mrs Varden insists, with her uncertain temper, on 'keeping 'em down', her husband remains passive, placid and suffering, responding by spoiling his daughter and ignoring the gesturings of his troublesome apprentice. As we see, the Protestant Manual has a share in the blame for the Riots which threaten to destroy Varden life and property as much as it does national, social, and religious tolerance, and it is only with this prospect realised that Gabriel makes a decisive movement which reasserts his control over affairs. He crushes the Protestant collecting box underfoot:

> So he dropped the red-brick dwelling-house on the floor, and setting his heel upon it, crushed it into pieces. The halfpence, and sixpences, and other voluntary contributions, rolled about in all directions, but nobody offered to touch them, or take them up.
>
> 'That', said the locksmith, 'is easily disposed of, and I would to Heaven that everything growing out of the same society could be settled as easily.'

Gabriel's gesture of self-assertion within the family mirrors the stand he is also prepared to take against the rioters themselves, bluntly refusing to accept Gordon's offer of protection. The establishment of order in the household suggests the order which *ought* to exist beyond the Varden family; we recognise the justice of Gabriel's stand, and the need for his new sense of purpose and will for reform, but the same justice is not apparent in the State's judicial prosecution of those responsible for the disturbances. With his wife finally under control, his daughter engaged to Joe Willet, and his troublesome apprentice and servant gone, Gabriel settles in to the character which we might assume to be rightfully his, that of 'the rosiest, cosiest, merriest, heartiest, best contented old buck, in Great Britain or out of it' (Chapter 80). It is at such moments that we should remind ourselves that though the society around him has built the prison, it was Gabriel who made the great lock of Newgate.

To complement this generally rosy picture of the domestic prospects of Gabriel Varden, the novel also ends with the lines of a happy future stretching before the newly married couples. Joe and Dolly succeed to the Maypole with a handsome sum in the bank and a brood of red-faced little Joes and Dollys, having provided a new ingle nook down the road for the now demented John Willet and his cronies. As significant, however, is the union of Edward Chester and Emma Haredale, a marriage which serves to heal a breach between families and faiths. Catholic and Protestant interest is united, and though families have been divided from each other and within each other, the end of the story asserts the new harmony of family life. Even for Barnaby there is a gradual recovery and a 'greater steadiness of purpose' once the traumatic shock of Gordon and his divisions has passed over and been healed.

Although *Barnaby Rudge* ends with *rapprochement*, its middle is taken up with a more effective evocation of strife and violence than Dickens ever again achieved. The novel has many fools amongst its characters, but two dominate it, and Dickens carefully establishes a parallel between the historical Gordon and the fictional Barnaby as victims of the situation into which their *dementia* has drawn them. The novelist's tolerant treatment of Gordon might owe something to a Scott precedent, but we see the man as pardonable simply because he is also shown as exploitable in his very instability. When we first see him his manner and attire suggest an inner turmoil only barely disguised:

> . . . his very bright large eye . . . betrayed a restlessness of thought and purpose, singularly at variance with the studied composure and sobriety of his mien, and with his quaint and sad apparel. It had nothing harsh or cruel in its expression; neither had his face, which was thin and mild, and wore an air of melancholy; but it was suggestive of an indefinable uneasiness, which infected those who looked upon him, and filled them with a kind of pity for the man: though why it did so, they would have had some trouble to explain.
>
> (Chapter 35)

Gashford, onto whom Dickens transfers both the blame and his venom, has a contrasting manner, 'smooth and humble' but 'very sly and slinking'. He wears an aspect of a man 'who was always lying in wait for something that *wouldn't* come to pass'. We have two distinct kinds of unease, one nervous and pitiable, the other calculated and disturbing. If Gashford's 'lying in wait' manages to achieve something of its end, the view of Gordon as a man more sinned against than sinning is maintained; during the height of the riots he is without authority or will, bigotted certainly, but unconscious of the results of his persecuting crusade. The novel's last chapter traces, amongst other things, his final lurch into insanity and Dickens offers him a generous tribute which nonetheless points a useful general moral:

Many men with fewer sympathies for the distressed and needy, with less abilities and harder hearts, have made a shining figure and left a brilliant fame. He had his mourners. The prisoners bemoaned his loss, and missed him; for though his means were not large, his charity was great, and in bestowing alms among them he considered the necessities of all alike, and knew no distinction of sect or creed. There are wise men in the highways of the world who may learn something, even from this poor crazy lord who died in Newgate.

The portrait of Gordon is one of the more striking and successful elements in *Barnaby Rudge*; the same cannot be said of the characterisation of Barnaby himself. There is a similar restlessness, but it proved to be a far more difficult challenge to Dickens to capture the wildness and strangeness of a mental defective. The novelist himself acknowledged that 'the absence of the soul is far more terrible in a living man than a dead one', and that in the unfortunate, living Barnaby 'its noblest powers were wanting'. But Barnaby is never really alive enough. Dickens has to persuade us of both a childlike simplicity, and an eeriness and essential blankness, and at times the attempt almost succeeds, as when we see the Rudges confronted by the rabid Tory Squire in Chapter 47 (another of Dickens's hits at the myth of Merry England). Elsewhere Barnaby's scenes hover as near to bathos as Wordsworth does in 'The Idiot Boy'. His involvement in the Riots is intended to show us an innocent exploited by the unscrupulous, and his arrest and conviction to persuade us that it is the poor that habitually get the blame, but the effect is spoilt by the very quality of the victim. Barnaby is so often mute, or able to express himself only in snatches, that his rare moments of coherence seem mawkish and unreal. The dialogue between mother and son in prison is sentimental and stilted:

'They will not harm you,' she said, her tears choking her utterance. 'They never will harm you when they know all. I am sure they never will.'

'Oh! Don't be too sure of that,' cried Barnaby, with a strange pleasure in the belief that she was self-deceived, and in his own sagacity. 'They have marked me, from the first. I heard them say so to each other when they brought me to this place last night; and I believe them. Don't you cry for me. They said that I was bold, and so I am, and so I will be. You may think that I am silly, but I can die as well as another. – I have done no harm, have I?' he added quickly.

'None before Heaven,' she answered.

'Why then,' said Barnaby, 'let them do their worst. You told me once – you – when I asked you what death meant, that it was nothing to be feared, if we did no harm – Aha! mother, you thought I had forgotten that!'

(Chapter 73)

Barnaby's cheeriness here has a ring of composed sanity that both counters our former impression of his imbecility, and manages to undermine the intended pathos. His confusion has vanished suddenly with the phantoms and nightmares which once haunted him, and neither reader nor novelist appears to know where such stoicism has been bred.

Barnaby is not Dickens's only important simple-minded character; Smike precedes him and we look on his like again in Mr Dick, Miss Flite, and Little Dorrit's Maggie, but none of his successors has quite his prominence or his symbolic function. As a central character he is far too insipid and Dickens never really manages to establish him as a positive asset to his moral scheme. His child-like innocence is too often confounded by his sheer stupidity for the odd moments of vision or insight to counter the worse madness of so many of his elders and betters. The effect Dickens aims at is much more succinctly and powerfully caught when he tells us of the legal retribution after the end of the Riots:

Two cripples – both mere boys – one with a leg of wood, one who dragged his twisted limbs along by the help of a crutch, were hanged in this same Bloomsbury Square. As the cart was about to glide from under them, it was observed that they stood with their faces from, not to, the house they had assisted to despoil; and their misery was protracted that this omission might be remedied. Another boy was hanged in Bow Street; other young lads in various quarters of the town. Four wretched women too, were put to death. In a word, those who suffered as rioters, were, for the most part, the weakest, meanest, and the most miserable among them.

(Chapter 77)

The flatness and the baldness of the horror are allowed to speak for themselves without the cloak of theatricality which conceals the impact of Barnaby's simplicity.

Although Gordon, Barnaby, and the unnamed, but factual, wretches hanged in the streets are seen as the victims of circumstance, they are countered by sufficient villainy in the mob and beyond it. Gashford manipulates and settles personal vendettas, but even he loses control at the height of the Riots. The disturbances, the novel suggests, are rooted in pre-existent, though unspecified, grievances; the rioters themselves are variously confused, envious, hungry, drunk, vicious or simply ignorant. The rallying call of 'No Popery' is eventually lost in the confusion. The grotesque Dennis believes that he is fighting for the ancient right to hang, while Hugh, the more truly villainous of the pair, offers, in error, the real motive of many of those involved:

> 'No Popery, brother!' cried the hangman.
> 'No Property, brother!' responded Hugh.
> 'Popery, Popery,' said the secretary with his usual mildness.
> 'It's all the same!' cried Dennis. 'It's all right. Down with him, Muster Gashford. Down with everybody, down with everything! Hurrah for the Protestant religion! That's the time of day, Muster Gashford!'

> (Chapter 38)

It is a confusion which must have been echoed in urban riots, sectarian or otherwise, in many ages, and it frightens the novelist. Hugh has a delight in undoing, and he is given ample opportunity in the story to express his talent, but he is also the product of a deforming environment. His world is narrow, cruel, dirty and deprived, but it comes as no surprise to learn of his parentage.

As the obfuscating Lord Mayor suggests to Haredale, 'There are great people at the bottom of these riots'. Dickens might not go far in his analysis of the political implications of the events, but he hints darkly as to the benefits derived by men like Sir John Chester from civil disruption. In Chester, Dickens concentrates his distaste for Augustan sophistication, a sophistication which is conservative, aristocratic and pre-eminently selfish. Chester's snobbishness offends Dickens's English middle-class sensibilities, and it looks forward to the more dangerous political privilege of Monseigneur in *A Tale of Two Cities*; both men represent a corrupt and corrupting order, and both are rejected by heirs who seek a destiny away from privilege.

Chester's supercilious comment on his son's relationship with Emma
Haredale types him utterly:

> 'In a religious point of view alone, how could you ever think of
> uniting yourself to a Catholic, unless she was amazingly rich? You
> ought to be so very Protestant, coming of such a Protestant family
> as you do. Let us be moral, Ned, or we are nothing. Even if one
> could set that objection aside, which is impossible, we come to
> another which is quite conclusive. The very idea of marrying a girl
> whose father was killed, like meat! Good God, Ned, how
> disagreeable!'
>
> (Chapter 15)

Sir John rejects his son later in much the same 'moral' tone, sending
him to the devil while he dispassionately cracks a nut. When we see
him just before the Riots, he is meditating in the manner of a stage
Machiavel on the destruction of his enemies, while avoiding active
and incriminating involvement:

> 'Now really, to foment his [Gordon's] disturbances in secret,
> through the medium of such a very apt instrument as my savage
> friend here [Hugh], may further our real ends; and to express at all
> becoming seasons, in moderate and polite terms, a disapprobation
> of his proceedings, though we agree with him in principle, will
> certainly be to gain a character for honesty and uprightness of
> purpose, which cannot fail to do us infinite service, and to raise us
> into some importance. Good! So much for public grounds. As to
> private considerations, I confess that these vagabonds *would* make
> some riotous demonstration (which does not appear impossible),
> and *would* inflict some little chastisement on Haredale as a not
> inactive man among his sect, it would be extremely agreeable to
> my feelings, and would amuse me beyond measure. Good again!
> Perhaps better!'
>
> (Chapter 40)

It is hardly a subtle soliloquy, but it does show us another side to the
social evil rampant in the novel. Dickens let Chester appear, by
implication, the manipulating great man at the bottom of the Riots;
having fathered the bastard, Hugh, he disclaims responsibility; having
fostered the Riots in which Hugh plays so active a part, he stands
aside, sneering, and quietening his 'accommodating conscience' with

the assistance of the 'numerous precedents that occurred to him'.

Chester's cynicism condemns him, for it reveals a control over circumstances which is rare in *Barnaby Rudge*. The novel has a reiterated theme of madness, a theme which emerges through events as much as through characters. Any reader is likely to come away from the book impressed not so much by its characters as by the spectacular success of its descriptive passages which present an account of the progress of the Riots in London and its suburbs. The description of the burning of the Warren, for example, employs the idea of a world turned topsy-turvy and savage:

> It was not an easy task to draw off such a throng. If Bedlam gates had been flung wide open, there would not have issued forth such maniacs as the frenzy of that night had made. There were men there, who danced and trampled on the beds of flowers as though they trod down human enemies, and wrenched them from the stalks, like savages who twisted human necks. There were men who cast their lighted torches in the air, and suffered them to fall upon their heads and faces, blistering the skin with deep unseemly burns. There were men who rushed up to the fire, and paddled in it with their hands as if in water; and others who were restrained by force from plunging in, to gratify their deadly longing. On the skull of one drunken lad — not twenty, by his looks — who lay upon the ground with a bottle to his mouth, the lead from the roof came streaming down in a shower of liquid fire, white hot; melting his head like wax. When the scattered parties were collected, men — living yet, but singed as with hot irons — were plucked out of the cellars, and carried off upon the shoulders of others, ,who strove to wake them as they went along, with ribald jokes, and left them, dead, in the passages of hospitals. But of all the howling throng not one learnt mercy from, or sickened at, these sights; nor was the fierce, besotted, senseless rage of one man glutted.
>
> (Chapter 55)

The account derives much of its own ferocity and justified rage from its evocation of a reversal of human and natural values; flowers become tortured men, men animals, bodies and heads wax. The frenzy of destruction seizes minds and sears them into a madness far worse than that of a Gordon or a Barnaby. Here the horror implicit in the early stages of the novel becomes explicit, realised in the assaults on nature, twisting flower stalks as if they were necks, and paddling in fire as though it were water. The madness even has its appropriate elements of religious fanaticism, as pain is divorced from usual sensation, but Christian moral values themselves are reversed as mercy is abandoned and unlearnt, and the dead are vainly stirred with ribaldry. But the excess evoked here is given a consistency as details, each worse than the one before, are worked into a rushing, blazing movement which reflects the new movement in the novel as a whole. Dickens's creative imagination is fully at work, and if we are to consider *Barnaby Rudge* truly as 'A Tale of the Riots of 'Eighty', it is most fearfully and wonderfully so once the relatively sluggish unwinding of the private destinies of characters is transfigured by a public world of violence and madness.

This early experiment with a bipartite structure was not to be repeated when Dickens returned to historical fiction some seventeen years later. Dickens himself believed *A Tale of Two Cities* to be the best story he had written. [12] His use of the word story should be taken as indicative of his pride in a carefully considered, tight, and straightforward plot. Unlike *Barnaby Rudge* the plot of the second historical novel is developed as an argument which balances opposites and exploits parallel characters and situations. Perhaps as a consequence *A Tale of Two Cities* has proved to be amongst the most consistently popular of all his novels, and its concluding sentence is probably the most quoted in his entire work, even though its familiarity may be indirectly due to stage and screen adaptations. Amongst modern critics, however, the novel's esteem is somewhat lower; Angus Wilson, for one, regards it as Dickens's 'great middlebrow success', and others, with similar reasoning, have denied it a place with the other late novels in the shifting canon of acknowledged masterpieces. [13] It has been accused of melodrama, of underdevelopment, and of imbalance. Most frequently it is criticised not for what it is, but for what it fails to be. It is said to lack humour and animation, to be deficient in dialogue and imagery, and to be without a properly Dickensian diversity of character.

Dickens twice refers to the idea that his novel was 'picturesque', once in his Preface, and once in a letter to John Forster in August 1859. In this same letter he again stresses the importance of plot: '. . . *a picturesque* story, rising in every chapter with characters true to nature, but whom the story itself should express, more than they should express themselves, by dialogue. I mean . . . that I fancied a story of incident might be written . . . pounding the characters out in its own mortar, and beating their interests out of them.' [14] We should consider *A Tale of Two Cities*, even more so than *Barnaby Rudge*, as a story in which the line of plot suggests both motive in characters and a means of grasping a social and moral dialectic. The plot offers a scheme by which we can understand personal decision and the meaning of an historical crisis. Although it has been criticised for being un-Dickensian, we should in fact look at the novel as another Dickensian experiment, an experiment in which the novelist may be as much out of his intellectual and emotional depth as he was in the much praised *Hard Times*. Both stories attempt to describe and criticise a diseased state of society which was foreign to Dickens's own immediate experience; but, at the same time, the industrial North and Revolutionary Paris emerge as powerful imaginative images, images conveyed in a dramatic framework which had required exceptional invention on the part of the author. In both stories Dickens offers what might be considered to be a simplified analysis of a complex and confused social situation, but in both he counters any such tendency by presenting us with a fictional critique of society which is the more forceful for its exaggeration. The consequences of social disease are observed, not with an analyst's detailing, but with an imaginative rigour which conveys a far deeper understanding of an underlying human dilemma than we might at first have supposed.

A *Tale of Two Cities* is both a return to historical fiction and to the problem of mob violence. Much attention has been given to the use of the crowd and to the effect of revolutionary activity in the novel, but such attention has tended to blind us to the fact that the storming of the Bastille is really only incidental to the true line of the plot's development, and that, as opposed to *Barnaby Rudge*, the accounts of mob violence are controlled and limited to serve a particular function. Dickens avoids dwelling on the September massacres, and the worst excesses of the French Revolution, when they are described, are used so as to give particular emphasis to aspects of the carefully moulded 'picturesque' plot. Violence is in fact as much part of the *ancien régime* as it is of the Revolution. The summary executions of de Launay and Foulon, though clearly intended to shock us, are introduced to show us a purposeful vengeance on the crowd's part, and especially on Mme Defarge's part. In this they differ considerably from the scenes in *Barnaby Rudge* which suggest the arbitrary nature of a leaderless mob; the destruction of the Evrémonde château, unlike the burning of the Warren, is described impersonally and unemotionally; its destruction is an act of retribution, not of mindless fury. The crowd scenes in *A Tale of Two Cities* may be less vivid than those in its forerunner, but they are incorporated into a tighter and more artificial structure. The crowd is often more thematic than actual; a realisation of the running footsteps which echo into Dr Manette's Soho retreat, and an instrument of Fate seeking vengeance for historic injustice.

Dickens has not only diminished the splendid excess of the picture he had earlier given of the Gordon Riots, he also seems to have acknowledged that he had no real need to outwrite Carlyle. As he tells us in his Preface, he could not hope to add to Carlyle's philosophy, nor, one might assume, did he find it necessary to add to the prose *tours de force* of *The French Revolution*, already familiar to many of his prospective Victorian readers. Carlyle is at his most spectacular as a prose-writer in the very scenes which Dickens may well have contemplated imitating. The novelist's aim was not to remake *The French Revolution* as a work of fiction, but to add 'something to the popular and picturesque means of understanding that terrible time'. It is through the development of theme and character, and through the development of character through the action, that Dickens offers his own insight into 'that terrible time'. The historical events, and the crowd's part in them, are effectively incidental to the progress of a fictional story through which the novelist develops his own assertion of a faith in life and progress.

No historical figures appear as major characters in *A Tale of Two Cities*, although some, like Foulon, are observed on the margins of the main plot. As a consequence no attempt is made to interpret events through comment on the motives of a real actor. Dickens thus stands apart from the example of Scott, and of his friends Ainsworth and Bulwer, and even from his own *Barnaby Rudge*. History is examined not by a marrying of factual with fictional characters but by placing a purely fictional group into a given historical situation. Dickens has no real need to include real events during the Revolution, but when he does so he gives a greater actuality of his fiction. Thus Defarge's active involvement in the Fall of the Bastille, though it gives the reader a grasp of the popular political significance of the event, is, in terms of the plot, crucial only to the future development of Dr Manette's story. Defarge's chief interest in the storming of the prison appears to be the retrieval of the Doctor's papers rather than an attack on a symbol of royal oppression. It is through the past sufferings of Manette, the present sufferings of his family, and the final sacrifice of Sydney Carton, that we interpret the nature of the Revolution. A dialectic is established not from ideas drawn from historical events, but from an opposition of fictional characters – Darnay against Evrémonde, Manette against Defarge, Miss Pross against Mme Defarge. Reconciliation and love are placed against vengeance and hatred.[15]

As in *Barnaby Rudge*, Dickens has taken care to remind us that his story is set back in the past. We are given the date of the novel's opening – 1775 – in the third paragraph of its first chapter; at the beginning of the second Book the date 1780 is mentioned three times in as many pages. Once the pace of the story quickens during the Reign of Terror we are again reminded of particular dates and of specific events linked with that particular phase of the Revolution. This determination to fix the story in a given period effectively distinguishes the novel from its predecessor, *Little Dorrit*, and its successor, *Great Expectations*, where dates and historical circumstances once again become indeterminate, but vaguely Victorian.

Nevertheless, Dickens's concern with the details of an historical period does not extend far beyond the obvious; there is little concern with descriptions of costume, diet, speech, or manners, a concern which so obsessed Bulwer and Reade and which was to haunt George Eliot in *Romola*. Apart from the opening chapters with their comments on the state of the roads and the authorial barbs directed against the law or the unthinking prejudices of the past, there is not much sign of an interest in everyday historical detail. Dickens is not expressing his supposed contempt for history by any such indifference, for such ephemeral details as Thackeray employs in a novel like *Henry Esmond* would be out of place in one like *A Tale of Two Cities*. He is preoccupied with telling a tightly-knit story, not with seeing historical man *en déshabille*.

But the so-called scorn for the eighteenth century is perhaps reflected in one particular omission from the picture of France in the novel. Although we are shown the blatant and unpleasant consequences of Monseigneur's power and influence we are given no suggestion of his culture or his taste. Dickens probably overstates his case against the *droits du seigneur* (there is at least none of Beaumarchais' subtlety), but the positive evil committed by the Evrémondes becomes important as a sign of the festering sores of the *ancien régime*. The chapter 'Monseigneur in Town' has a satirical edge reminiscent of the descriptions of the social gatherings at Chesney Wold in *Bleak House*, but the bite of the satire is here heightened by the look forward to the certain retribution held in the future. Monseigneur is served his breakfast chocolate by four liveried lackeys, and proceeds to his morning levée, and Dickens, very much in Carlyle's manner, directs his criticism at the 'Dandiacal Body':

> . . . all the company at the grant hotel of Monseigneur were perfectly dressed. If the Day of Judgement had only been ascertained to be a dress day, everybody there would have been eternally correct. Such frizzling and powdering and sticking up of hair, such delicate complexions artificially preserved and mended, such gallant swords to look at, and such delicate honour to the sense of smell, would surely keep anything going, for ever and ever. The exquisite gentlemen of the finest breeding wore little pendant trinkets that chinked as they languidly moved; these golden fetters rang like precious little bells; and what with that ringing, and with the rustle of silk and brocade and fine linen, there was a flutter in the air that fanned Saint Antoine and his devouring hunger far away.
>
> (Book II, Chapter 7)

The exquisite gentlemen are held by their gold chains until Saint Antoine is ready for them, but like Tom-all-Alone's, he will have his revenge, sweeping away the sham and the 'leprosy of unreality'. But Dickens's remarks on the outward trappings of the French aristocracy avoid any direct reference to their artistic taste. Although the novelist himself probably found the received visual image of Monseigneur's world morally objectionable, to many of his contemporaries, from prince to parvenu, it was an image that had proved appealing since the 1820s. The *ancien régime* had chosen to picture itself, as on the one hand Elysian and pastoral, and on the other as lettered and delicately sophisticated; the impression survived not of a decaying despotism, or of an unworkable government, but of a delightfully mandarin culture rejoicing in its own urbanity. That the image was so firmly rejected both by Carlyle and Dickens is not a sign of their insensitivity to the visual arts but of the clarity of their moral vision. The attendant charms of Versailles and the salons of Paris are lost in the stark reality of a view of economic oppression and social injustice. The rococo idyll is dismissed as another of Monseigneur's perverse and leprous whims.

This disregard of the visual charms of the world of the *noblesse* allows Dickens to develop an unadorned balance of defined rights and wrongs, for throughout the book the Revolution is seen as the consequence of past and unreformed evil. The Marquis has persecuted Mme Defarge's family, and, by extension, Dr Manette, who has dared to protest at the double and un-Christian standards of a divided and stratified society. Through the relationship between the Marquis and his democratic nephew, Charles, however, Dickens suggests that there might have been a more peaceful transition between the old order and the new. Though the Revolution is a reaping of the harvest sown by Monseigneur and his order, it is Charles, the admirer of Washington and the willing relinquisher of his aristocratic rights, who shows a proper and more humane means of change. Even Dr Manette, the bourgeois surgeon and the character who has suffered most, becomes aware in the course of the novel of the healing power of reconciliation; for Manette, who has reason enough to curse the Evrémondes, his daughter's marriage to a member of his persecutor's house represents the supremacy of love over hatred, of private forgiveness over a demand for public vengeance.

The entire plot of *A Tale of Two Cities* is ordered around themes of reconciliation, sacrifice and resurrection, themes which proved to be of far less importance in *Barnaby Rudge*, but which were to be explored again, and with similar emphasis, in *Great Expectations* and *Our Mutual Friend*. *A Tale of Two Cities* shows us not simply Charles Darnay's renunciation of privilege, but also the more profound renunciation of the privileges of a revenger on Dr Manette's part, and of self-interest on Sydney Carton's. It is Carton's sacrifice which dominates the closing stages of the novel, the restless dissolute becoming the resolved instrument of grace. The fact that Dickens places these themes against a background of deep hatreds and social disorder gives some indication of the faith he places in mankind capable of redemption from the chaos it has created.

Death and resurrection run variously, but Christianly, through *A Tale of Two Cities* just as they do through *Our Mutual Friend*. The word death is repeated with something of a poetic force, and the physical phenomenon is real enough in the deaths of characters, from Barsad to Carton, and in the violence of both the *ancien régime* and the Revolution. The father of the child crushed under the wheels of Monseigneur's carriage can only repeat the single word 'dead' in his despair, while the burst wine cask in Chapter 5 of the first Book presents an image of the coming bloodshed in the same Parisian streets. It is not idly that Dickens thrice quotes the Revolutionary motto – 'Liberty, Fraternity, Equality, or Death' – noting the irony of the inclusion of its last clause. But the deaths in the novel are not purely physical, for the story opens with the mysterious idea of

Dr Manette's 'recall to life', and, throughout, prison represents, as so often in Dickens, an exclusion from life. Release into the outer world is a real resurrection for the blinking Bastille prisoners, emerging from their tomb 'all wondering and amazed, as if the Last Day were come'.

Death looms larger and more brutally than in any other of Dickens's novels, but it is here integrally linked to the idea of resurrection. Both Manette and Barsad are presumed dead before their respective recalls to life, and the idea is grimly parodied when young Jerry Cruncher is seen discovering that his father makes a second living as a 'resurrection man'. For Sydney Carton, who tells Lucie that he is 'like one who died young. All my life might have been', the idea of regeneration becomes realisable in a sacrifice of his wasted life. When he remembers the words of the burial service he has his first intimations of immortality, and Dickens intends us to take his resolution with full Christian force:

These solemn words, which had been read at his father's grave, arose in his mind as he went down the dark streets, among the heavy shadows, with the moon and the clouds sailing on high above him. 'I am the resurrection and the life, saith the Lord: he that believeth in me, though he were dead, yet shall he live: and whosoever liveth and believeth in me, shall never die.'

In a city dominated by the axe, alone at night, with natural sorrow rising in him for the sixty-three who had been that day put to death, and for to-morrow's victims then awaiting their doom in the prisons, and still of to-morrow's and to-morrow's, the chain of association that brought the words home, like a rusty old ship's anchor from the deep, might have been easily found. He did not seek it, but repeated them and went on.

(Book III, Chapter 9)

John Gross surely distorts this passage by seeing only death in Carton's surroundings and peace in his mind.[16] The two states have, as Dickens suggests, a chain of association; the death that Carton sees around him is that of a society unhinged by revenge and violence, and the half-quotation from *Macbeth* reinforces the view of the nullity of such a world. Unlike Macbeth, Carton sees a way forward in personal decision and conviction, and his sacrifice is to be positive and creative. Carton's understanding of the scriptural quotation follows Jesus's explanation of his meaning to the questioning Nicodemus; resurrection is a rebirth, one which requires the death of the old life in order to put on a new spiritual life. As such, Carton's final resolve can be seen to parallel the rebirths of Raskolnikov, Pierre Bezukhov and Prince Neklyudov in novels written, in part, under Dickens's influence. Carton's resurrection marks a reaching out to a new life, but for *A Tale of Two Cities* as a whole it is a testimony to society, and it is to be taken with full Christian force.

Carton's example is a pattern for the redemption of society. The Revolution, though the product of centuries of injustice, creates in its turn its own injustice, and works its own particular damnation. Carton redeems his wasted life by laying down that life for his friend and for the woman loved both by the friend and by him; through him, the Manette/Darnay family are able to go on to continue the process of loving reconciliation. Dr Manette forgives, not simply by forgetting his buried life in the Bastille, but also by accepting an Evrémonde as the husband of his redemptrix-daughter. In this there is some resemblance to the pattern of a Scott novel, but Dickens requires of Charles Darnay a rejection of France, rather than, as Scott might have done, a commitment to the new order. As elsewhere in Dickens there is hope for future progress, but there seems to be some lack of will in the principal characters in involving themselves in political action. Withdrawal into private benevolence and family security seems to offer more hope than an attachment to society as a whole, however corrupt that society may have appeared to be within the fictional framework. Charles's political sympathies are clearly liberal, but there is scant indication of his attitude to what is going on in France, and certainly no hint of a desire to involve himself in Revolutionary reform. It is the 'loadstone rock' of his past, the inevitability of his aristocratic fate, and personal obligation, which take him back to France. In the end he and Lucie withdrew again to relatively peaceful England, and to the quiet domestic bliss which Sydney Carton prophesies for them.[17] *A Tale of Two Cities* is an affirmative novel, but it is mutedly so. If it proclaims the supreme importance of the individual in the historical process, it shows him better able to contribute to that process by private resolve than by public action.

The reasons for this muted affirmation here are perhaps similar to those that one might adduce from the similar endings to *Bleak House, Little Dorrit* and *Great Expectations*. Society in the novel has appeared too corrupted for the redeemed individual to purge alone; he can but take a stand, play his small role, and affirm that there is hope for humanity. *A Tale of Two Cities* ends in an assertive Christian tone, but there is no indication amidst the serenity that there will be an imminent eschatological solution to the ills of the world. Throughout, Dickens has contrasted emotions and convictions, and especially love and hate, as though they had an importance beyond the temporal. When Miss Pross manfully struggles with Mme Defarge, like Christian with Apollyon, we are told that her final victory comes through the 'vigorous tenacity of love, always stronger than hate'. It is a positive force against a negative one, creation against destruction. The struggle is elemental in that neither woman understands the other's language, but both respond to a deep, intuitive, and totally possessing emotion, and of Miss Pross, as of Sydney Carton, a sacrifice is required to prove the strength of love.

The Defarges are impelled only by the uncreating force of hatred, even though the novel fully justifies the depth of their passion. Like Estella, Mme Defarge is an impressive and chilling character, educated from childhood to take her revenge. The iron entered her soul early on:

> There were many women at that time, upon whom the time laid a dreadfully disfiguring hand; but, there was not one among them more to be dreaded than this ruthless woman . . . imbued from her childhood with a brooding sense of wrong, and an inveterate hatred of a class, opportunity had developed her into a tigress. She was absolutely without pity. If she had ever had the virtue in her, it had quite gone out of her.
>
> (Book III, Chapter 14)

She is a product of evil circumstances and times, and in her Dickens concentrates his belief that retribution follows cruelty; through her he expresses his belief that hate, however justified it might be, distorts the human soul into the bestial. The reference to the tigress in her surely reminds us of Shakespeare's Queen Margaret; her lack of pity of Lady Macbeth. She has de-humanised and de-sexed herself, and, like her friend, la Vengeance, she has become the principle by which she lives. With pity dead in her, she is incapable of differentiation between the innocent and guilty, between the letter and the spirit of her controlling laws, and she is prepared to seek the blood of the Evrémondes even to the second and third generation until the greater force of Miss Pross's loving devotion prevents her.

In *The Dreamer's Stance*, Taylor Stochr criticises the intrusion of 'metaphor' into *A Tale of Two Cities* and he quotes what he considers to be a significant 'metaphoric' passage from the novel's last chapter: 'Crush humanity out of shape once more, under similar hammers, and it will twist itself into the same tortured forms. Sow the same seed of rapacious licence and oppression over again, and it will surely yield the same fruit according to its kind.' Stoehr comments on this passage: 'The oratorical tone that is so unpleasant here marks the author's withdrawal from the story in order to grind his own axe, his rather conventional moral indignation, a declaration of authorial intentions.'[18] Such a criticism stems from a misreading of Dickens's novel. The line of plot suggests how we should interpret what happens, and the authorial comment here seems to be quite apposite to his larger intentions. In no sense has the novelist withdrawn from his story, rather, he is deliberately directing us to grasp his meaning.

The directness of *A Tale of Two Cities* was stressed by John Forster in his review in the *Examiner* in 1859:

> This novel is remarkable for the rare skill with which all the powers of the author's genius are employed upon the conduct of the story. In this respect is is unequalled by any other work from the same hand. . . . It is written throughout with an energy that never wanders from its aim, a strength that uses with the subtlety of genius the resources of a studied art.[19]

It is extravagant praise, but Forster seems also to be hinting that, because of its tight, unfaltering structure there is some distinctively Dickensian ingredient missing. If *Barnaby Rudge* is a novel of transition in that it shows a darkening of themes and a deepening of Dickens's social awareness, we should not seek for the fulfilment of its intensity in the later historical novel. Despite Forster's praise, *A Tale of Two Cities* offers nothing directly comparable to the combination of energy, humour, poetic insight, diversity of character, and social criticism of the other, more extended, late novels. If Dickens's real strength as a novelist lies in his depiction of the vitality and diversity of life, his historical novels lack the breadth of his best work. This can only be explained by suggesting that history held in it nothing for Dickens quite as compelling as the present, and that the need to remedy the ills of the modern world seemed infinitely more pressing than a study of the shortcomings of the past. The earnestness of the historical novels derives from a belief that man must advance, but that he is constant in his hopefulness, his faith, and his charity. What we miss is the delight in the play of light which the novelist took for granted when he wrote about his own world, for in history the shades of the prison house seem to stretch lengthily and menacingly. Dickens was not a particularly profound or original historical novelist, but he made the historical novel his own, and through *Barnaby Rudge* and *A Tale of Two Cities* he expanded and developed the range of his own vast creativity.

5 Clio's Heroes and Thackeray's Heroes: *Henry Esmond* and *The Virginians*

No man can be a *Grand-Monarque* to his valet-de-chambre. Strip your Louis Quatorze of his king-gear, and there *is* left nothing but a poor forked radish with a head fantastically carved; – admirable to no valet. The Valet does not know a Hero when he sees him! Alas, no: it requires a kind of *Hero* to do that; – and one of the world's wants, in *this* as in other senses, is for the most part want of such.

> Carlyle: *On Heroes, Hero-Worship and the Heroic in History*;
> Lecture V: 'The Hero as a Man of Letters'.

The ancients have passed down to us examples of epic poems in which the heroes furnish the whole interest of the story, and to this day we are unable to accustom our minds to the idea that history of that kind is meaningless for our epoch.

> Tolstoi: *War and Peace*, Book III, Part 2, Chapter 19.

In March 1862 Thackeray moved into the house he had designed and built for himself at Kensington Palace Green on what were still the western fringes of London. Despite its modest classical proportions, and its sedate red brick, the house was striking and original. Like Sir Walter Scott before him, Thackeray regarded his new residence as a symbol of his success, a visible testimony to his status as an artist and a gentleman. Abbotsford had established Scott as a country landowner, as a rich man in his castle, and it had set the fashion for the Scottish baronial style which was to spread across Europe and America in the wake of the Waverley novels. Thackeray's London house would scarcely remind one of Abbotsford, but its regular and urbane façade was to have, like its designer's novels, a special impact on a city whose modern buildings tended to be Italianate and stuccoed or virulently Gothic. A particularly virulent Goth, and a co-resident in Kensington, William Burges, was later to write: 'It has been said and with great truth that the real restorer of mediaeval art was Sir Walter

Scott — in the same way, Thackeray, by means of his writing has made Queen Anne's style popular.'[1] Like Scott, the author of *Henry Esmond* was to find only a transient happiness in his new home, but, surrounded by the bric-à-brac of his favourite century in his favourite suburb, he was able to enjoy the last year of his life as a robust Victorian reflection of a quizzical Augustan man of letters.

Thackeray's fondness for Kensington and its past was nothing new, however. He had rented a house in Young Street, off Kensington Square, in 1846, when the parish had few pretensions to fashion and was little more than an adjunct to William III's rambling Palace. Streets, houses and gardens, familiar enough to his eighteenth-century characters, when a genteel enclave had flourished around the royal presence, had become daily reminders to the novelist of the object world of the reigns of Queen Anne and the first three Georges. The Castlewoods have their town house in Kensington Square in both *Henry Esmond* and *The Virginians*, and the house proves convenient for 'their service at the Palace hard by', and for their clandestine service to the Pretender to the throne. In the Palace gardens is laid the memorable, if fictional, meeting of the last Stuart Queen with her proscribed Stuart brother; at the Kensington Tavern Henry Esmond's 'love of ten years' falls down dead on the spot. When, at the end of his life, Thackeray himself contemplated continuing Macaulay's *History of England* into the reign of Anne, and providing a factual parallel to his fictional account of the period, he was able to look out over the royal palace from the upper windows of his own town house.

Thackeray's affection for the eighteenth century was not simply nostalgic, sentimental or professional; in some ways, as his long residence in Kensington suggests, it was as real as was his attachment to his own time. When he was writing *Henry Esmond* in the self-congratulatory year of the Great Exhibition, he told his mother that his novel preoccupied him 'to the exclusion of the 19th Century', but, as he also knew, the nineteenth century continued to provide him with a real and hard-earned success. His ability to translate himself backwards in time might, however, explain the ease with which Thackeray employs historical detail in his work, without there being any disquieting sense that it is an intrusion into a fluent narrative. He had a scrupulously researched picture of the historical period he described, but he also had a serious, considered, and informed view of history. Unlike Bulwer-Lytton, or even George Eliot, he was also able to take history easily. If he professed to prefer the eighteenth century to the nineteenth, it is also clear that in his stories he examines the past with the same detached, critical, satirical eye with which he studied the society of his contemporaries; he loves and hates, supports and undermines, two worlds which are more alike than they are disparate. All of Thackeray's novels are equally deficient in heroes, and those 'heroes' of the past elevated by conventional historians into supermen, are, from the novelist's viewpoint, as open to criticism as any fictional character. The great and the humble exhibit moral foibles as much as they share more destructive vices or considerable virtues. He sees man everywhere as equal, and in the round, whether as the subject of Anne or George IV or Victoria, and regardless of his position on a social or philosophical ladder. It is an egalitarian vision which sees the past as vividly as the present, the sovereign as critically as the subject, and history itself as a series of questionable and unheroic human decisions.

The formal opening of *Henry Esmond* is in some senses a substitute for an epic invocation of Clio. It is in marked contrast to the direct beginnings of *Vanity Fair* and *Pendennis* and even to the fabular opening of *The Newcomes*, but like them it presents us with ideas which are to be considered, developed and qualified in the course of the narrative. To Thackeray's narrator, Clio appears in disguise and untrue to herself; she is addressed indirectly:

> The Muse of History hath encumbered herself with ceremony as well as her Sister of the Theatre. She too wears the mask and the cothurnus, and speaks to measure. She too, in our age, busies herself with the affairs only of kings; waiting on them, obsequiously and stately, as if she were but a mistress of Court ceremonies, and had nothing to do with the registering of the affairs of the common people.
>
> (Book I)

Esmond demands that the Muse be raised from her courtly knees, and be led from palaces and theatres into the clear light of the world beyond, a world where masks and costumes can be seen for what they are. Posterity, we are told, will judge an age differently from myopic contemporaries, and critical detachment will reveal the nature of human frailty. Historical 'truth' has been distorted by the hero-worshippers: 'In a word, I would have History familiar rather than heroic: and think that Mr. Hogarth and Mr. Fielding will give our children a much better idea of the manners of the present age in

England, than the *Court Gazette* and the newspapers which we get thence.' Henry Esmond is echoing his creator's sentiments. Much as Fielding had referred to Hogarth for a parallel or for clarification of a visual point, Thackeray refers us to both the painter and the novelist to stress that art gives a truer picture of life than the conventional historical account. The novel does not simply amplify or outdo history, as it does for Bulwer-Lytton, it is to be preferred as a more trustworthy guide. The novel, Thackeray implies through his fictional narrator, records in detail the minutiae of human experience and shows them to be equal to the grand gestures. Joyce was to experiment in a different way with a similar fictional idea. The great man and his actions are to be rendered equivalent to the daily routine or to the imprecision of humble resolve; the hero, rendered human and fallible, plays his part in the same pattern as the fool and the coward. As a consequence, our judgement of Thackeray's fiction, and especially of his historical fiction, must be relative to his belief in human equality and human imperfection.

Thackeray's faith in art and his distrust of conventional history had been publicly outlined in his 'Lectures on the English Humourists' and it is these Lectures which contain the germ of *Henry Esmond*. In his introduction to Steele, who appears later as a prominent character in the novel, Thackeray outlines his suspicion of history books and historical memoirs:

> I doubt all autobiographies I ever read except those, perhaps, of Mr. Robinson Crusoe, Mariner, and writers of his class. *These* have no object in setting themselves right with the public or their own consciences; these have no motive for concealment or half-truths; these call for no more confidence than I can cheerfully give, and do not force me to tax my credulity or to fortify it by evidence. . . . Out of the fictitious book I get the expression of the life of the time. . . . Can the heaviest historian do more for me?[2]

This assertion begs many historical questions, but puts forward an independent and radical viewpoint which is amplified in the fiction. Scott's dramatisation of history, and his grasp of the relationship between the individual and society, had had a considerable impact on historians like Macaulay and Carlyle. Although Thackeray much admired Macaulay's complex expository scheme, he was determined that his own historical fiction should advance beyond a broad study of the cultural and political aspects of a given period. His reaction to

Carlyle is similar, for though Carlyle had seen history as composed of innumerable biographies, and history itself as the 'Biography of Great Men', Thackeray does not simply expose the 'sham' hero by discovering truer ones; he shows 'heroism' itself to be a false and distorting concept. He is arguing something more radical than either of his contemporaries – that history is better understood through the unbiased and critical eyes of a novelist. Detail can be legitimately verified from proven sources, but the real spirit of an age eludes all except the artist who, unlike the historian, neither seeks to draw conclusions from what he observes, nor necessarily finds a moral pattern in the process he describes.

Georg Lukács's criticism of *Henry Esmond* relates it both to the Waverley novels and to the wider European tradition, but his comparison with Scott is especially pointed in that both novelists deal with Jacobitism and the attendant threat of social disorder. Lukács sees Scott as offering 'a broad and *objective* picture both of the historical forces which lead to the Stuart rebellions and those which inevitably foredoom them'. Thackeray, on the other hand, 'does not see the people', he reduces his story to 'the intrigues of the upper classes' and thereby dispels 'historical objectivity'.[3] Lukács's method of contrasting a fictional analysis of the individual to a broader historical and political perspective results in the conclusion that Thackeray's example is ultimately less significant to the history of the novel than the work of Scott or Tolstoi, and, given the premises of his critical argument, such an opinion has a certain validity. Alternatively, however, *Henry Esmond* can be seen not as a critique of an historical crisis in social terms, but as a radical examination of the individual within society. For Thackeray, and for Henry Esmond, and George and Harry Warrington, taking sides in a political conflict is as much a private decision as a public one, and no decision is clear-cut and unbiased. The development and climax of *Henry Esmond*, for instance, is as dependent on Harry's love for Beatrix as it is on his disillusion with the character and cause of the Jacobite Pretender. The novel does not assert moral positives against such negatives, it constantly challenges positives and easy socio-historical assumptions. Harry's ultimate acknowledgement of his love for Rachel Castlewood, though it has been suggested throughout and though it marks the end of Harry's emotional development, hardly resolves the political problem posed by the novel. At the end Harry, like the Pretender, bows out of the political arena, and moves physically, as much as symbolically, to a new world. It could be argued, with some justice, that Lukács simply misses Thackeray's point. His statement that the novelist counters an exposure of false heroism with an emphasis on 'a genuine, inner nobility of simple morality' seems wide of the mark, as does his assertion that Thackeray turns his good characters into 'tedious, insufferable paragons of virtue'. The questioning of heroes extends as much to the narrator as it does to the Pretender or to Marlborough, and it is the very nature of this questioning which gives the novel its distinctive, if sometimes disconcerting, stature.

In no sense does the novelist look back on the past in search of a lost innocence or an ideal civilisation. like Fielding before him he acknowledges that though clothes, manners and expressions change, man himself remains recognisable, physically and morally, in whatever century he is observed. Elements in such a view of the past can perhaps be related to Gordon Ray's assertion that 'a knowledge of forebears is more essential in understanding William Makepeace Thackeray than any other English novelist'.[4] The belief that a grandfather of his had married a descendant of General Webb's certainly determined the generous treatment of the General's character in *Henry Esmond*. A preoccupation with ancestors and families, however, runs through all of Thackeray's works. Ray also cites the case of a contemplated novel, to be set in in the time of Henry V, 'which would be his *capo d'opera*, in which the ancestors of all his characters, Warrington's, Pendennis's, and the rest would be introduced'.[5] Even without this projected novel there are sufficient blood links between books to justify the assertion, the most significant being the continuation of *Henry Esmond* into *The Virginians*. Through passing reference to 'Sir Wilmot Crawley, of Queen's Crawley' (*Henry Esmond* Book 1, Ch. 5) a simple link forward to characters in *Vanity Fair* is made. Thackeray is not simply playing a game with his readers, as Trollope may be accused of doing, nor is he trying to make his novels into a loose family chronicle, he is demonstrating an intimate connection between the past and the present. The interplay of fictional and factual references within the narrative suggests that we must accept the 'reality' of the whole imagined situation in a complex manner. The imagined world is not an escape from modern reality; it is seen to be as open to criticism as any other world, real or unreal. The eighteenth-century novels are in this way at least of the same 'type' as those set in Thackeray's own age; his criticism does not extend over two different societies, but over an England which is substantially unchanged despite shifts in political and social fashions.

Henry Esmond is, however, as much a new development of the historical novel as it is an extension of Thackeray's own art as a novelist. The individual quality of his art is suggested by Anthony Trollope, perhaps his most dedicated Victorian admirer, in his comment on *Vanity Fair*: 'The nature of the tale . . . was altogether unlike that to which readers of modern novels had been used. No plot, with an arranged catastrophe or *denoument* (sic), was necessary.'[6] To Trollope, *Henry Esmond*, was 'the greatest work that Thackeray did'; more ambitiously planned than any of Thackeray's preceding novels, and a self-conscious attempt to imitate the style and manner of the fiction of the previous century. It was planned as a unit, and was published in three volumes instead of the monthly parts to which Thackeray and his readers were accustomed. The original format was impressive and contrived to a particular effect; the volumes were printed in old type face, with running titles at the head of each page, and without illustrations.[7] No clearer visual link with Defoe, Fielding and Richardson could have been established. Although a significant emotional distress influenced the style and shape of the tale, it was written at a leisurely pace, without the imposed strains of serial publication.[8] As a consequence *Henry Esmond* is in most senses the most artfully worked of Thackeray's novels, and, as its epigraph insists, it pursues the development of a single dominant character more consistently than any other of his works. This 'consistency' and the single, involved narrator are vital elements in Thackeray's distinctive approach to historical fiction in *Henry Esmond*; the diminishing of their importance in *The Virginians* seems to me to contribute to its comparative failure as a novel.

In a review of *Henry Esmond* published in the *Spectator* in 1852 the critic George Brimley contrasts Thackeray's manner with Sir Walter Scott's. Brimley was disturbed by Thackeray's habit of 'looking at the actors in life from the side-scenes and in the green room rather than from before the footlights'.[9] As if in anticipation of Lukács, Brimley is disquieted by the lack of epic sweep in *Henry Esmond*. Scott's resolution of fictional and historical problems, through a guidance of his characters to a state of emotional and political maturity, depends upon the reader's acceptance of, and sympathy with, his heroes; if the sympathy fails, so does the proper resolution of the historical issue discussed in the novel. Neither *Vanity Fair* nor *Henry Esmond* leads to that variety of moral conclusion in which all the elements of the plot fall into a positive perspective. Nothing is proved, at least in terms of a thesis to which the novel is directed.

Unlike Scott, Thackeray is a disconcerting writer; shades of good and bad, determination and vacillation, honour and selfishness, are to be found everywhere, not because the novelist himself vacillates but because he sees his characters as being capable of doing so.

Unlike many Victorian historical novels, *Henry Esmond* is neither a *roman à thèse*, nor a study of social development, though much of its action is dependent upon the concept of loyalty to the legitimate sovereign, and upon the acceptance of a *de facto* dynasty as expressive of the will of the majority. Thackeray starts not with the Whig prejudices of his time, even Macaulay's, but with a dissenting hero whose ultimate conformity results from a confusion of motives, private, public and political. Ultimately, Thackeray comes close to the norm of *Waverley, Rob Roy, Woodstock* or *The Heart of Midlothian* in his interpretation of the social consequences of revolution, independence and advance; what divides him from Scott is the choice of emphasis.

In *Henry Esmond*, and later, to a lesser extent, in *The Virginians*, the process of rendering history 'familiar rather than heroic' takes precedence over Scott's method of humanising an historical situation. As a consequence the 'great men' figure far less vividly than do the fictional characters, although Thackeray clearly enjoyed and saw the importance of introducing historical persons on the periphery of his novels. In *Henry Esmond* there are brief episodes concerning Queen Anne, Addison, Swift and General Webb, and more extended studies of the characters of the Pretender, Marlborough and Steele. In *The Virginians* Washington and General Wolfe make significant and, to some Victorians, vexing appearances, while George II, the Prince of Wales, Richardson, and Dr Johnson are glimpsed critically by fictional observers. Further to this, the very structure of *Henry Esmond* could be said to be an expansion on the idea of a 'familiarisation' of history. Clio's heroes, the historical celebrities, are seen, by virtue of the autobiographical narrative, through the narrator's eyes; his personal limitations, likes, dislikes and tastes, and not necessarily those of the novelist, account for the particular treatment of any one of the celebrities. Harry objects personally to Marlborough as an acquaintance and as a general, and to Swift as an acquaintance and a satirist; the picture the novel gives us of the two men is founded purely on Harry's jaundiced opinion. The great men are seen publicly and privately by a biased but observant contemporary; the reader of the novel is free, however, both to add to the picture his knowledge of a character from another source (either history or biography) and in turn to recognise and judge Harry's prejudices.

The political crisis of the novel's concluding chapters is as dependent on Harry's personal interest as on the appearance and disappearance of the Pretender. Through his eyes and by means of his memory, we observe events upon which the future destiny of England depends. The Royalist and Jacobite cause has been a feature of the novel from its second chapter, which traces the fortunes of the Esmond family and their attachment to the Stuarts. Throughout the novel the Jacobite interest has been the centre of Harry's romantic, national and royalist aspirations, even though he warns us at the very beginning that not all political exiles are as worthy of respect as Addison's Cato. The introductory remarks of the narrator emphasise the unheroic nature of a 'fugitive Cato fuddling himself at a tavern with a wench on each knee' but the full import of the remark is left until we are eventually shown the Prince in the flesh and witness with the narrator the squandering of the philandering Prince's throne.

In the early stages of the novel, the Stuart cause has the romance of being a lost one, and a dangerous one. The presence of Fr Holt gives it a slightly sinister edge, but the machinations of old Lady Castlewood are dramatic if comically inefficient. The young Harry is increasingly aware that he is a member of a household overshadowed by intrigue and by an emotional adherence to the old order:

> . . . they were in the deepest state of dejection, for King James had been banished, the Prince of Orange was on the throne, and the direst persecutions of those of the Catholic faith were apprehended by my lady. . . . My Lord and lady were in a manner prisoners in their own house; so her ladyship gave the little page to know, who was by this time growing of an age to understand what was passing about him, and something of the characters of the people he lived with.
>
> (Book I, Ch. 5)

Harry's judgements are evidently sharpening. Although the influence of Fr Holt wanes, and Harry's opinions develop independently, he is never able fully to excuse the Churchills for their unfaithfulness while the Esmonds suffer for their loyalty. Harry matures politically, but his adherence to the Stuart dynasty remains until the end a romantic illusion of right and virtuous acting. Even though he comes to admit (in Book II, Ch. 3) that King William has proved to be 'the wisest, the bravest, and the most clement sovereign whom England ever knew', he is constrained to add that 'loyalty to the exiled King's family was traditional . . . in that house to which Mr. Esmond belonged'.

This Jacobitism is periodically re-asserted, and, as the second great political crisis of the novel develops – that concerning the Hanoverian succession – Harry is in no doubt as to where true loyalty leads him. The prospect of a German heir being preferred to the Stuarts by a self-interested parliament stretches the true-born Englishman's faith in legitimacy and natural justice:

> That a foreign despotic prince, out of Germany, who happened to be descended from King James the First, should take possession of this empire, seemed to Mr. Esmond a monstrous injustice – at least, every Englishman had a right to protest, and the English Prince, the heir-at-law, the first of all. What man of spirit with such a cause would not back it? What man of honour with such a crown to win would not fight for it?
>
> (Book III, Ch. 1)

Harry's very words betray his prejudice, though, as Thackeray must have sensed in giving them to him, the reader may well be approaching the political situation with different prejudices and be judging Harry accordingly. To the Esmonds, the reception of 'the English Prince, the heir-at-law' is a matter of honour; the consequence of their action is not only temporary public dishonour, but a private slight brought upon the house by the Prince's uncontrolled sexual passion. At the end of the novel its various strands are moulded with great subtlety; and we are aware increasingly of the confused passions and motives which are leading Harry to a conflict with himself. Harry even appears to find it difficult in retrospect to distinguish clearly between love and conviction. His political hopes face disillusion while his tortured and entangled love for Beatrix is put to its final, decisive test. The 'English Prince' proves to be only a Frenchified roué who fails to show the least sign of honour or heroism; his political moment is squandered through sexual indiscretion and it is his hosts who suffer the double indignity of his action.

Henry Esmond's terse description and interpretation of the concluding scenes convey both his initial confusion and his subsequent determination. The 'King' is compromised, by a fine touch of irony on Thackeray's part, by Beatrix's note in the *Eikon Basilike* –

'the image of the King' — and the Royalists' chief means of beatifying Charles I. The Pretender bows his way out while Harry's love for Beatrix collaspses finally with painful, but inevitable abruptness:

> But her keen words gave no wound to Mr. Esmond; his heart was too hard. As he looked at her, he wondered that he could ever have loved her. His love of ten years was over; it fell down dead on the spot, at the Kensington Tavern, where Frank brought him the note out of the *Eikon Basilike*. The Prince blushed and bowed low, as she gazed at him, and quitted the chamber. I have never seen her from that day.
>
> (Book III, Ch. 13)

The sudden switch to the first person from his habitual use of the third person emphasises Harry's continuing involvement and his commitment to the events he later describes. The movement is final, but it is also the last stage in the process of maturing for the narrator. The Stuart Pretender proves himself unworthy both of private respect and of public loyalty. If this knowledge does not alter the compromised position of the Esmonds, it at least marks their awareness of the shabby reality.

It is essential to Thackeray's approach to history that we witness the débâcle through Harry's eyes, and that Harry is emotionally involved with the events he recalls. His disillusion is sudden, but it signals the painful achievement of significant experience. The failed revolutionary is one with the scorned lover, and embarrassed by what happens. The episode is also the climactic event of Harry's life: 'With the sound of King George's trumpets, all the vain hopes of the weak and foolish young Pretender were blown away; and with that music too, I may say, the drama of my own life was ended.' (Book III, Ch. 13) The narrator points to the immediacy of the memory again by lapsing into the first person. The use of the word 'Pretender' here insists that Harry has ceased to acknowledge him as King, and he now recognises the 'pretence' of the Jacobite claim. Harry's use of the word 'drama' also recalls his opening warning of the twin deceits of Clio and Melpomene; Harry's emotional defeat at this point is no more really 'tragic' than the Pretender is 'heroic'. The final mood is one of regret which underlines a new sense of self-knowledge and awareness of human frailty. Human emotions, Thackeray implies, rarely rise to the heightened pitch of the Classical stage. Henry

Esmond's 'drama' has not been plotted or willed by Fate, rather he has drifted into a melancholy love affair, and merely followed a family bias in his loyalty to the Stuarts; he publicly suffers little for either. Much as Scott's heroes do, he reaches a point of decision and achieves as a result some new kind of balance and reward. In Thackeray's scheme, however, the analysis of the historical and social evolution is countered by the demands of the novelist's particular view of realism. The grand design of Epic is avoided as much as are the attendant heroics. The final stress is on Harry's gain of private contentment, and on his withdrawl into voluntary exile away from a political and cultural centre. He avoids involvement in the new order or Georgian England. Life in Virginia is not untroubled or serene, but at least its pressures and conflicts can be seen clearly and more maturely than could those which marked the 'drama' which appears to have ended.

Henry Esmond concludes in a mood of resignation, with a deliberate underplaying of the final union of Harry with his 'mistress'. Thackeray has frequently been accused of giving insufficient indication of the growth and realisation of their love. In 1852, for example, G. H. Lewes found the love of Harry and Rachel *'vrai'* but not always *'vraisemblable'*. John Forster's doubts were deeper; even Thackeray's clear hints as to the proper conclusion, he wrote, 'cannot induce us to accept or tolerate such a set of incidents as these. The thing is incredible, and there's an end on't'.[10] The root of such disquiet lies surely in a basic misunderstanding of Thackeray's conception of the character of his narrator. The criticism that the novelist throws away the end of his novel in hurried and confused incident also stems from a misreading of the manner in which the story is told. The success or failure of *Henry Esmond* is as dependent upon the reader's acceptance of Harry as autobiographer, as an acceptance of the extraordinary events in *Jane Eyre* is dependent upon a belief in the narrator's veracity. Thackeray has conceived his narrative as the autobiographical recollections of a fictional character involved in the events he recounts and the novel is more of a study of a single central character than is any other of his works. Harry not only 'makes' the plot by witnessing all that passes, he is also the unifying factor, bringing into a single line of narrative disparate events of a remembered life. Scott's detachment is here supplanted by the personal involvement of the central character who is the sole guide to what happens. The proper reading of *Henry Esmond* both as an historical novel and as an independent work of fiction, depends therefore upon our assent to the autobiographical form which Thackeray chose to employ.

The importance of the novel's epigraph has not always been acknowledged. The original title page, on which the novelist's name does not appear, testifies that the 'history' is by Esmond himself. To this is added a Latin quotation, in the eighteenth century manner, taken from Horace's *Ars Poetica*. Rendered in full, the quotation translates as 'If you . . . are so bold as to invent a new character, be sure that it remains the same throughout as it was in the beginning, and is entirely consistent'. (Si . . . audes/Personam formare novam; servitur ad imum/Qualis ab incepto processerit, et sibi constet. *Ars Poetica* 125–7.) This very idea of 'consistency' surely refers us both to the unity of the narrative, and to the conception of the character of the autobiographical narrator. From Harry come not only the novel's shape and style, but also its mood.

As work progressed on *Henry Esmond* one thought dominated Thackeray's references to the novel in his letters. He wrote to Lady Stanley of 'a book of cutthroat melancholy suitable to my state', and, a month later, in a letter to his mother, he describes the first volume as being 'frightfully glum'. After receiving Charlotte Brontë's comments on a part of the manuscript he assumed that her criticism of the novel as 'admirable and odious' again related to its 'melancholy'. Perhaps most revealing are the novelist's remarks to his mother; the book is again described as 'grand and melancholy' while Harry himself is 'as stately as Sir Charles Grandison . . . a handsome likeness of an ugly son of yours'.[11] The link back to Richardson, and to a man torn between two women, perhaps clarifies the essentially un-Byronic nature of Harry's melancholy but the link with the novelist himself has been more open to misconstruction. Gordon Ray has rightly observed personal elements in the novel's plot and has stressed the manner in which the sorrows of young Esmond reflect those of the young and the mature Thackeray. It is also clear from the novelist's letters that the book was written at a time when the pains of the love affair with Jane Brookfield were most affecting his emotional state. It is clear that the gloom which hangs over the opening parts of the novel echoes the novelist's depression, and that the central character shares his creator's melancholy. There the parallel ends. Harry's melancholy is the determining feature in the development of both the private and the public themes of the book, but his mental state is a constant which scarcely reflects the ebullience of Thackeray's other novels, or of his other major characters. Harry's psychological

condition gives him a certain world-view which is appropriate to the
events and dilemmas he describes. The 'consistency' of the historical
viewpoint thus depends upon the 'consistent' conception of the
narrator as a melancholic.

Harry, whom the Pretender characterises, with rare perception, as
'le grand sérieux', reveals himself throughout as a depressive. His
memoirs form a meditation on his past life by a character whom
others note as being pensive and withdrawn. To his fellow under-
graduates Harry is 'Don Dismallo', while the Coffee House set in
London see him as a kind of Don Quixote, a 'knight of the sorrowful
countenance'. To Beatrix, in pique, he is 'Graveairs'. Harry is inclined
to dwell on wrongs inflicted upon him, forgiving a Marlborough or a
Swift with his reason not with his heart; the narrator's critical opinion
of both is accordingly coloured unfavourably. His love for Beatrix is
unrequited and agonising, but it is fostered even when there is no
hope; his love for Rachel remains unconscious, real enough, but
seemingly unrealisable. Like David Copperfield and Jane Eyre, Henry
Esmond is a lonely child who longs to love and be loved; like them his
heart needs discipline, but, like David (and Arthur Pendennis), he
learns late in his story the true direction for his love. As a child Harry
moves from house to house, guardian to guardian, language to
language, religion to religion. Even though he seems to share less of a
sense of desertion than David or Jane, he experiences a greater
emotional, temperamental, moral and educational upheaval than
they do. He shares their critical intelligence, but lacks their achieved
self-confidence and self-assurance.

Harry's separation from his parents, his early ignorance of them,
and his consequent belief that he is a bastard, fosters his sense of being
an outsider, and of being detached from, and unsure of, his
relationships. He is as much the consistently thwarted lover as he is a
thwarted conspirator. He achieves some modest success as a writer, as
a soldier, and as a friend, but we are aware that he develops
emotionally as he experiences. He writes retrospectively from an
achieved position of maturity. The lonely, politically involved child,
is father to the man who only slowly grasps the meaning of his
experience. He describes his sense of rejection while in prison:

At certain periods of life we live years of emotion in a few weeks —
and look back on those times, as on great gaps between the old life
and the new. You do not know how much you suffer in those
critical maladies of the heart, until the disease is over, and you look

back on it afterwards. . . . Esmond thought of his early time as a
noviciate, and of this past trial as an initiation before entering into
life. . . .

(Book II, Ch. 1)

Though his childhood seems to be a 'noviciate' as he describes it, his
adult life also forms a further period of preparation for his acceptance
of Rachel and of the emptiness of his political aspirations. Like Jacob,
he has to prove himself worthy of his love for a Rachel. Harry relives
his depression as he writes, even though he will on occasion remind
us, in an interpolated Virginian reflection, of a future understanding
of past experience. He records events as they happened, but in spite of
the retrospect of his impersonal use of the third person, a degree of
confusion is apparent.[12] Much in his account works by inference or
suggestion, little by self-analysis. His love is divided and sometimes
secret, and like his political opinions it is strained, ambiguous and
compromised.

There is no authorial voice in *Henry Esmond* which prompts or
interprets for us. What promptings there are, are ambiguous. The
ambiguity stems from an element in the character of the narrator;
Harry's ambiguity, his involvement as well as his detachment, are
vital to the novel's historical viewpoint as much as they are to its view
of character. Other characters are developed through a seemingly
random selection of incidents, each one of which qualifies or clarifies
our understanding. Our impression of Beatrix in particular is built on
contraries and on opposed insights. The difference between the
authorial treatment of a Becky Sharp or an Arthur Pendennis on the
one hand and Beatrix on the other is that our view of her is recorded
by an increasingly involved narrator and not by an observant and
critical puppet-master. Beatrix is seen growing from the spoilt child,
of whom Harry is able to record that she will 'always forsake an old
friend for a new one' (Book I, Ch. 2), into the temptress of such 'a
dazzling completeness of beauty' upon whom he dwells so lovingly.
He records adverse comment, but chiefly remembers her physical
presence, in glances, or in the blaze of her eyes, even after the passage
of years. She is the enthraller of Amadis, she is Euridice, and she is
Helen, but she is still an object of passion and unreasoning adoration:

Esmond's mistress had a thousand faults beside her charms: he
knew both perfectly well! She was imperious, she was light-
minded, she was flighty, she was false, she had no reverence in her

character; she was everything, even in beauty, the contrast of her mother, who was the most devoted and the least selfish of women. Well, from the first moment he saw her on the stairs at Walcote, Esmond knew he loved Beatrix.

(Book II, Ch. 15)

The ambiguity of Harry's emotion is here deftly suggested, even his use of the word 'mistress' (the term by which he usually refers to Rachel). Beatrix's faults are excused by the lover who seems, even in retrospect, to love the vision he saw at Walcote, yet amidst the recall comes an immediate comparison and contrast with the mother. It is this doubleness both in Beatrix, and in Harry's love, which indicates the narrator's limited self-knowledge, for his melancholy defeatism blinds him to the implications betrayed to the reader by his words.

Akin to Harry's tendency to introspection and self-absorption is his passivity. It too contributes to his 'un-heroic' pose in the novel. Harry is, for the most part, a passive observer; things happen to him without his striving to make his heroic destiny. Like Tom Jones or Daniel Deronda he begins with the assumption that he is a noble bastard, but, having found out the truth of his birth by a mid-point in the novel, he gives up all claim to his rightful inheritance and attempts to conceal the true facts out of a sense of obligation to the Esmond family. His action, we sense, is selfless and virtuous, and it shows how different is his quest from those of Fielding's and George Eliot's heroes. No fortune depends upon his marrying well, nor does the mystery of his birth lead to any new spiritual insight. By the beginning of Book III he is 'if not rich at least easy for life' by means of the dowager Lady Castlewood's legacy; at the end of the novel he accepts, and enjoys, exile. Thackeray seems deliberately to avoid employing any device which might keep the reader in suspense as to Harry's worldly prospects for fame and fortune, or for his achievement of Beatrix. She may at times seem as unobtainable as Sophia Western, but both the narrator and reader acknowledge that no lasting satisfaction is to be found with her, and that Harry's dilemma is not to be resolved in such a marriage. His love for Beatrix is deep and romantic, for Rachel it is deeper still, yet unconscious. The love which exists for the two women leads him to deny his legal rights, and to reject his proper station in society. Happiness, Thackeray suggests, lies beyond the claims of honour and title, and beyond heroics and ultimately, the 'unhistorical acts' have, as in George Eliot's fiction, the greater and profounder significance. In the end, it is love 'immeasurably above all ambition, more precious than wealth, more noble than name' which leads Harry and Rachel to the Indian Summer of the New World and the relative placidity of the closing pages of the novel.

The major characters withdraw from Hanoverian England and from their position in the new political and social framework. It is surprisingly unlike the gestures with which Scott so often chooses to end his historical novels. Harry is seeking a new beginning; his future will not necessarily be easy, but it is at least a-political, and the society he chooses to join is as yet untroubled by a long historical memory. Despite Lukács' strictures, the final withdrawl does not serve to stress just the 'inner nobility of simple morality'; it is the proper extension of Harry's former rôle in English Society. He has been an outsider from childhood, not only as a presumed bastard, but as a sensitive melancholic. He is, at the beginning, isolated from the national Church — both as a Huguenot and as a Papist — and isolated from the surrounding community by the political opinions of his adopted family. Even with them he is separated by his youth and his intelligence from the intrigues which surround him; he observes both sides as culpable — the Viscountess clumsily conceals papers in her bed, while the soldiers who discover them have insufficient Latin to decipher them. Later Harry comes clearly to acknowledge the flaws in both the Jacobite creed and in the Jacobite Pretender, but feels drawn by ties of blood to the historic loyalty which keeps him separate from the Whig mainstream in English politics and the arts. Again Harry sees both parties at fault; a Marlborough is balanced politically by a Swift, but both are time-servers. Harry's world is as corrupt and corrupting as the Regency England of *Vanity Fair*, but he never fully attaches himself to any social group, party or institution. He involves himself, for the most part, where he chooses, as a soldier, or a writer, or an intriguer, but in all he keeps an independent and critical mind, more concerned with his love for women than with a wider social commitment. As he remarks in the second chapter of the third book, all men aim for some goal, but the goal shifts according to the man:

> There's some particular prize we all of us value, and that every man of spirit will venture his life for. With this it may be to achieve a great reputation for learning; with that, to be a man of fashion, and the admiration of the town; with another, to consummate a great work of art or poetry, and go down to immortality that way; and

with another, for a certain time of his life, the sole object and aim is a woman.

Harry is speaking at this point of his passion for Beatrix, but we are shown in the end that his search ends in Rachel and that his love for her is the one that conquers all. In his happy marriage lies the security and peace of mind which have eluded him elsewhere and which counters the hollowness he has found in all other human activity. The quiet tone of the novel's almost terse conclusion stresses both this achieved content, and the importance of a detached and impartial view of man, his society and his history. The world, as we were reminded after the death of Beatrix's betrothed, the Duke of Hamilton, is indifferent to human suffering — 'night and day pass away, and tomorrow comes, and our place knows us not'. At the end of the novel the lovers show themselves to be indifferent to the outward show of the world, but still involved in living their lives together. Any possible impact they may have had on 'history' consequently seems irrelevant.

The conclusion of *Henry Esmond* emphasises Thackeray's belief that fictional autobiography, like Robinson Crusoe's had a greater significance than did the biography of the 'great man'. Human endurance counts for more in the long run than a title or a remembered name, and endurance is constant in all ages. From fiction comes 'the expression of the life of the time' and it is ultimately timeless, and truthful. Thackeray is not merely composing fiction in *Henry Esmond*, he makes his narrator a conscious and artful writer. Like David Copperfield, Harry is a man of letters, and as Carlyle had informed the audience of *On Heroes and Hero Worship*, the man of letters was 'our most important modern person'. We hear of Harry as a moderately successful dramatist and poet; 'The Faithful Fool, a Comedy' is actually performed, despite its sentiment, and we see an example of his work as an essayist, but we are continually aware of him as autobiographer. He is consciously arranging and analysing his experience, part of which was, and perhaps remains, ambiguous. Recall is often painful, but it is necessary to the faithful representation of the complex life of one man:

> Who in the course of his life, hath not been so bewitched, and worshipped some idol or another? Years after this passion hath been dead and buried, along with a thousand other worldly cares and ambitions, he who felt it can recall it out of its grave, and

admire, almost as fondly as he did in his youth, that lovely queenly creature. I invoke that beautiful spirit from the shades and love her still; or rather I should say such a past is always present to a man; such a passion once felt forms a part of his whole being, and cannot be separated from it; it becomes a portion of the man of today, just as any great faith or conviction, the discovery of poetry, the awakening of religion, ever afterwards influence him; just as the wound I had at Blenheim, and of which I wear the scar, hath become part of my frame and influenced my whole body, nay, spirit subsequently, though 'twas got and healed forty years ago. Parting and forgetting! What faithful heart can do these? Our great thoughts, our great affections, the Truths of our life, never leave us. Surely, they cannot separate from our consciousness; shall follow it whithersoever that shall go; and are of their nature divine and immortal.

(Book III, Ch. 6)

At other points Harry suggests the painful or surprising tricks of memory. At the very end of the first Book he remembers the fireside tile, showing Jacob cheating Esau of his birthright, lit up with the flame of the burning paper which holds the truth of his own birth. He feels young again as he recalls Beatrix as a paragon of whom 'no single movement of hers but was beautiful', and he hears the delightful music of her voice again as he remembers her laughing exchanges with the Pretender. The very shape of the memoirs is due to the shaping art of Henry Esmond as he orders his experience. In this way we see the historical events recounted in the novel as part of the life of one man. An opinion of history is expressed which relates the experience of the individual to the broader notion of human experience. Thackeray's idea of history is thus developed by a complex narrator who both exposes the idea of 'heroism' and imposes upon history his own 'familiar' pattern. There is a single time-scheme — that of the narrator's past experience — but within it remembered time becomes inseparable from chronicled time. The historical events included in the narrative give Thackeray a crucial further dimension to his already subtle play with the moulding of Esmond's knowable and remembered past.

It is the un-heroic qualities in Harry which guide the history on its 'familiar' course. The emphases, as well as the omissions, in the historical perspective are Harry's own. The great creators of complex plots, Jonson, Fielding, or, to some extent, Dickens, order experience within a pattern which in some way resolves the emotional and moral problems posed within a story. Thackeray is a moralist of a different order; he presents his subject in a 'realist' manner which apparently disguises a tidy shaping pattern and an easy moral. Positive virtues are nowhere embodied in single figures, and virtue rarely appears to be positively rewarded. Vices, both smaller and greater, are prevalent in a whole range of character and incident. In *Henry Esmond* Thackeray presents a scrupulously 'invented' picture of life, yet the invention itself represents the arbitrary and ambiguous nature of human experience. Events seem casual or indecisive, characters ambivalent or flawed. But this is not to imply that Thackeray is a negative moralist, or a pessimist. In *Henry Esmond* at least he shows himself to be more of a realist than those historical novelists who set out to be didactic or interpretive, for he feels unable to draw conclusions where there seems to be no valid conclusion to draw.

In terms of its family links, certain prominent themes, and its constant reference back to the earlier story, *The Virginians* is properly the sequel to *Henry Esmond*: in terms of its narrative structure and invention it is no such thing. The radical device of an autobiographical narrator in an historical novel is all but abandoned, and historical events appear to be merely incidental to the main line of the plot in spite of the fact that the two chief protagonists take political sides more unequivocally than does any character in *Henry Esmond*. Quite as many historical celebrities enter the story, but they seem to have little impact on the progress of the plot, based as it is on the divergent careers of two brothers. *The Virginians* lacks the consistency and unity of its predecessor. Gordon Ray perhaps over-reacts in seeing the novel as 'the acme of formlessness', but its plot certainly rambles, and Thackeray seems to have been content to have let it do so. [13] Characters find themselves, and lose themselves again, amidst the complications of Georgian society on both sides of the Atlantic, and Thackeray returns, rather clumsily, to his earlier satirical mode in pointing to the shortcomings and inconsistencies of the 'bo monde'. Although he dispenses with a single, determining narrator, the novelist introduces letters exchanged by characters to vary the narrative style, and to relate it back to the eighteenth-century epistolary novel. It is a device which nevertheless damages the unity of the story. Only the last quarter of the book is given over, somewhat uneasily, to George Warrington's first person account of the American War, and it is this part alone which reflects the subtlety of *Henry Esmond* in considering the ambiguity of the individual caught in political divisions.

During his trip to America in 1852– 3 Thackeray had made a point of visiting the region he had imagined as the site of the Esmond estates in Virginia. 'It gave me', he wrote, ' a queer sensation to see the place, and I fancied the story was actually true for a minute or two. . . .'[14] Although, as Madame Esmond's Preface to the earlier novel shows, Thackeray had already indicated the main lines of a future plot, his American trip provided much useful visual and social material for the opening sections of his new story. *The Virginians* was to discuss the conflicting loyalties of an Anglo-American family at the time of George Washington, and it was to consider and reaffirm the close emotional, racial and historical ties between the United States and Britain, between Jonathan and John Bull. The illustrated wrapper to the monthly parts, an image Thackeray repeated as the frontispiece to his second volume, introduced this supposedly dominant theme to his readers. The two brothers are shown in uniform; the American officer grasps the hand of his departing British brother who carries in his other hand a furled Union Jack while behind the figures floats the Stars and Stripes of the new Republic.

Nevertheless, despite this pictorial statement of intent, the novel's treatment of such important historical ideas is decidedly limited. The greater part of *The Virginians* is set in England, and the trans-Atlantic balance is lost. Apart from the two opening chapters, the American sections seem to be little more than an introduction and a coda. Thackeray divides his story equally between the careers of Harry and George Warrington, but his main concern seems to be to recount their divergent fortunes in the England of George II. Only the occasional letter from their mother in Virginia reminds the brothers of their home, and of the civil discontent brewing there. The potential for a comic reflection on the idea of the American abroad, which might have come through the black servant, Gumbo, is largely deflected into a delight in Gumbo's receptivity to the decadent values of the Old World. The ultimate involvement of George and Harry on opposing sides in the American War of Independence con- sequently seems to come about arbitrarily rather than as the inevitable conclusion to a developed central argument. Only the brothers' names, George for the loyalist, Harry, like his grandfather, for the revolutionary, suggest where Fate and principle will lead them. If Thackeray was aiming again at his own distinctive kind of realism, with the arbitrary nature of events and human decisions made significant, he more often simply suggests disorder in both the private and public realm. The shaping which Henry Esmond gives to his memoirs is here replaced by a complicated displacement of characters whose motives add to the confusion without clarifying it in personal terms.

The involvement of the chief characters in *The Virginians* in the making of the United States emerges chiefly as a concern with family property. At the end of the novel, where it most resembles *Henry Esmond*, we are not so much conscious of the tensions of history as of the relative placidity within the Esmond family group. George, however, becomes as much a prey to melancholia as his grandfather had been. He is independent of society and of social niceties, and his dark moods make him an outsider from the groups he finds unsympathetic:

> As for my wife, all the world liked her, and agreed in pitying her. I don't know how the report got abroad, but 'twas generally agreed that I treated her with awful cruelty, and that for jealousy I was a perfect Bluebeard. Ah, me! And so it is true that I have had many dark hours; that I pass days in long silence; that the conversation of fools and whipper-snappers makes me rebellious and peevish, and that, when I feel contempt, I sometimes don't know how to conceal it, or I should say did not. I hope as I grow older I grow more charitable.
>
> (Chapter LXXXV)

George's dark moods are, however, never as integral to the story, or to the nature of the story, as are those of his grandfather, though they help to provide the novelist with an unexpected and successful end to his novel. Thackeray shows Harry Warrington reassuming his Virginian responsibilities, while in England the American *parvenue*, Miss van den Bosch, married into the Castlewood family, apes the more unpleasant manners of the old aristocracy. The final irony of the novel, and the one the melancholic George resignedly reports to us, concerns the very Virginian estates where Henry Esmond had enjoyed his Indian Summer and his descendants' story had begun. Esmond's American Castlewood, like James's Poynton, is burned, and its surrounding land has to be rescued from the acquisitive designs of the new van den Bosch-Esmonds. With this final and effective gesture Thackeray again reminds us of the inconsistency and duplicity of mankind, and of the impermanence of temporal possessions. Title, rank, prestige, home and fortune had been eschewed before, now even the Virginian alternative can be seen as subject to change, to threat and to destruction. Henry Esmond had withdrawn from faction and division to the relative obscurity of an American plantation. *The Virginians* comes to a point of rest in a similarly resigned mood, with America no longer obscure, but with private placidity and the strength of human love posed against the transcience of earthly ambitions. It is mutedly implied that, as for Esmond, a gain in self-knowledge counts for more than a place in recorded history, and that the possibility of a fulfilled love is the only way of mastering time, fate, and the indifference of the world.

Thackeray has no obvious conclusions to draw from history. Despite his strong and emotional attraction to the eighteenth century, the choice of a period setting for his two truly historical novels is determined, for the most part, by a belief that the present is no real improvement on what has gone before, and that there is little reason to assume that the future will improve matters much. Macaulay's, Dickens's, or Lukács's notion of progressive historical advance is challenged by the observation that unheroic mankind is constant only in its shortcomings. The past, like the present, offers a complex web to the novelist; it can be satirised or analysed, but it is not easily or innocently interpreted. 'Society', Thackeray wrote in the Preface to *Pendennis*, 'will not tolerate the Natural in our Art.' The 'natural', an observation of what seems to be there rather than what we would like to see, does not present easy solutions to problems, historical or modern. In his historical fiction Thackeray advances Scott's pattern of linking the public to the private by suggesting that the division between the two sectors is not easily determinable.

6 The Argument from Tradition: *Hypatia, Fabiola* and *Callista*

See! in the rocks of the world
Marches the host of mankind,
A feeble, wavering line.
Where are they tending? – A God
Marshall'd them, gave them their goal. –
Ah, but the way is so long!
Years they have been in the wild!
Sore thirst plagues them; the rocks,
Rising all round, overawe.
Factions divide them; their host
Threatens to break, to dissolve.
Ah, keep, keep them combined!
Else, of the myriads who fill
That army, not one shall arrive!
Sole they shall stray; in the rocks
Labour for ever in vain,
Die one by one in the waste.

Matthew Arnold, *Rugby Chapel*

'During the first quarter of this century a great poet was raised in the North, who . . . has contributed by his works . . . to prepare men for some closer and more practical approximation to Catholic truth.'[1] So wrote the already celebrated incumbent of the University Church of Saint Mary in Oxford, the Rev. J. H. Newman, in 1839, attributing to Sir Walter Scott the creation of a cultural mood favourable to a national religious revival. A year earlier a fellow Tractarian, the Rev. John Keble, had noted much the same thing, though with a slightly more political edge: '[Scott's] rod, like that of a beneficent enchanter, has touched and guarded hundreds, both men and women who would else have been reforming enthusiasts.'[2] Scott, both men imply, had made conservatism romantic, inspiring a new respect for the old order and the old faith: the Church, its ceremonial, its symbolism, and even its clergy, could be honoured as elements of an ancient and fruitful tradition. In the years which succeeded Catholic Emancipation and the 1832 Reform Bill, however, progressive change, shocking enough to many, was in the wind, and the established Church seemed too obese and decayed an institution to resist its blast for long. For the Oxford Tractarians the Church's real hope of survival lay in a new emphasis on its holiness and on its ancientness. For both Keble and Newman the cult of the Middle Ages, to which Scott's popularity had contributed so much, also contained fresh hope for the salvation of the Establishment; a romantic sense of history could rescue creeds and clergy from the dangers of radical reform by directing men towards 'catholic truth'. The interference of Parliament in the affairs of the Irish Church had been the occasion of Keble's Assize Sermon of 1833, on the subject of 'National Apostasy', the anniversary of which was kept solemnly by Newman and his disciples as marking the beginning of what was to be called the Oxford Movement. It is the impact of that Movement on the Victorian historical novel that this chapter will consider. If it produced no supreme masterpieces, it at least made three prominent churchmen into popular novelists and into apologists in fiction for the divergent causes they found themselves defending. The Oxford Movement temporarily divided the Church of England, and contributed both to the strength and to the unpopularity of the Church of Rome, but it also succeeded in turning religious niceties into the stuff of widespread national debate.

The Church, the Oxford men argued throughout the 1840s, was not an appendage of the state, but the very source of European civilisation and the protector of a nation's highest ideals and aspirations. Newly assertive, or newly converted, English Roman Catholics found themselves arguing the same case for their own faith. The past held the secret of the present and the future, and the Church, having both experience and the advantage of a long memory, could best interpret history to a troubled and doubting age. The Tractarians in particular had early realised the importance to their cause of re-editing and translating the works of the early Christian Fathers in order to promote their image of the links and parallels between the primitive and the modern Church.[3] But scholarly enterprise, even in an English translation, was of necessity accessible only to the educated few. Newman's secession to Rome and the Pope's 'aggressive' establishment of Roman sees in England brought religious affairs to the fore, remarkably so in a country never particularly noted for the fervour of its devotion or for the niceness of its theological opinions. In the 1850s old prejudices resurfaced to complement new ones; deep-seated Protestant suspicion of convents and confessionals was confronted by a determined advocacy of both by Anglican Ritualists and Romans alike. Priests of both persuasions claimed an infallibility derived from the Apostolic Succession. It was, given the literary and ecclesiastical fashions of the time, inevitable that the debate should become the substance of novels favourable to one party or another. Fiction reached the faithful and the faithless alike, and if statesmen, noblemen, lawyers and soldiers wrote novels there seemed no reason, except perhaps that of propriety, why churchmen should not follow suit by putting an argument derived from history into the form of a popular historical novel.

A prominent anti-Tractarian and a violent anti-Romanist, Charles Kingsley, established a style for scholarly early-Christian fiction with his *Hypatia* in 1852–3. He was followed, and to some extent replied to, by Nicholas Wiseman, the new Cardinal-Archbishop of Westminster, in his sentimental *Fabiola, or The Church of the Catacombs* in 1854, and more trenchantly in 1855 by *Callista, A Sketch of the Third Century* by John Henry Newman, now a priest of the Birmingham Oratory. But the three men were not simply intent on out-flanking each other by adjusting Scott's methods to their theological ends; they were strangely united in reacting against the account given of the first Christian centuries by Edward Gibbon. To Cardinal Wiseman and to Newman, if not to the residually radical Kingsley, Gibbon was as sinister a product of the Age of Reason as the modern clamour for rational reform, but to all three, just as it proved to be, though for different reasons, for Mr Boffin, *The Decline and Fall of the Roman Empire* was chiefest among the many 'Scarers in Print'. Gibbon had consistently and maliciously shown Christians in an unflattering light; he had described the Church vindictively destroying the last remaining virtues of Roman-ness, and readily taking upon itself the worst vices of an Empire it had once seemed intent on ignoring; worst of all, he was marvellously persuasive. Charles Kingsley's clerical distaste is evident in his reference in the preface to *Hypatia* to a 'shadow . . . sneerer'. While still an Anglican, Newman had anathematised the Gibbonian position in his sermon 'The Contest between Faith and Sight', condemning the temptation which induces men to think themselves gods, so 'intoxicated by their experience of evil' that they consider that they possess wisdom. Newman acknowledged Gibbon's 'real abilities', but argued that his 'cold heart, impure mind, and scoffing spirit' had made him 'one of the masters of a new school of error, which seems not yet to have accomplished its destinies'.[4] By the mid-nineteenth century the 'new school of error' showed few signs of decline, and many and various signs of vigorous life, and there had still been no effective popular refutation of Gibbon's slanders. The post-*Waverley* prestige of the historical novel, however, suggested a new form of polemical warfare to Christians on the defensive; the debate could be taken out of the universities and the pulpits into the circulating libraries and drawing-rooms of the ordinary reader. For Kingsley, Wiseman and Newman the novel seemed apt and ready to assume a new propagandist moral role.

Charles Kingsley was a man of strong opinions, many of which were directed against men with whom he strongly disagreed. He was a faithful clergyman of the Broad Church school, and a loyal son of the part of the Church of England which best suited his understanding of the Gospel. He was already a well-known preacher, despite his stutter, and despite those who suspected him of sedition as the Chartist 'Parson Lot' and as the author of *Yeast* and *Alton Locke*, but he was respectably Protestant enough for Prince Albert to have approved of his attack on celibacy in *The Saint's Tragedy*. Kingsley had also already begun to emphasise those aspects of his social philosophy which were soon to be nicknamed 'muscular Christianity'; he was a Carlylean hero-worshipper, but his normative military heroes were Joshua and David, Alfred the Great and Sir Philip Sidney.

The sub-title of *Hypatia*, 'New Foes with an Old Face', made it plain to Victorian readers that this, Kingsley's first historical novel, was to be more of a tract for the times than a sketch of a lost Golden Age. As in *The Saint's Tragedy*, there was a clear modern warning embodied in a study of the past; it was intended to be a rebuttal both of agnostic rationalism, and of the Tractarian and Roman claims for the purity of the age of the Church Fathers. If they claimed consanguinity, Kingsley aimed to prove that it was at the peril of their souls. If the contemporary fracas over Ritualism and 'Papal Aggression' may have rendered Thackeray's comment on Jesuitry in *Henry Esmond* especially pointed, there seemed an even clearer reflection of modern problems in the turmoil described in *Hypatia*. One reviewer of 1853 noted a similarity between Kingsley's Cyril of Alexandria and the 'living reality in lawn' of Henry Phillpotts, the controversial High Church Bishop of Exeter. The same reviewer went on to assume that Porphyry, who 'aspires to be a religious man without being a Christian', was in fact modelled on Newman himself. One twentieth-century critic has suggested that Cyril is instead a portrait of the then vastly unpopular Wiseman.[5] But if the old faces have proved difficult to identify, Kingsley made sure that their theological opinions rang true to both ancient and modern ears.

Despite the obvious implications of 'New Foes with an Old Face' Kingsley was chiefly determined to give an accurate description of the face and voice of fifth century Alexandria. In her biography of her husband Mrs Kingsley quotes the comments of a friend who saw something of the preparatory research for the novel: 'I was struck not only with his power of work, but with the extraordinary pains he took to be accurate in detail. We spent one whole day in searching the four folio volumes of Synesius for a fact he thought was there, and which was found there at last.'[6] Kingsley even re-read *The Decline and Fall of the Roman Empire* in order to determine where his own unflattering emphases should fall. In the Preface to the novel he tells us that his pursuit of information reflected an historian's quest for factual accuracy: 'I can only say that I have laboured honestly and industriously to discover the truth, even in its minutest details, and to sketch the age, its manners and its literature, as I found them.' This labour to be 'realistic' as well as accurate suggested the introduction into the narrative of a very creditable translation of some 110 lines of Homer, an imitation of an Eddaic poem for his Goths, and even part of a sermon for St Augustine. *Hypatia* is a far livelier novel than anything by Bulwer-Lytton, and far more intellectually alive than any other of Kingsley's own historical novels. He did not have it in him to be an unprejudiced observer, especially when it came to religious matters, but for once his private obsessions and his public crusade managed to combine vividly and carefully. He aimed at historical realism, but his subject enabled him to be involved, critical, various, and digressive. It rapidly emerges that he has more sympathy with the lost Classical age which precedes the one he is describing, and with the Dark Ages which will succeed it, than he has with fifth-century Alexandria, but his distaste seems to have stimulated him into a rare neutrality towards his characters. *Hypatia* has as much of the delight in physical action as *Westward Ho!* or *Hereward the Wake* but it has far less of the arrogance and bluster.

When he had finished his novel Kingsley was pleased to discover what he considered to be a resemblance between his own method of 'reproducing a past age' and that of 'the most learned dramatist we ever had' – Ben Jonson. [7] He was probably thinking of Jonson's considerable echoes and borrowings from Latin writers in his tragedies, sources which Jonson had proudly annotated for the sake of any less learned reader. Despite this valid, but not always flattering, parallel, the real influence on the shape of Kingsley's historical novels remained Sir Walter Scott. The major characters in *Hypatia* are invented, but their adventures bring them into contact with the prominent historical figures of their time. The action of the novel is largely recounted from Philammon's point of view, and it is through his innocent candour that Kingsley most tellingly comments on the corruption of Alexandria. Philammon is far more than a choric figure. The novel is shaped around his journey from the desert to the city, and then back to the desert, and his journey, we sense, proved to be both physical and spiritual. Hypatia, ostensibly the central figure, and an historical character like Cyril, Synesius and Augustine, is really less notable for her growth towards faith, than for her impact on the invented Philammon.

Despite his antipathy to fifth-century Alexandria, the novelist regarded the age in which his story was set as 'one of those critical and cardinal eras in the history of the human race', marking a transition between a declining Mediterranean culture and a newly forceful Gothic North. Once the North of Europe, with its tribes untainted by Rome, had been won for Christ, new vistas opened for the future. Gibbon had mourned the last remnants of a Classical civilisation overturned by an ignorant Church; Kingsley looks to the future. Given this important distinction between the philosophies of the two writers, it remains true that there are many points of contact between *Hypatia* and the forty-seventh chapter of *The Decline and Fall of the Roman Empire*. Gibbon describes the murder of the Platonic philosopher Hypatia by fanatic monks and unequivocally blames the Church; Kingsley too sees the Church at fault, but he adds the salve that Hypatia is reaching out for a pure and rational faith. The account of the philosopher's death in Gibbon is brief, but it dramatically and effectively points his moral:

> In the bloom of beauty and in the maturity of wisdom, the modest maid refused her lovers and instructed her disciples; the persons most illustrious for their rank or merit were impatient to visit the female philosopher; and Cyril beheld, with a jealous eye, the gorgeous train of horses and slaves who crowded the door of her

academy. A rumour was spread among the Christians that the daughter of Theon was the only obstacle to the reconciliation of the prefect and the archbishop; and that obstacle was speedily removed. On a fatal day, in the holy season of Lent, Hypatia was torn from her chariot stripped naked, dragged to the church, and inhumanly butchered by the hands of Peter the reader and a troop of savage and merciless fanatics: her flesh was scraped from her bones with sharp oyster shells, and her quivering limbs were delivered to the flames. The just progress of inquiry and punishment was stopped with seasonable gifts; but the murder of Hypatia has imprinted an indelible stain on the character and religion of Cyril of Alexandria. [8]

The last phrase has a useful ambiguity, but it is plain enough that to Gibbon, as much as to Kingsley, Hypatia is a martyr, if in a different cause. To the historian she is murdered by a jealous, contentious, superstitious, and political Church which regards her as a threat; to Kingsley she is working towards the kind of faith which finds no place in Alexandria, a simple Reformation Christianity. Her death proves a final disillusioning revelation to Philammon, and it drives him back to solitude and negation, incapable, unlike the unthinking Goths, of coping with the serious divisions in his world.

Clearly the novel was not suggesting that Hypatia's death would be repeated in Victorian England, but it was warning of the dangers of intolerance and superstition. For Kingsley the worst flaw of Christian Egypt lay in its inability to come to terms with human sexuality. The old order is self-indulgent and profligate; the new unnaturally elevates celibacy as a prime Christian virtue. To the novelist both are tantamount to 'effeminacy', a betrayal of manhood and the ideal of monogamy, an ideal which obsessively haunts all of his subsequent writings. Protestant England, quiescent amid a revival of monasticism, should note the spiritual and moral vices of the ancient world, and contrast them with its own. Kingsley draws a stark distinction between the joys of the flesh and the evils of celibacy, even though he allows only one character in the story, the convert Jew, Raphael, to achieve the kind of married bliss so dear to the novelist himself. It is almost as if he were implying that the world was not yet ready for the ideal. The novel opens in a community of hermits in the Nubian desert, but in Chapter III, Philammon, the innocent *en route* for Alexandria, encounters a woman for the first time:

A woman of some two-and-twenty summers, formed in the most voluptuous mould of Grecian beauty, whose complexion showed every violet vein through its veil of luscious brown. Her little bare feet, as they dimpled the cushions, were more perfect than Aphrodite's, softer than a swan's bosom. Every swell of her bust and arms showed through the thin gauze robe, while her lower limbs were wrapped in a shawl of orange silk, embroidered with wreaths of shells and roses. Her dark hair lay carefully spread out upon the pillow, in a thousand ringlets entwined with gold and jewels; her languishing eyes blazed like diamonds from a cavern, under eyelids darkened and deepened with black antimony; her lips pouted of themselves, by habit or by nature, into a perpetual kiss; slowly she raised one little lazy hand; slowly the ripe lips opened; . . .

Kingsley is evidently relishing her effect as much as his ingénu. In spite of the Rossetti lips, this is the kind of titillation in classical drapery loved later in the century by Leighton and Alma-Tadema. Pelagia, reclining in the Goths' Nile barge, awakens Philammon sexually, but the novelist carefully limits him to what his eyes alone can enjoy. It in fact turns out that Pelagia is his long-lost sister and she is to end her days with him as a penitent in the desert.

The moral laxity of the Alexandrians, however, succeeds in further destroying Philammon's peace of mind. As the novel progresses, Kingsley introduces encomia on married love, and, although he denies the state to his hero, he at least gives him a perception of its bliss. In Chapter XIV, for example, Philammon meditates on his newly conceived passion for the virginal Hypatia, and the novelist coyly interpolates his own thoughts, inspired he claims by St Augustine, into the reverie. The love which links 'youth to youth, or girl to girl', he tells us, only reaches its full perfection 'between man and woman'. In Chapter XXI Raphael is observed debating the merits of monogamy with Bishop Synesius, a subject to which Raphael returns when we hear that his own marriage to a girl he was rescued from the threat of a convent has been blessed by Augustine himself. Through the wavering Raphael we guess that Kingsley is suggesting that in certain cases Christian marriage can even be efficacious in saving a soul.

The early parts of the novel are built around stark but effective contrasts of landscapes, men and manners. They also contain some of Kingsley's best descriptive prose. Take, for example, the desert contemplated by Philammon in the opening chapter:

> Behind him the desert sand-waste stretched, lifeless, interminable,
> reflecting its lurid glare on the horizon of the cloudless vault of
> blue. At his feet the sand dripped and trickled, in yellow rivulets,
> from crack to crack and ledge to ledge, or whirled past him in tiny
> jets of yellow smoke, before the fitful summer airs. Here and
> there, upon the face of the cliffs which walled in the opposite side of
> the narrow glen below, were cavernous tombs, huge old quarries,
> with obelisks and half-cut pillars, standing as the workmen had left
> them centuries before; the sand was slipping down and piling up
> around them, their heads were frosted with the arid snow;
> everywhere was silence, desolation – the grave of a dead nation, in
> a dying land.

Kingsley is suggesting not simply a geographical gulf between
England and Egypt, but also the grand time-scale of Egyptian history.
The fifth-century monk, a citizen of the dying Roman Empire, is able
to contemplate the long-dead Empire of the Pharaohs a full thousand
years before a British Empire was possible. Philammon's landscape is
empty of living men, and marked by their desolate monuments; the
monks who have sporadically inherited the wasteland have withdrawn from the world. Kingsley's view of the desert monks in the
first chapter is surprisingly tolerant, especially so when we see it in
contrast to his attitude to the urban monasticism of Alexandria, for
though he criticises the Abbot's automatic connection of the female
with sin, he is prepared to admit that there is valid enough Scriptural
precedent for withdrawal. This opening chapter finely conveys a
sense of emptiness, slow movement, and decay, but it also gives us a
disquieting feeling of unnaturalness.

Beyond the Nubian desert is another world, urban, unredeemed,
and rotten. Before he leaves on his journey down the Nile, the Abbot
instructs Philammon in the full horrors, both Christian and Pagan, of
what he is likely to encounter:

> 'Eunuchs the tyrants of their own sovereigns. Bishops kissing the
> feet of parricides and harlots. Saints tearing saints in pieces for a
> word, while sinners cheer them on to the unnatural fight. Liars
> thanked for lying, hypocrites taking pride in their hypocrisy. The
> many sold and butchered for the malice, the caprice, the vanity of
> the few. The plunderers of the poor plundered in their turn by

worse devourers than themselves. Every attempt at reform the parent of worse scandals; every mercy begetting fresh cruelties; every persecutor silenced, only to enable others to persecute him in their turn: every devil who is exorcised, returning with seven others worse than himself; falsehood and selfishness, spite and lust, confusion seven times confounded, Satan casting out Satan everywhere – from the emperor who wantons on his throne, to the slave who blasphemes beneath his fetters.'

One might expect a hermit to rant thus about a degenerate society from which he has retreated, but we see that Kingsley, like Gibbon, generally assents to his condemnation. But the Abbot's tone is of despair, not that of a Muscular Christian whose aim is to change the world by involving himself in reform. The decadence of Alexandria 'compared with which Paris is earnest and Gomorra chaste', might not yet be paralleled in modern England, but the warning stands.⁹

The novel's second chapter – 'The Dying World' – serves to justify the warning. The stillness of the first pages is contrasted with confused activity; characters come and go, and voices and tones clash. Here the images of death are different; the sand and the tombs are replaced by an opposition of cultures and the smell of decay. But the Alexandria that we first glimpse retains elements of a chaster past. It is dominated by its great Hellenic library, and in its lecture halls, 'decorated in the purest Greek style', Hypatia is speaking as the representative of a great classical culture. The Greek reverie is broken by the intrusion of the Roman prefect, nominally a Christian, but overdressed and overscented, and the discussion between the philosopher and the prefect rapidly destroys any illusion of refinement and civilised unity. Alexandria is in fact torn apart by racial and religious antagonism and by mutual envy and suspicion; it is a battleground for Greeks and Egyptians, Romans, Jews, Goths, sectarian Christians and self-interested tradesmen. The picture of a cultural and racial imbroglio is redeveloped in Chapter V when a porter who leads Philammon astray accompanies his misdirections with a diatribe against Christianity. Some Victorian readers must have been disturbed by such reminders that the world of Homer and Euclid had died so ignominious a death, and had been replaced not by a simple Apostolic faith but by a corrupt sect from the slums of a Mediterranean port; eventually the great library is burned, and Hypatia, its guardian and the last of the ancient sages, is dismembered by the successors of the Apostles. Rather than offering a riposte to Gibbon,

Kingsley is obliged to admit the justice of his argument that Greco-Roman civilisation was fiercely emasculated by the Church; he differs only in emphasis.

In this sense at least *Hypatia* remains an extraordinary novel for a Victorian clergyman to have written. Criticism of prelates, or of the silliness of the faithful, may mostly be given to characters antipathetic to Christianity, but the strength of the case is only barely challenged by examples of good-living, thinking Christians. Bishops appear as intriguers, sybarites and sycophants, surrounded in their turn by flatterers and fools; laymen are by turns bigots, apostates, cowards or cynics. Toleration, as we see it, has brought few spiritual blessings, for, as Peter the Reader admits, 'Emperors and courtiers have given up burning and crucifying us, and taken to patronising and bribing us instead' (Chapter VII). Even Cyril who, if hardly saintly, is certainly above the average in his virtues, sees the Church's corruption and ignores it, even to the extent of exploiting abuses for his own political advantage, in the knowledge that 'there is no use flighting with those whom you cannot conquer'.

The only really admirable and amiable ecclesiastics in the story are Synesius, Bishop of Cyrene, and Augustine of Hippo, though both make only brief appearances. Synesius is a character built up from the evidence of his surviving writings – 'a man of magniloquent and flowery style, not without a vein of self-conceit: yet withal of overflowing kindliness, racy humour and unflinching courage, both physical and moral'. Kingsley's ideas of him as 'the Squire-Bishop' is no mere Barsetshire jest; it types him, as does the suggestion that he is happily married, as a Muscular Christian before his time. Much the same is true of Augustine, a character established as the likely author of the *Confessions* but who has little impact on the novel's plot. His physiognomy suggests a complex spirit:

> . . . a tall, delicate-featured personage, with a lofty and narrow forehead, scarred like his cheeks with the deep furrows of many a doubt and woe. Resolve, gentle but unbending, was expressed in his thin close-set lips and his clear quiet eye; but the calm of his mighty countenance was the calm of a worn-out volcano, over which centuries must pass before the earthquake-rents be filled with kindly soil, and the cinder-slopes grow gay with grass and flowers.

> (Chapter XXI)

This somewhat laboured paragraph lacks the deftness which Kingsley can occasionally show in his descriptions of character, but he is attempting to present a figure known, by name at least, to most readers, who must be seen as part of the fallen age in which he lives, though towering above its defects. Kingsley sees Augustine's rejection of the lax morals of Carthage for an active life in the service of God as the one good deed in the naughty world of fifth-century Africa, and it must have been something of a relief to have been able to include some small reference to it.

Hypatia constantly questions the assumption that the modern Church should be proud of its descent from a corrupt Patristic age, even though two of the Fathers themselves emerge with some credit. Kingsley confidently remains Christian in his own assumptions and prejudices, but he seems to want his readers to look to themselves for justification, not to the past. Tradition, as we see it in the novel, is invalidated as a prop to faith, and there is a real danger in imitating the errors of history. *Hypatia* is not a pessimistic novel, but what affirmation it offers is confined to a speculation about the future, a future which is to be decided by the untutored Goths who are intent on destroying the last vestiges of Roman power. Once Christianised, it is implied, these same destroyers will become the new civilisers. The Preface is quite explicit about this:

And the new blood, at the era of this story, was at hand. The great tide of those Gothic nations, of which the Norwegian and the German are the purest remaining types, though every nation of Europe, from Gibraltar to St Petersburg, owes to them the most precious elements of strength, was sweeping onward, wave over wave, in a steady south-western current, across the whole Roman territory, and only stopping and recoiling when it reached the shores of the Mediterranean. Those wild tribes were bringing with them into the magic circle of the Western Church's influence the very materials which she required for the building up of a future Christendom, and which she could find as little in the Western Empire, as in the Eastern; comparative purity of morals; sacred respect for woman, for family life, law, equal justice, individual freedom, and, above all, for honesty in word and deed; bodies untainted by hereditary effeminacy, hearts earnest though genial, and blest with a strange willingness to learn, even from those whom they despised; a brain equal to that of the Roman in practical power, and not too far behind that of the Eastern in imaginative and speculative acuteness.

As always Kingsley eulogises brute force, though he puts moral rectitude and racial predestination beside it. The first phase in Christian history is coming to an end; the second is about to be born in the North to grow into the Reformation. As both *Hereward the Wake* and *The Roman and the Teuton* later emphasise, Providence is guiding the advance of the Teutons for its special redemptive ends.

The novel ends, not with this triumphant future in sight, but with a matured and sorrowing Philammon returning to the solitude of the desert. The final paragraph recalls the theme stated so boldly in the Preface, but so often lost in the variousness of the novel itself:

> I have shown you New Foes under an Old Face – your own likenesses in toga and tunic, instead of coat and bonnet. One word before we part. The same devil who tempted these old Egyptians tempts you. The same God who would have saved these old Egyptians if they had willed, will save you, if you will. Their sins are yours, their errors yours, their doom yours, their deliverance yours. There is nothing new under the sun. The thing which has been, it is that which shall be. Let him that is without sin among you cast the first stone, whether at Hypatia or Pelagia, Miriam or Raphael, Cyril or Philammon.

As this jumble of Biblical quotation suggests, Kingsley's view of history is moralistic but confused. It is not simply that he sees the flaws of the human character as constant, he seems to be suggesting that the confusions of the distant past are exactly repeatable, and that progress is only viable as an idea once it is linked to God's scheme of salvation for the entire human race. But Kingsley's confusion in *Hypatia* is, paradoxically, a strength, for it frees him from the clearly divided rights and wrongs, and blacks and whites, of his clumsier work. The final effect is the one he aimed at – a picture of a frenzied and decaying civilisation awaiting regeneration. Kingsley has neither the will, nor the artistic subtlety, to draw a careful and convincing parallel with his own society, but his sketch of Alexandria remains the prime imaginative success of the novel. We guess that the novelist himself is on the side of the angels, even though many of his fellow-Christians, as we see them in the story, seem not to be. The murder of Hypatia, just as she is moving towards a Platonic acceptance of Christ, is the dramatic climax of the plot, but after it the other elements seem naturally to fall apart. Kingsley seeks to prove nothing more, leaving us only with further evidence of the inability of the old Egyptians to save themselves from the pit. He does not end with easily tied knots, marriage or family relationships, or any other sign of temporal and spiritual well-being; we are left in the unnatural and empty silence of the desert. The disturbing, open-ended quality of the story was intentional; it was a questioning of easy assumptions which Kingsley was, for once, content to achieve.

Hypatia certainly vexed Kingsley's clerical antagonists. When his name was proposed for the Oxford D.C.L. by his former pupil, the Prince of Wales, in 1863, Dr Pusey led a noisy campaign against the granting of the degree, labelling *Hypatia* in particular as an immoral book, evidence of its author's profligacy and false doctrine. Under the threat of Pusey's *non placet* the University was obliged to accept Kingsley's withdrawal.[10] Amongst Roman Catholics the response was somewhat more positive and creative, for in 1854 the first volumes of 'The Popular Catholic Library' appeared, an attempt at presenting the layman with doctrinally sound and devoutly in-structive reading matter. If *Hypatia* was regarded as pernicious, no such accusation could have been levelled at stories and histories with such titles as *Missions in Japan and Paraguay, Heroines of Charity* and *Alice Sherwin; A Tale of the Days of Henry VIII*. Most prominent among the historical novels in the series were Wiseman's *Fabiola* and Newman's *Callista*; though both appeared anonymously, little attempt was made to keep the names of the authors a close secret. In Rome it was not at first considered proper that a Cardinal should eccentrically stoop to fiction, but the vast international success of *Fabiola* stilled most doubts. 'It was the first good book', commented the Archbishop of Milan later, 'to have the success of a bad one.'[11]

The genuine and widespread popularity of the story exceeded even Wiseman's expectations; it was gradually translated into most European languages, and, at one point, surprising as it might now seem, adapted for the stage. The main Catholic journal, the *Dublin Review*, proclaimed confidently in 1856: 'What the Waverley Novels and their imitators have done for modern and mediaeval history, "Fabiola" has done with the most perfect success for the history of the early church.'[12]

The Cardinal himself, said to be the original of Bishop Blougram, remained modest enough about his achievement. He wrote to a friend soon after the novel's appearance: 'I have done nothing but deposit in the little book the thoughts and feelings which, gathered in early youth at the tombs of the martyrs, have never lost their freshness in my mind and heart.'

Fabiola had, however, achieved what it had set out to achieve by winning itself a sympathetic, and not exclusively Catholic, audience. Wiseman was delighted to note that it was 'creeping in among Protestants', and was gratified that even the Lutheran King of Prussia had been reading it 'like Assuerus' Tale'.[13]

Fabiola is little more than a sensational, ultramontanist account of an unlikely concitation of martyrs. Historically, it is interesting for its author's sake, not for any intrinsic merits. Little enough effort in fact went into its composition; the novel was started by the energetic but over-worked Cardinal during a visit to Rome in the winter of 1853, and finished the following summer in the somewhat less august surroundings of Filey, and Wiseman's biographer records that there was scarcely a need 'to consult a book or a monument' during composition, so familiar was the author with his material.[14] As the alternate title suggests, *Fabiola* attempts to tell the story of 'The Church of the Catacombs', weaving the lives of the martyrs whose names are recited in the Canon of the Mass into a devout adventure. Generally, the story lacks precision, scholarship and inventive characterisation, though the novelist had been prepared to hint at this in his Preface:

> It consists rather of a series of pictures than of a narrative of events. Occurrences, therefore, of different epochs and different countries have been condensed into a small space. Chronology has been sacrificed to this purpose. The date of Dioclesian's edict has been anticipated by two months, the martyrdom of St. Agnes by a year; the period of St. Sebastian, though uncertain, has been brought down later.

Such an admission would have been anathema to most nineteenth-century historical novelists to whom accuracy had become a point of honour as well as of legitimate art; but perhaps, as Kingsley was to argue so disastrously later, truth, for its own sake, was proving itself never to have been a virtue with the Roman clergy.

Fabiola is really only hagiography re-dressed as Victorian fiction. Most of the fourth-century characters have some basis in historical records, either as Saints or as figures named in inscriptions found in the catacombs, but none of them is sufficiently realised to withstand psychological analysis, or even a questioning of motives. The odour of sanctity is strong enough to offend the nose of any doubter. In the second chapter, for example, the boy Pancratius (more familiar, if less patrician, as St Pancras) tells his mother of his school exercise:

> 'The subject was "That the real philosopher should ever be ready to die for truth". I never heard anything so cold and insipid (I hope it is not wrong to say so), as the compositions read by my companions. It was not their fault, poor fellows! what truth can they possess, and what inducements can they have, to die for any of their vain opinions? But to a Christian, what charming suggestions such a theme naturally makes! And so I felt it.'

Pancratius is priggish and self-righteous, and Wiseman fails to persuade us that he is in earnest, or that there is a real enough martyrdom to be embraced, a martyrdom quite without 'charming suggestions'. Neither Pancratius, nor Agnes, nor Sebastian, emerge as the stuff of martyrs, simply because they do not seem to have sufficient life in them to lay down for their faith. The Cardinal had tried to make his saints human by giving them, as far as he dared, the voices and opinions of virtuous Victorians, but like the villains of the novel they are really only stereotypes hidden under togas. One villain in particular, Fulvius, 'the new star of society', owes more to the 'silver fork school' than to Martial or Juvenal:

> Young, and almost effeminate in look, dressed with most elaborate elegance, with brilliant rings on every finger, and jewels in his dress, affected in his speech, which had a slightly foreign accent, overstrained in his courtesy of manners, but apparently good-natured and obliging, he had in a short time quietly pushed his way into the highest society of Rome.
>
> (Chapter VI)

It is like a reminiscence of a salon of the 1840s, though even Count D'Orsai might have felt at home amongst Wiseman's well-born and privileged Romans. Only one prominent character, the blind girl Caecilia, is poor enough to need the freely-given charity of the patrician martyrs, but though the Church of the Catacombs clearly does contain many more of the deserving poor, the novelist seems far happier in describing their patrons, and presenting them as representative of a respectable and aristocratic institution, already socially worthy of its great future.

With very little to win our sympathy for the characters, the deficiencies of the plot seem even more glaring. The novel relies heavily on coincidence which the novelist happily confuses with the workings of Providence. When the servant girl, Miriam, tells her life-story to the newly converted Fabiola, parts of her tale make even *Candide* probable by comparison. Wiseman habitually interferes with the flow of his narrative in order to interpret events retrospectively, to prophesy some future happy development or to explain the relevance of the Breviary. Often he seems to be contemplating not ancient Rome, but the glory that shall be Roman Catholic. His attempts at irony tend to misfire, his judgements are vindictive, and his concept of justice as gauche and as cruelly pagan as Kingsley's. Just as his villains hunt down proscribed Christians, so Wiseman pursues and destroys those who persecute the elect of God. Almost the last event of the novel is the death of Corvinus, a character whose name betrays his nature; Corvinus contracts hydrophobia from a panther penned in the Colosseum, and the novelist treats his last agonies as merited, and this death of an unrepenting sinner as worthy of one who has rejected the water of baptism.

Fabiola was intended to be an instructive novel, and, just as Ainsworth had done, Wiseman makes sure that we take his point by inserting superfluous information on Rome and its relics wherever it seems advantageous. Archæological facts are most frequently interpolated, and an entire chapter (Part II, Chapter II) is given over to 'What Diogenes [a character] could not tell about the catacombs', in which the novelist presents us with a concise history of explorations and finds, adding footnotes recommending standard reference works. Later on in the novel there are wood-cut plans of tunnels and chambers, and accounts of particular inscriptions, drawings and tombs. Something of this confident didacticism had also been announced in the Preface:

It is indeed earnestly desired that this little work, written solely for recreation, be read also as a relaxation from graver pursuits; but that, at the same time, the reader may rise from its perusal with a feeling that his time has not been lost, nor his mind occupied with frivolous ideas. Rather let it be hoped, that some admiration and love may be inspired by it of those primitive times, which an over-excited interest in later and more brilliant epochs of the Church is too apt to diminish or obscure.

But the 'more brilliant epochs of the Church' seem in fact to determine the light in which 'those primitive times' are viewed. The body of Christians is always referred to as 'the Catholic Church', suggesting that it is to be identified with its modern successor. We are told in Chapter 22 of Part II that the doctrine of the Real Presence, 'undoubtedly' held in the fourth century, has remained unchanged ever since, and in Chapter 33 of the same book, Miriam treats her converted mistress to a purple passage of Mariolatry. References to the authority and dignity of the Papal See are quite explicit; we are told, for instance, of the chair 'whence commands should issue, to reach worlds unknown to Roman sway, from an immortal race of sovereigns, spiritual and temporal', without there being the least glimmer of a suggestion that no early Bishop of Rome could have dreamed of usurping the earthly role and titles of his persecutors, the Caesars. As far as Wiseman is concerned in his novel, Catholic history is an uninterrupted and glorious movement forward, and a movement in which a primitive simplicity finds an exact reflection in the nineteenth-century Church.

Despite the uniformity in their attitudes to the ancient dignity of the Roman Church, the temperamental differences which divide the assertive Wiseman from careful, nicely intellectual Newman are clear enough in their respective novels. *Callista* was published as the twelfth volume of the Catholic Popular Library in 1855, and Newman describes his novel in the Advertisement as 'an attempt to imagine and express, from a Catholic point of view, the feelings and mutual relations of Christians and heathens at the period to which it belongs, and it has been undertaken as the nearest approach which the Author could make to a more important work suggested to him from a high ecclesiastical quarter.' The high ecclesiastical quarter was Wiseman himself, anxious that the project for instructive Catholic fiction should not founder. The Cardinal had hoped for a series of novels springing from *Fabiola* and tracing the development of the Church from the age of persecution through 'the Church of the Basilicas' and 'the Church of the Cloister' to the 'the Church of the Schools', but, typically, Newman had not chosen to concur with so obvious a scheme. His own 'sketch of the Third Century' is set, not in Rome, but like *Hypatia* in North Africa.[15] Having written appreciatively but vaguely to Wiseman of the 'instruction and interest' in *Fabiola*, he had then, with a characteristic wilfulness, gone his own way.

Callista is a much more direct response to *Hypatia* than Wiseman's undemanding little tale. Although the public collision of Kingsley and Newman was still some eight years in the future, the latter must have been fully aware of Kingsley's hostility to his religious opinions, and particularly those on the Patristic tradition, to his development and to his adoptive Church. But the roots of the novel do not lie exclusively in a present controversy, more in personal association and memories. In the Postscript Newman tells us that a great part of Chapters 1, 4 and 5, as well as a sketch of the character and fortunes of Juba, had been written as early as the spring of 1848, that is in the period immediately following the completion of *Loss and Gain*. Given the literary fashions of the day it would have been easy enough to transfer his thoughts from a contemporary novel, dealing with the problems of apostasy and conversion, to an historical novel with a similar theme. In 1839 he had written the preface to the edition of Cyprian's *Treatises* published as part of the 'Library of the Fathers', and had actually glimpsed the landscapes he describes in the novel during a Mediterranean voyage undertaken with the Froudes in 1832. Seeing the remains of Carthage *en route* for Italy his imagination had been quickened not just by thoughts of the Phoenicians, of Tyre and the Punic Wars, but also by 'Cyprian, and the glorious Churches now annihilated'.[16]

To Newman history remained a real and living force, a continuous and progressive realisation of the purposes of God; though the study of the past revealed decay, the present was both a development from it, and a temporary realisation of its potential. As an Anglican controversialist, he had learnt to argue from history even to the extent of arguing himself out of Anglicanism and the *Via Media*. In the *Apologia Pro Vita Sua* he describes the crucial process:

> There was an article in [the *Dublin Review*] on the 'Anglican Claim' by Dr. Wiseman. . . . It was on the Donatists, with an application to Anglicanism. I read it, and did not see much in it. . . . The case was not parallel to that of the Anglican Church. St. Augustine in Africa wrote against the Donatists in Africa. They were a furious party who made a schism within the African Church, and not beyond its limits. It was a case of Altar against Altar, of two occupants of the same see, as that between the Non-

jurors in England and the Established Church; not the case of one Church against another, as of Rome against the Oriental Monophysites. But my friend . . . pointed out the palmary words of St. Augustine, which were contained in one of the extracts made in the Review, and which had escaped my observation. 'Securus judicat orbis terrarum.' He repeated these words again and again, and, when he was gone, they kept ringing in my ears. 'Securus judicat orbis terrarum'; they were words which went beyond the occasion of the Donatists: they applied to that of the Monophysites. They gave a cogency to the Article, which had escaped me at first. They decided ecclesiastical questions on a simpler rule than that of Antiquity; nay, St. Augustine was one of the prime oracles of Antiquity; here the Antiquity was deciding against itself. What a light was hereby thrown upon every controversy in the Church! . . . 'Securus judicat orbis terrarum!' By those great words of the ancient Father, interpreting and summing up the long and varied course of ecclesiastical history, the theory of the *Via Media* was absolutely pulverised.[17]

The revelation was 'like a spirit rising from the troubled waters of the old world, with the shape and lineaments of the new', and through it the Church of England appeared aberrant, cut off from the main stream of history. It was no longer a matter of presenting a plea for a restoration of a primitive order, it became necessary to pursue the logic of the idea of development by assenting to a developing Church. If history was progress, and the Apostolic Church the sole gate to salvation, then it seemed that the only way was securely forward with an authoritative Church.

Hypatia had shown new foes with old faces; *Callista* attempts to show both friends and foes, and to describe the process of conversion proceeding in a particularly relevant figure from the past. Newman chose to consider the third century not the fifth, and to contrast paganism with Christianity, not schism with order, but he aimed to make his historical novel a reflection of the troubled waters of modern controversy. For the Catholic of the nineteenth century there seemed to be as great a need to proclaim certainty to a hostile world as there had been in the third century of pagan North Africa. Kingsley's Christians inherit the decadence of the late Roman Empire; Newman's are a light amid the encircling gloom of intolerance and conventional indifference. Reviewing the novel, *The Christian Remembrancer* found its subject rather too disquietingly reminiscent of recent history: 'Callista herself is evidently an allegory: her doubts, weariness, yearnings and discontents, out of character as they are to a girl of seventeen, are understood, when we take them to be the history of another career, one with the landmarks of which we are all familiar, and the course of which has been noted with continual minute introspective observation.' The reviewer believes that he is dealing with a veiled autobiography, and his assumption leads him to draw a disturbing conclusion: 'We own it jars on our patriotism to see . . . a Briton born satirise England as heathen Rome, and not very obscurely prophesy for her the same doom.'[18]

The Christian Remembrancer assumes too far and too much. Devoutly as Fr Newman may have prayed for the conversion of England, it must be conceded that his novel does not attempt to draw exact parallels between the old world and the new, a dead one and a living one; it merely observes a soul struggling for direction in a perennial dilemma. Despite his view of history as development, Newman sees man and his nature as unchanging, and determined not by a social reality but by a spiritual one. He finds Callista's dilemma familiar, but his is a familiarity based both on his own experience, and on his sacerdotal assumption that the human soul aspires equally to truth in all ages. Much as he had persuaded himself to see it, the Roman Church emerges for Callista as the sole repository of a truth that reveals more of itself as man progresses to a fuller revelation of the Divine purpose.

In spite of its grand underlying themes, *Callista* remains a disappointing novel, awkward and unrealised even as an account of the changing spiritual perceptions which lead characters from doubt to certainty and through the difficult process of conversion. In contrast to both *Fabiola* and *Hypatia* it develops slowly and undramatically, though like them it ultimately fails to probe the heart of the problem it investigates. Newman aimed at some degree of ordinariness, as if he were deliberately countering the sensationalism of Kingsley's and Wiseman's stories, and he sets his novel not in cosmopolitan Carthage, but in the second city of Proconsular Africa, Sicca. His characters too are provincial and drawn mostly from amongst artisans, merchants and small landowners. The novel opens not with an evocation of the gorgeous east but with a picture of a friendly and useful landscape:

The immediate neighbourhood of the city was occupied by gardens, vineyards, cornfields and meadows, crossed or encircled here by noble avenues of trees or the remains of primeval forests, there by the clustering groves which wealth and luxury had created. This spacious plain, though level when compared with the northern heights by which the city was backed, and the peaks and crags which skirted the southern and western horizon, was discovered, as light and shadow travelled with the sun, to be diversified with hill and dale, upland and hollow; while orange gardens, orchards, olive and palm plantations held their appropriate sites on the slopes or the bottoms.

This suggestion of general well-being is reinforced by a quotation from the account of the creation of vegetation in *Paradise Lost*, serving both to imply the bounty of a Creator and to set the African landscape in the context of a Classical pastoral tradition. But these opening impressions prove deceptive; the prosperity of the Province encourages little amongst its inhabitants except an indifference to spiritual values and when the balance of nature is shifted by a natural disaster, the population switches to zealously persecuting the religious minority in its midst.

Newman is far better at describing landscapes than he is at characterisation, or at picturing ordinary human activity. His story requires him to give accounts of day-to-day transactions, of casual conversations, of dinner parties, and even of a widespread riot, but in none does he manage to bring the scene to life or allow his characters to act easily and naturally. When it comes to describing the riot against the Christians the novelist affects a lack of verbal skill, acknowledging his own limitations:

It would require the brazen voice which Homer speaks of, or the magic pen of Sir Walter, to catalogue and to picture, as far as it is lawful to do either, the figures and groups of that most miserable procession.

(Chapter XVII)

But generally he avoids straining his resources, and embarrassing any squeamish reader, by simply remaining vague about any activity beyond the cerebral. The most memorable section of the novel, and one of the most striking passages in Newman's entire *oeuvre*, however, is the vivid account of the swarm of locusts which descends on Sicca. There is a precision here, a mastery of mood, and an imaginative creation. Newman is drawing on the horrors of the

Plagues of Egypt, but he manages to achieve a Latinate resonance in his evocation of the strangeness of the visitation:

> The swarm to which Juba pointed grew and grew till it became a compact body, as much as a furlong square; yet it was but the vanguard of a series of similar hosts, formed one after another out of the hot mould or sand, rising into the air like clouds, enlarging into a dusky canopy, and then discharged against the fruitful plain. At length the huge innumerous mass was put into motion, and began its career, darkening the face of day. As became an instrument of divine power, it seemed to have no volition of its own; it was set off, it drifted, with the wind, and thus made northwards, straight for Sicca. Thus they advanced, host after host, for a time wafted on the air, and gradually declining to the earth, while fresh broods were carried over the first, and neared the earth, after a longer flight, in their turn. For twelve miles did they extend from front to rear, and their whizzing and hissing could be heard for six miles on every side of them. The bright sun, though hidden by them, illumined their bodies, and was reflected from their quivering wings; and as they heavily fell earthward, they seemed like the innumerable flakes of a yellow-coloured snow. And like snow did they descend, a living carpet, or rather pall, upon fields, crops, gardens, copses, groves, orchards, vineyards, olive woods, orangeries, palm plantations, and the deep forests, sparing nothing within their reach, and where there was nothing to devour, lying helpless in drifts, or crawling forward obstinately, as they best might, with the hope of prey. They could spare their hundred thousand soldiers twice or thrice over, and not miss them; their masses filled the bottoms of the ravines and hollow ways, impeding the traveller as he rode forward on his journey, and trampled by thousands under the horse-hoofs. In vain was all this overthrow and waste by the road-side; in vain their loss in river, pool, and watercourse. The poor peasants hastily dug pits and trenches as their enemy came on; in vain they filled them from the wells or with lighted stubble. Heavily and thickly did the locusts fall; they were lavish of their lives; they choked the flame and the water, which destroyed them the while, and the vast living hostile armament still moved on.

> (Chapter XV)

The repeated words, and the short, almost breathless phrases serve to emphasise the impossibility of stemming such a tide of destruction, and the unpleasantness of Sicca's experience is redoubled as the swarms die as suddenly as they had come, leaving the stench of their foetid carcasses on the ground they had stripped of life. Nothing else in *Callista* has the same drama and vividness as this chapter, despite the fact that we have only reached a mid-point in the novel. Although the pace of the plot quickens, and the destinies of the characters become more involved, there is an unfortunate sense of anti-climax in all that remains to be worked out.

The latter half of *Callista* considers the process by which the heroine thinks herself into Christianity, only to end up a martyr for the cause she espouses. As a consequence the novel is notably more of a dramatised thesis than it is a *Bildungsroman*; Callista learns intellectually, not emotionally, and the novel is constructed, like a rather flat and two-dimensional play, out of dialogue and discussion. Newman provides us with plentiful information about the social, cultural and economic background to his story, but often the conversations between characters serve to tell us more about their environment than about the men and women themselves. For relatively obscure provincials they seem surprisingly well-educated, able to quote the Latin poets with ease, knowledgeable about history and politics, and alert to the main trends in the thought of their time. It is at times almost as if Sicca were the Oxford of *Loss and Gain* translated through time and space like a populous Holy House. Callista is a Greek, a maker of images for the numerous pagan cults of North Africa, but we soon sense that she has a remarkably alert and restless mind. She is 'yearning after some object', yet unable to fall back upon 'that drear, forlorn state, which philosophers call wisdom, and moralists call virtue' (Chapter XI). Her objections to the outward forms of paganism are not the result of a sudden revelation but of a philosophical distaste; like Sue Bridehead, another image-maker, she is a Platonist, but Newman sees *his* heroine's quest as a progressive and disciplined acceptance of monotheism, not an attempt to escape into the freedom of polytheism or unbelief. Callista is perhaps closest to Newman's own experience in the period of transition between the loss of one pattern of belief and the acceptance of another. He interprets her state of mind by offering us an analogy:

> She was neither a Christian, nor was she not. She was in the midway region of inquiry, which as surely takes time to pass over, except there be some almost miraculous interference, as it takes

time to walk from place to place. You see a person coming towards you, and you say, impatiently 'Why don't you come faster? – why are you not here already?' Why? – because it takes time. To see that heathenism is false, – to see that Christianity is true, – are two acts, and involve two processes. They may indeed be united, and the truth may supplant the error; but they may not.

(Chapter XXIX)

Once the end of the spiritual journey has been reached, and the conviction realised, Callista allows her head to persuade her heart in following its logic. Her martyrdom is seen as an act of love, in which she greets her mystical bridegroom in a happy acceptance of final union.

But for Callista and all the other Christians in the story the determination to serve Christ alone entails a separation from the values and norms of the pagan world in which she lives. Newman insists that the temptations to conform are strong, simply because they are the means of finding acceptance and advancement within the social group; the outsider is suspect and anti-social. In the fifth chapter of the novel we are treated to a eulogy of Roman-ness by a guest at Jucundus's feast who has recently returned from the Imperial capital, proud to be a citizen of so great an Empire. This 'cockney of the Imperial period' sees only majesty in the pageants of Rome, and a promise of the eternity of her institutions, and through him Newman suggests that modern cockneys might be just as blinkered. But the problem of conformity to the unifying Imperial idea is treated more urgently later in the novel. In Chapter XXVIII the heroine is reproached by a fellow Greek for challenging the first principle of the State, its uniform cult of the Emperor. Rome, Polemo tells Callista, tolerates all other national sects provided they incorporate reverence to the divinity of the Caesars. Christians seem to be wilfully and unnecessarily threatening treason:

I love Greece, but I love truth better; and I look at facts. I grasp them, and I confess to them. The whole earth through untold centuries, has at length grown into the imperial dominion of one. It has converged and coalesced in all its various parts into one Rome. This, which we see, is the last, the perfect state of human society. The course of things, the force of natural powers, as is well understood by all great lawyers and philosophers, cannot go further. Unity has come at length, and unity is eternity. It will be for ever, because it is a whole. The principle of dissolution is eliminated. We have reached the *apotelesma* of the world.

Polemo is using pseudo-science, a science which, despite its Aristotelian base, stands in antithesis to Newman's own idea of development. Polemo sees Callista and her fellow Christians as pitting her will against that of the centuries, but Newman is making the argument between the two a more subtle response to Gibbon than either Wiseman or Kingsley could have managed. History for Newman does not stand still, and the outward signs of decay are for him evidence of a new and better creation which is still being forged. Callista's faith is not a denial of a unifying idea, it is an assertion of the integrity of the individual within a wider *apotelesma*, one which is still in the making. The novel is broadening out an ancient debate, not narrowing it down to ancient or modern instances. Callista's death is part of a grander process than Polemo can understand – a separation from the world in order to submit to the will of the Creator of the world.

It would have required the resources of a far greater imaginative writer than Newman adequately to suggest the character of a saint or a saintly hero, set apart, like Milton's Samson, by a determination and a special vision. Ecstasy is an uncommon state, and needs an uncommon invention to convey something of its fervour and mystery, but Newman has neither sufficient passion nor sufficient freedom as a novelist to render Callista's martyrdom at once climactic and cathartic. He attempts instead to be dispassionate, even commonplace:

> A few minutes sufficed to put the rack into working order. She was laid down upon its board in her poor bedimmed tunic, which once flashed so bright in the sun, – she who had been ever so delicate in her apparel. Her wrists and ankles were seized, extended, fastened to the moveable blocks at the extremities of the plank. She spoke her last word, 'For Thee, my Lord and Love, for Thee! . . . Accept me, O my Love, upon this bed of pain! And come to me, O my Love, make haste and come!' The men turned round the wheels rapidly to and fro; the joints were drawn out of their sockets, and then snapped in again. She had fainted. They waited for her coming-to; they still waited; they got impatient.
> 'Dash some water on her,' said one. 'Spit in her face, and it will do,' said a second. 'Prick her with your spike,' said a third. 'Hold your wild talk,' said a fourth, 'she's gone to the shades.' They

gathered round, and looked at her attentively. They could not bring her back. So it was: she had gone to her Lord and her Love.

(Chapter XXXIV)

The scene is a static drama, though perhaps here there is more of the stasis of a mediaeval painting than of a play. Each of the soldiers takes a different formal pose, but Newman disturbs the effect by unsuccessfully adding pathos. He manages hints at the eroticism implicit in the passions of early virgin martyrs, but he avoids physicality, and quickly passes over any painful details. Callista's death is handled tersely enough, and many Victorian readers must have felt relieved that it was described with such tactful 'good taste', but the account is flat, evasive and ultimately both unreal and unspiritual. Certainly there is little enough in it to bring an atheist to his knees.

The 'cold heart, impure mind and scoffing spirit' of Edward Gibbon had very naturally suspected the motives behind the alacrity with which so many early Christians embraced martyrdom. While he is unable to find much to say against the death of Callista's contemporary, St Cyprian, Gibbon takes the opporunity of suggesting disagreeably selfish promptings amongst Cyprian's fellow prelates:

> It is not easy to extract any distinct ideas from the vague, though eloquent, declamations of the fathers, or to ascertain the degree of immortal glory and happiness, which they confidently promised to those who were so fortunate as to shed their blood in the cause of religion. They inculcated with becoming diligence, that the fire of martyrdom supplied every defeat, and expiated every sin; that, while the souls of ordinary Christians were obliged to pass through a slow and painful purification, the triumphant sufferers entered into the immediate fruition of eternal bliss, where, in the society of the patriarchs, the apostles, and the prophets, they reigned with Christ, and acted as his assessors in the universal judgement of mankind. The assurance of a lasting reputation upon earth, a motive so congenial to the vanity of human nature, often served to animate the courage of the martyrs.[19]

But for Newman, Callista, the type of an early martyr, is fulfilling her private destiny, not seeking reward or reputation. The novel also suggests that she is affirming the right of the individual to follow the dictates of a reasoning conscience, and that, in doing so, she is attuning her temporal will to that of the eternal. The martyrdom might seem an affirmative end to a novel only in a limited Christian sense, but, in a way, Newman also wants us to see it as the direct consequence of pursuing an idea to its heroic conclusion, regardless of the cost. Though the novel fails to demonstrate the full force of the example, *Callista* is about convictions, and it shows a third-century woman treading a path charted by a nineteenth-century convert to Rome. Like Newman himself she gives up 'much that (s)he loved and prized and could have retained, but that (s)he loved honesty better than name, and Truth better than dear friends'.[20] In her sacrifice we are meant to see a triumph not a failure, and a hope for the future not an historical despair.

For Newman, as much as for Wiseman and Kingsley, history traces the gradual growth of mankind towards God, and it is a process providentially guided and enlightened by a line of Patriarchs, Prophets, Apostles and Martyrs. All three considered themselves to be the inheritors of an historical wisdom, and wrote novels as priestly guardians of an ancient mystery. But in spite of the religious prejudices they shared, each approached the history of the Church from different and entrenched positions. To Kingsley the age of the Fathers was an intellectual, spiritual and social nightmare, a dark night of the soul dimly lit here and there by prophetic minds, but otherwise a troubled sleep from which Europe would only wake at the Reformation. The Christian tradition was invalid and fragmentary except where it expressed a view of the Church similar to Kingsley's own. To Wiseman, however, the modern Roman Church is consistent with the Church of the Catacombs he so sentimentally pictured in his story; its creeds, formularies, and observances are virtually identical, though its worldly circumstances have altered for the better. A Pope sits holily and infallibly in the chair of Peter, and rules a vast spiritual empire from the city of Romulus and Augustus, because the Holy Spirit has willed it so. To Wiseman the Church represents continuity, certainty and power; it is the fulfilment of history, the sole gate of salvation, and the protector of the tombs of the martyrs. Past and present are one because the successors of Peter have a unique understanding of, and power over, the progress of the human soul. Newman's view of history is more complex, more radical, and far more subtle and intricate, but, despite the clarity of his thought, his novel shows little evidence of real originality and rather less of life. All three writers claim to know the meaning and relevance of the past to the present, but none managed to find the appropriate fictional embodiment of their vision. Perhaps only Kingsley, the bluntest and least flexible thinker, succeeded best in his experiment, simply because he saw historical certainties as challengeable, and the Christian tradition as sullied and suspect. *Hypatia* has a tension behind its preaching which *Callista*, for all its arguments, lacks, and which *Fabiola* never attempts. If Kingsley does not speak with a steady voice, he at least manages at times to echo some of the inflexions of the finest Victorian historical fiction and to put flesh and blood on the skeletons of his old foes.

7 Last of the English: Charles Kingsley's *Hereward the Wake*

'Is it what you call civilisation that makes England flourish? Is it the universal development of the faculties of man that has rendered an island, almost unknown to the ancients, the arbiter of the world? Clearly not. It is her inhabitants that have done this: it is an affair of race. A Saxon race, protected by an insular position, has stamped its diligent and methodic character on the century. . . . All is race; there is no other truth.'

Benjamin Disraeli, *Tancred*, Book II, Chapter XIV

RICHARD	As we have quite done with the Saxons, I wish, mamma, you would be so good as to tell us all you recollect about them.
MRS MARKHAM	Indeed, my dear, you have set me no easy task. I will, however, try to execute it as well as I can; but I must first tell you, you are a little mistaken in supposing you have quite done with the Saxons. Your Papa and I are Saxons.
MARY	You a Saxon, mamma! Why I thought you were an Englishwoman!
MRS MARKHAM	So I am; but, as the Saxons continued in the country after the Conquest, and were much more numerous than the Norman settlers, we are still almost all of us chiefly of Saxon descent; and our language, and many of our habits and customs, sufficiently declare our origin.

Elizabeth Penrose, *Mrs Markham's History of England*
Chapter VII

Charles Kingsley published six full-scale novels in the course of a career in which he managed to combine and confuse the roles of clergyman, poet, essayist, novelist, naturalist, socialist, social reformer, historian and tutor to the Prince of Wales. For each aspect of his life there is an appropriate, if unequal, literary expression. As an antagonistic reviewer of *Westward Ho!* grudgingly admitted in 1855,

Kingsley was one of the most remarkable and voluminous writers of his age with, as he put it, 'no small infusion of quicksilver' in his veins.[1]

The appearance of *Hypatia* in 1852 began a new phase in Kingsley's work as a novelist, what seemed at first sight to be an abandonment of a committed social fiction for a story set in a remote and foreign past. But for the novelist new foes had old faces and old divisions had a fresh modern relevance. *Hypatia*, like *Westward Ho!* and *Hereward the Wake*, was not a rejection of a literature which reflects the nature and concerns of society, but an extension and a reconsideration of problems touched upon, with such radical conviction, in *Yeast* and *Alton Locke*. Most twentieth-century critics, if they have considered Kingsley at all, have concentrated on the two early novels as important examples of stories relating directly to the 'condition of England question' of the 1840s and 1850s. The historical novels have gradually been relegated to the status of boys' adventure stories.

Kingsley's once considerable reputation as a novelist has been largely eclipsed by those of his contemporaries and there have been few serious attempts to restore his critical fortunes. In 1895, however, Frederic Harrison still found it fitting to treat Kingsley in one of a series of articles on mid-century novelists, noting that the vogue for all of them, including Dickens and George Eliot, was passing away. Retrospectively, he sees Kingsley's novels as typical of their period, presenting 'a striking example of that which is so characteristic of recent English literature – its strong, practical, social, ethical or theological bent. It is in marked contrast with French literature.' Harrison emphasises that, perhaps more so than his contemporaries, Kingsley was pre-eminently a didactic novelist who saw his fiction as an extension of his other professional concerns: 'He was novelist, poet, essayist and historian, almost by accident, or with ulterior aims. Essentially he was a moralist, a preacher, a socialist, a reformer and a theologian.'[2] There is much justice in the comment, though it suggests an undervaluation both of Kingsley's power of invention and of his personal dedication to his art. The preacher and the story-teller are inseparable, though the balance of exemplum to instruction does shift considerably between novel and sermon. The real weakness in Kingsley's work lies not in the end to which the stories are directed, but in the failure of the novelist to think lucidly. The novels fail ultimately because they lack intellectual precision, and because they never manage to show a working out of the full implications of either the plot or the characters. *Hypatia* ends provocatively, with a rare balance of contraries and an open moral; its successors also discuss historical rights and wrongs, but they treat issues according to a predetermined and often muddled moral scheme. *Westward Ho!* and *Hereward the Wake* leave us with an impression of an author convinced of his own self-righteousness, but wavering and liable to withdraw sympathy and judgement at crucial moments.

The illogicality and lack of consistency of Kingsley's thought has led many readers to distort his opinions into an unflattering consistency, isolating his prejudices as though they revealed the whole man or the whole writer. Even the young Henry James, a critic scarcely free of literary prejudice, tended to caricature a novelist so temperamentally different from himself. Kingsley, he wrote in 1877, 'appears to us a man of an extremely vigorous temperament and a decidedly simple intellect. . . . It seems to the reader . . . a striking anomaly that fortune should have forced him into the position of a philosopher or intellectual teacher. Even literature, with him, was amateurish.'[3] James qualifies his dismissal of Kingsley the novelist with a real appreciation of Kingsley the naturalist and delineator of nature, but we are still left with an impression of a man of limited gifts who had somehow blundered into novel writing. It would be a thankless task to attempt to re-assess his philosophy, though at times, especially in his Christian Socialist phase, Kingsley does emerge as a courageous and advanced thinker, but the historical novels deserve to be acquitted of the charge of 'amateurism', despite their very obvious flaws. *Hereward the Wake* is hardly a reflective or profound masterpiece, but it does present a vivid and at times well-ordered action, an interesting variety of characters, and an effective recreation of an unfamiliar period. Above all it manages to carry, as none of Bulwer's tired narratives do, the force of a conviction that mediaeval history can be painful as well as exciting, complex as well as limited in its horizons, and alive in fiction when it touches perennially familiar issues. Kingsley was determined to use the novel both as an art form and a vehicle for popular education; this is not a sign of 'amateurism', but rather of a particular, if narrow and un-Jamesian, view of the form and end of fiction.

Hereward the Wake was Kinglsey's last novel, though two further historical stories, both dealing with religious issues, were projected but never completed. It is the culmination of many lines in its author's thought, though its ambitions betray more muddle and emotion than one might expect from what purports to be an imaginative but carefully considered study of the major crisis in English history. In

Hereward Kingsley is dealing, as Bulwer had before him, with the material of a national epic. Both novelists, in common with many prominent contemporary historians, most notably the Frenchman, Augustin Thierry, considered the Norman Conquest to be a decisive turning-point in modern history, the pivot on which all subsequent events, political, social, and religious, turned. The Conquest opened doors for provincial Saxon England, letting in light from the Continent, and letting out a spirit of adventure which would embark on a crusade to master the world beyond. To Kingsley the Norman Invasion represented the last phase in the long process of the transformation of England from a Romano-British culture to an emphatically Teutonic one and the Normans themselves are to be seen as descendants of the same Vikings who had already remade Northern and Eastern Britain. Although it was still popularly, if naively, held that the Normans had destroyed the primitive liberties of Saxon England and had brought with them feudalism and hereditary kingship, many Victorians had persuaded themselves that 1066 merely represented a temporary subjection which forced a new vigour to spring up in ineradicable English institutions. A similar case was later to be persuasively, consistently and bluntly restated as the central theme in the work of the Oxford historian Edward Augustus Freeman.[4]

Hereward the Wake describes a guerrilla struggle for national independence, albeit a struggle which was both remote and futile. Bulwer had dealt specifically with the events of the Conquest in his *Harold*; Kingsley did not attempt to imitate or outdo his predecessor; he chose to change viewpoints, and take as his hero not the defeated Saxon king, but the wayward leader of armed resistance to the invader.[5] Kingsley's real trouble lay in the fact that his sympathies were divided, for, unlike Bulwer, he was not inclined to mourn passing orders. He firmly believed, and told us that he believed, in the rightness of the Conquest as part of a strategy of Providence, but he also attempted to show that Hereward's resistance to the new regime was to be identified with the free Norse-Saxon spirit of the nation. Scott was far more able to cope with the implications of historical necessity, a faith in progress, or a nationalistic rebellion. The final acceptance of a Norman dynasty by Cedric of Rotherwood, though fortuitous, at least serves to suggest that he has come to terms with reality. In Kingsley's story Hereward's homage to William the Conqueror is a sign of the hero's demoralisation, and, though the novelist may here be following his historical sources, he is clearly ill at ease with his hero's compromise. A real disquiet with the novel as a whole arises once one asks the questions – What was Hereward fighting for? and what did he achieve? Kingsley may have been aiming at a subtle contrast of opinions and conflicting loyalties, with his hero compromised but still noble, but he provides us with insufficient evidence in the course of the story to reach so pointed a conclusion at its end. Indeed, neither the characters nor the plot suggest that there has been much room for subtlety.

In Kingsley's 'modern' novels – *Yeast, Alton Locke* and *Two Years Ago* – we are led to understand and interpret the story through the reactions, deliberations, and decisions of the central character. *Alton Locke* for example traces the experience of its hero through an alertness to the problems of society to an acceptance of a Christian answer to those problems. The novel establishes a pattern for the 'muscular Christian' heroes who follow. The historical novels show an even greater need for, and dependence on, heroes, men set apart by their valour, their moral uprightness, or their superior understanding, qualities which could be interpreted as indicative of Kingsley's waning radical interest in popular democracy. The process is more developed in *Westward Ho!* and *Hereward the Wake* than in the earlier *Hypatia*, where Philammon emerges as a kind of *tabula rasa*, an essentially passive observer marked by the saints and sinners with whom he comes in contact. From the very opening of *Hereward*, however, it is obvious that the novel will be dominated by a man of action rather than a contemplative. But Kingsley's interest is divided, just as his sympathy is divided, between the heroic Hereward and the heroism implicit in the treatment of Hereward's antagonist, William the Conqueror. We thus have a double stress, but one which does not detract from the centrally expressed faith in supermen; the supermen forge history, and, in being demanded by the times, readily respond to their calling. Kingsley's debt to Carlyle is nowhere clearer than in *Hereward the Wake*, but Carlyle had been able to keep his argument steady and single-minded in studying the Conqueror's heroic progress. By contrast Kingsley wants us to see history proving William right, while at the same time the same historical process can be seen to justify his enemy. He is playing a double game, while he has none of Tolstoi's or Thackeray's perception that perhaps history proves nothing, or that modern man can dispense with the concept of heroism.

Hereward, like Amyas Leigh, is a rough-hewn 'muscular Christian'. In a series of sermons on the subject of King David, delivered in the University of Cambridge, Kingsley employed the term, already associated with his name, somewhat coyly, linking it to the wider concept of 'chivalry'. Chivalry, he asserted, proclaimed 'the possibility of consecrating the whole manhood . . . to God', a consecration which he saw as truly heroic and standing opposed to the monastic ideal which he so detested.[6] Kingsley once told an acquaintance that Queen Victoria had mentioned to 'a certain Professor' (evidently himself) that the young men of her reign were 'losing the spirit of romance and chivalry' and were too prone 'to laugh at anything earnest'; it seems hardly coincidental that the subject broached by the Queen should have been considered in a subsequent sermon in the Chapel Royal at Windsor. 'The age of chivalry', he told his august congregation, 'is never past so long as there is a wrong left unredressed on earth, or a man or woman left to say, I will redress that wrong, or spend my life in the attempt.'[7] It is this broad concept which determines the heroism of *Hereward the Wake* and which relates its themes forward to Victorian England. The novel shows a metamorphosis; Hereward grows from a loutish delinquent, albeit a justified one, to a fully Christian knight, the protector of the weak, defender of the right, the redresser of wrongs. At a mid-point in the story he is reconciled to his family, submitting to their will and acknowledging himself to be of a sounder mind than heretofore. In his act of submission he enacts a deed worthy of a true knight, but he goes on to proclaim himself unworthy of the title until he has 'mightily avenged the wronged and mightily succoured the oppressed' (Chapter XX). He emerges into the light of a newly consecrated life, a penitent sinner worthy of the task of delivering his homeland from the oppressor.

If Kingsley was conscious of a model for his hero it was probably the subject of his Cambridge sermons, King David. As Mrs Kingsley records, the novelist named David as his favourite character in history in one of those questioning autograph books of which the Victorians were so fond. At the same time he announced that his favourite motto or proverb were the words 'Be strong'.[8] Like David, Hereward the Wake is a rebel against his lawful but tyrannous king, and like him he is to be identified with a national struggle for independence and godliness. The parallel is even more striking in that both heroes sin by committing adultery, David with Bathsheba, Hereward with Torfrida, and both are punished for their sin by failure. But Kingsley's attraction to the two men is not founded on their sinfulness (which he tends to view as red-bloodedness), but on their prowess, their strength and their flawed, but godly, valour. If modern readers tend to balk at the novelist's delight in physicality and violence, or at his adulation of the strong man, Kingsley would have argued that he was merely reflecting the way of life of the period he describes, and offering parallels to scenes which had proved acceptable enough to readers of the Old Testament. When challenged for his support of Rajah Sir James Brooke, the dedicatee of *Westward Ho!*, he compared Brooke's actions in Borneo to those of the champions of Israel: 'Do you believe in the Old Testament? Surely, then, say, what does the destruction of the Canaanites mean? If it was right, Rajah Brooke was right. If he was wrong, then Moses, Joshua, David were wrong.'[9] Kingsley seems to be suggesting that once a divine right has been proved, then ends justify means. For him the study of history reveals the processes of God, showing the hero as the instrument of God, and, by extension, as the true representative and hero of his race.

Kingsley's view of European history, and its providential progress, was publicly stated in the lectures which he gave as Professor of Modern History in Cambridge in 1860, some six years before the publication of *Hereward the Wake*. He chose to speak on a theme which had obviously interested him at the time of *Hypatia*, the decline of the Roman Empire and the compensating expansion of the influence of the Goths. The Cambridge professorship allowed him to elaborate his sketchy thesis into a supposedly coherent interpretation of the divine mission of the Teutons. To many of his contemporaries, much as to the new Professor, the growth of Britain's colonial Empire, the westward expansion of the United States, and the pursuit of German re-unification, suggested that the future destiny of the world lay in the capable hands of the Germanic races. To Kingsley the assumption could be further justified from history, and by indicating that there was a logic behind seemingly random events in the distant past.

The opening lecture of the series reveals the extent of Kingsley's debt to certain aspects of Carlyle's thought, but it also suggests that he was approaching the study of history as a story-teller first, and an historical analyst second. He begins with the announcement that biography and autobiography provide the best means of responding to the men of the past. 'Fill your minds', he told his enthusiastic undergraduate audience, 'with live human figures; men of like passions with yourselves; see how each lived and worked in the time and place in which God put him.'[10] Thackeray would have

wholeheartedly approved. But Kingsley goes on to make a considered and sweeping statement of intent which divides him both
from Thackeray and from the orthodox historians of the nineteenth
century; history, he asserts, traces a moral pattern not an intellectual
one:

> For not upon mind, gentlemen, not upon mind, but upon morals,
> is human welfare founded. The true subjective history of man is
> not of his thought, but of his conscience; the true objective history
> of man is not that of his inventions, but of his vices and his
> virtues. . . . In proportion as a nation is righteous . . . will
> thought grow rapidly, securely, triumphantly; will its discoveries
> be cheerfully accepted, and faithfully obeyed, to the welfare of the
> whole commonweal.[11]

Kingsley sees God as the sole mover and judge of nations, the weaver
of the diverse threads of time and race, and he proposes that we see
history as the process of God educating Man, a notion which he
claims is no hypothesis but the 'observation of thousands of minds,
throughout thousands of years'.

It is a simple enough proposition, but once it is applied in the
subsequent lectures to a highly indeterminate situation, one rapidly
senses that it is no more than a vast and disturbing over-simplification.
He applies the techniques of the crudest exegesis of the Old Testament
to a series of events which have been thinly recorded and which the
lecturer himself has only barely grasped. The ideas are grafted onto
supposition, and the evidence adduced often seems to be at variance
with the interpretation. Kingsley seeks to prove that the Teutonic
invasions were a part of the grand 'strategy of Providence', though
he asserts categorically, argues weakly, and never gives us the 'live
human figures' who might have given some substance to his bold
outline. The over-simplification affects not just his philosophy, it
shapes the very heroes of the lectures, the Teutonic tribesmen who
established control over the remains of the despised Roman *Imperium*.
The Teutons, Kingsley tells us, were like children enduring a system
of education devised specifically for them by a benign Providence. To
familiarise us with this perverse notion he draws a modern
comparison:

> I wish to impress strongly on your minds this childishness of our
> forefathers. . . . The nearest type which we can see now is, I fancy,

the English sailor, or the English navvy. A great, simple, honest, baby – full of power and fun, very coarse and plain spoken at times; but if treated like a human being, most affectionate, susceptible, even sentimental and superstitious.[12]

The comparison reveals a sad lack of sympathy both for the circumstances of navvies and sailors, and for the culture which sustained the early Teutons. Though his adulation of the Goths in *Hypatia*, and of the Vikings in *Hereward*, approaches Wagner's passion for his Volsungs, there is little evidence in *The Roman and the Teuton* that Kingsley sees his heroes as anything other than puppets of alternatively good and evil forces beyond their ken.

The lectures were built around an opposition of Latinate to Germanic culture; the first has inherited and compounded decadence, the second, once Christianised, redeems Europe. It is the kind of divide of which Matthew Arnold was also fond, but for Kingsley ignorant armies clash not by night but under the sunny smile of the Almighty. *The Roman and the Teuton* shows a new and progressive order growing out of the fall of the Roman Empire, and it affirms that both the Reformation and the growth of the nation-state are the happy consequence of virtues inherent in Teutonism. Kingsley's confidence is quite Miltonic; God's hand has carefully separated the Saxon island of Britain in order to prepare it for a special mission; history can be seen to work in obedience to natural laws; the Dark Ages were really a vast campaign in which God has revealed himself to be the general. Kingsley ended his lectures with an astounding assertion, determined, he implies, by 'simple mathematical principles':

> While I believe that not a stone or a handful of mud gravitates to its place without the will of God; that it was ordained, ages since, into what particular spot each grain of gold should be washed down from an Australian quartz reef, that a certain man might find it at a certain moment and crisis of his life; – if I be superstitious enough, (as thank God I am) to hold that creed, shall I not believe that though this great war had no general upon earth, it may have had a general in Heaven? and that in spite of all their sins, the hosts of our forefathers were the hosts of God?[13]

To at least one reviewer, however, the lectures were 'feeble, confused and pretentious', though the lecturer was to develop his theme again in his novel about the decisive events of another Teutonic conquest.[14] If *Hereward the Wake* covers a comparatively limited episode in the history of the race, its implications are equally epic in Kingsley's eyes, and they reflect the same assumption that there is a peculiar Providence guiding the fates of nations.

The change of mood from the lectures to the novel results from a shift from the general to the particular, and from the loss of the simple outline which had at least given the theories some narrow logic. Particular instances seem instead to have encouraged Kingsley's tendency to confuse issues, for in the novel it seems as though Providence were building an already divided house. The story ranges widely, from Ireland to Friesland, and it mingles Saxon, Celt, Norman and Dane with abandon, but if it suggests a forward movement in history, it will not admit that Hereward's resistance to change might seem to be resistance to the blessed inevitability of progress. Kingsley seeks to give us an heroic biography, but he often seems to have lost sight of his object. Hereward's transformation from a soldier of fortune to a nationalistic guerrilla is casual enough, but it tends to suggest that his cause was equally casually espoused. Like Kingsley, we sometimes feel that we are not sure whose side we are supposed to be on.

The novelist approached his subject with the same careful scholarship that he had employed in preparing *Hypatia*, and the extensive footnotes offer proof of his efforts to root his story in recorded history. Two dynastic tables are included in order to explain family connections within the story and to outline the connecting ancestry of modern royal families. The first two chapters establish the novelist's credentials in regard to his use of factual evidence, and they place the story in a landscape and an historical period. Kingsley is, as he explains in his Dedication, fitting the Saxon Hereward for the modern drawing-room, and he is moulding historical evidence to provide the proper setting for his hero, one which is at the same time accessible and accurate. But despite Hereward's drawing-room disguise, Kingsley is careful to remind us that there are significant differences between the manners and beliefs of the eleventh and the nineteenth centuries. Unlike an Ainsworth, or even a Bulwer, he is open enough not to want to see his characters as Victorians manqués, and readers are not required to note precise reflections of one world in another. In the opening chapter, for example, Kingsley contrasts his hero's horizons to those of a modern reader:

Not to him, as to us, a world circular, round, circumscribed, mapped, botanized, zoologized; a tiny planet about which everybody knows, or thinks they know, everything; but a world infinite, magical, supernatural – because unknown; a vast, flat plain reaching no one knew whence or where, save that the mountains stood on the four corners thereof to keep it steady, and the four winds of heaven blew out of them; and in the centre, which was to him the Bruneswold, such things as he saw: but beyond things unspeakable, – dragons, giants, rocs, orcs, witch-whales, griffins, chimeras, satyrs, enchanters, Paynims, Saracens, Emirs and Sultans, Kaisers of Constantinople, Kaisers of Ind and of Cathay, and beyond them again of lands as yet unknown.

Hereward's is a world in which uncertainty outweighs certainty, in which credulity determines belief, and superstition knowledge, but it is also a world of wonder and infinite possibility. It is the kind of world-scape in which the Victorians placed their mythical Arthur, but for Kingsley it is a factually correct and fitting realm of quest and adventure for this historical hero who can prove himself and learn a moral discipline which gives order to the incomprehensible.

Kingsley's evident sympathy with his subject does not stem purely from his attraction to a tribal code, it comes too from a love of the English counties in which the story is set. He had spent an influential period of his childhood in the Cambridgeshire Fens, and he went back there in 1848, accompanied by F. D. Maurice, on a visit which Mrs Kingsley believed had inspired the novel. It is in fact the descriptive sections, and those passages which place the action in a particular setting, which are the most memorable parts of the book. Most readers will especially recall the account of the defence of Ely, and the drowning of the Norman besiegers in the surrounding mire, at the climax of Hereward's campaign. Elsewhere Kingsley evokes the wild beauty of the undrained Fens of his childhood. When Hereward returns to Crowland to begin his grand campaign the landscape through which he passes has a stillness and an expectancy expressive of his new determination, but it also contains a violence which foreshadows the nature of his struggle and his eventual death:

And they rowed away for Crowland, by many a mere and many an ea; through narrow reaches of clear brown glassy water; between the dark-green alders; between the pale-green reeds; where the coot clanked, and the bittern boomed, and the sedge-bird, not content with its own sweet song, mocked the notes of all the birds around; and then out into the broad lagoons, where hung motionless, high over head, hawk beyond hawk, buzzard beyond buzzard, kite beyond kite, as far as eye could see. Into the air, as they rowed on, whirred up great skeins of wild fowl innumerable, with a cry as of all the bells of Crowland, or all the hounds of the Bruneswold; while clear above all their noise sounded the wild whistle of the curlews, and the trumpet note of the great white swan. Out of the reeds, like an arrow, shot the peregrine, singled one luckless mallard from the flock, caught him up, struck him stone dead with one blow of his terrible heel, and swept his prey with him into the reeds again.

(Chapter XX)

It is such controlled and effective passages which make one miss a like conviction and sureness of touch elsewhere in the novel. If anything shows the sporadic nature of Kingsley's art it is the gap between, on the one hand, his meditative descriptive writing or his accounts of physical action, and, on the other, his failure to give his characters a comparably active and meditative inner life.

Despite the care which marks the background research and the use of landscape and wild nature in *Hereward the Wake*, the novel as a whole is an amalgam of confused elements lacking a central logic and direction. Kingsley has tried to relate his hero's private life to his historical role as the champion of Saxon England, but he tends to simplify, or to provide insufficient evidence in bringing the character to life. The most unresolved sections of the novel are those which are crucial to our impression of Hereward's emotional life, his relationship to his mistress/wife Torfrida. Their physical attraction to each other is at first well-handled, but once Torfrida indulges in the 'mechanical art' of magic to win her man the real nature of their love-affair becomes clouded and obscure. Kingsley hedges his bets as to the nature of this 'mechanical art', hinting at times that it is indeed potent, at others that it is merely another feminine wile. From such beginnings the relationship develops unsteadily, both because all the other characters seem to believe that Hereward is bewitched and because Kingsley himself seeks to persuade us that the love is doomed. We are told that Torfrida is passionate, and we are repeatedly shown that Hereward prefers action to meditation, but in basing the emotional decline and fall of his hero simply on an excess of restlessness we are given an insufficient understanding of the real depths of the characters of the lovers. The treatment of Torfrida's involvement in the defence of Ely, and of her withdrawal to a convent after her husband has deserted her, ring truer than does the account of Hereward's disillusion, largely because Kingsley is so awkward when it comes to considering the psychological flaws of his man of action. He even admits that he is unable to describe Hereward's passion after Torfrida's flight; 'There are moods of man', he tells us, 'which no one will dare to describe, unless like Shakespeare, he is Shakespeare, and like Shakespeare knows it not.' It is at such moments that one wonders at Kingsley's artistic ambitions.

The relationship between the hero and the heroine grows stale, but the reasons we are given seem somewhat hollow:

> Alas! for them. There are many excuses. Sorrow may be a softening medicine at last, but at first it is apt to be a hardening one; and that savage outlaw life which they were leading can never have been a wholesome one for any soul of man, and its graces must have existed only in the brains of harpers and gleemen. Away from law, from self-restraint, from refinement, from elegance, from the very sound of a church-going bell, they were sinking gradually down to the level of the coarse men and women whom they saw; the worse and not the better parts of both their characters were getting the upper hand; and it was but too possible that after a while the hero might sink into the ruffian, the lady into a slattern and a shrew.
>
> But in justice to them be it said, that neither of them had complained of the other to any living soul. Their love had been as yet too perfect, too sacred, for them to confess to another (and thereby confess to themselves) that it could in any wise fail. They had idolised the other, and yet been too proud of their idolatry to allow that their idol could crumble or decay.
>
> (Chapter XXXVI)

It is in what is left unsaid that the real crux lies. It might be argued that Kingsley feels constrained by a Victorian modesty not to go into further details of the savage outlaw life and its effect on character, but he does not even try to show us the couple's former intimacy, or their present lack of it. Beside *Romola* or *Sylvia's Lovers*, *Hereward the Wake* seems both evasive and crude. The avoidance of detail might have been less consequential were less stress laid on it as the chief cause of the failure of Hereward's military will. He deserts Torfrida for an advantageous political marriage to Alftruda, a match approved by the Conqueror, but the real implication of what is happening are suggested by a comparison with a later soldier:

> The truth was, that Hereward's heart was gnawed with shame and remorse; and therefore he fancied, and not without reason, that all men pointed at him the finger of scorn.
> He had done a bad, base, accursed deed. And he knew it. Once in his life – for his other sins were but the sins of his age – the Father of men seems (if the chroniclers say truth) to have put before this splendid barbarian good and evil saying, Choose! And he knew that the evil was evil, and chose it nevertheless.
> Eight hundred years after, a far greater genius and greater general had the same choice – as far as human cases of conscience can be alike – put before him. And he chose as Hereward chose.
> But as with Napoleon and Josephine, so it was with Hereward and Torfrida. Neither throve after.
>
> (Chapter XLI)

For Kingsley, Hereward's heroic stature, and the cause to which he is dedicated, are not destroyed by a superior political and military might but by a tragic moral flaw, or, more accurately, a sin. Once again history is said to trace a moral pattern, and Kingsley seeks simple causes and immediate effects. Though one might readily dispute the philosophy behind the argument, Kingsley could have constructed a better case for himself if he had given us a more convincing picture of his hero's moral decline, and had related Hereward's divided private life more closely to his public struggle. The argument of the novel as a whole suffers; initially, we were persuaded that Hereward embodied the best of the Norse-Saxon virtues of his race, and that with a just cause – the salvation of his nation from a ruthless invader – he was fighting for right against wrong; by the end Kingsley has changed moral horses and clumsily attempts to show us a Hereward defeated by his sense of guilt, not by the inevitable forces of progress and the Norman military machine.

Kingsley's muddle is nowhere better stated than in a paragraph in the novel's Prelude:

> We have gained, doubtless, by that calamity. By it England and Scotland, and in due time Ireland, became integral parts of the

comity of Christendom, and partakers of that classic civilisation and learning, the fount whereof, for good or for evil, was Rome and the Pope of Rome: but the method was at least wicked; the actors in it tyrannous, brutal, treacherous, hypocritical: and to say that so it must have been; that by no other method could the result (or some far better result) have been obtained, — is it not to say that men's crimes are not merely overruled by, but necessary to, the gracious designs of Providence; and that — to speak plainly — the Deity has made this world so ill, that He is forced at times to do ill that good may come?

What, then, does Kingsley mean? His final question suggests that a degree of doubt has crept into the once confident justification of the ways of God to his Teutons. He weighs the loss against the gain, and without suggesting that the gain is empty, he speculates on a possible difference in the means. One notion interferes with another, and Kingsley seems to have been incapable of charting a clear path through his conflicting sympathies and assumptions. But nothing stops him thinking both assertively and publicly, and attempting to give substance to his ideas by putting them into his story.

This tendency to equivocate also appears in the treatment of William the Conqueror, virtually the novel's second protagonist. We are consistently told of his genius, his wisdom, and his political, psychological and military skill. It is taken for granted that he is the man of the hour, and king of England *de facto*, *de jure*, and *Dei gratia*. Almost all the anti-Norman venom of the novelist is directed instead at Ivo Taillebois, without doubt the villain of the novel, and an ambitious and unscrupulous thug. By contrast, the Conqueror is a hopeful figure, a true Teuton, a man of force, who, despite the suffering occasioned by his policies, emerges almost as a 'muscular Christian' before his time, especially in his conduct towards Edgar Etheling:

The descendent of Rollo the heathen Viking, had become a civilized chivalrous Christian knight. His mighty forefather would have split the Etheling's skull with his own axe. A Frank king would have shaved the young man's head, and immured him in a monastery. An eastern sultan would have thrust out his eyes, or strangled him at once. But William, however cruel, however unscrupulous, had a knightly heart, and somewhat of a Christian conscience; and his conduct to his only lawful rival is a noble trait amid many sins.

(Chapter XVIII)

Later in the novel, when the disguised Hereward is brought before the king at Brandon, he looks into William's face and feels that 'it was the face of the greatest man whom he had ever met' (Chapter XXX). Kingsley himself never really manages to explain the real nature of this 'greatness'; he implies that the Conqueror has an innate talent, that he has achieved power through his talent, and that Providence has thrust further greatness on him, but, unlike Bulwer before him, he is uncertain of what might lie at the core:

There have been certain men so great, that he who describes them in words — much more pretends to analyze their innermost feelings — must be a very great man himself, or incur the accusation of presumption. And such a great man was William of Normandy, — one of those unfathomable master-personages who must not be rashly dragged on any stage. The genius of a Bulwer, in attempting to draw him, took care with a wise modesty, not to draw with in too much detail: to confess always, that there was much beneath and behind in William's character, which none, even of his contemporaries, could guess. And still more modest than Bulwer is this chronicler bound to be.

(Chapter XXV)

We tend to feel cheated by the 'wise modesty', especially as one of the chief 'live human figures' he had bidden his Cambridge audience to imagine fails to materialise where he is most needed — at the heart of a novel dealing with the events of the Conquest.

Kingsley's shadowy and elusive Conqueror does not, at least, come near to eclipsing interest in Hereward, but he does serve to reinforce the suspicion that the novelist is not sure of his bearings. If William stands for order and progress, Hereward's rebellion is disordering and anti-progressive and history proves him wrong. When Kingsley returned to the theme some eight years later, in the course of a series of lectures on the Vikings and America, his stance was once again clearly defined and Hereward has no place in an account of the happy advance of Norse influence:

England *was* to be conquered by the Norman; but by the civilised not the barbaric; by the Norse who had settled, but four generations before, in the North East of France . . . and . . . with that docility and adaptability which marks so often truly great spirits . . . [they] had become, from heathen and murderous Berserkers, the most truly civilized people of Europe. . . . So greatly had they changed, and so fast, that William, Duke of Normandy . . . was perhaps the finest gentleman, as well as the most cultivated Sovereign, and the greatest statesman and warrior in all Europe.[15]

William is now the unchallenged hero of his age, and a gentleman to boot, and the repeated references to his 'civilised' and 'cultivated' followers suggest that Kingsley was now content to let the troublesome soul of Hereward rest in his crude Saxon tomb. The 1874 lectures stress, like *The Roman and the Teuton* before them, that the devout study of history reveals that 'God's thoughts are not as our thoughts; nor His ways as our ways'. The suffering brought about by the Norman Conquest is transfigured in the knowledge that whatever is, is right. For the lecturer, proper understanding is based on the simple paradox that *Hereward the Wake*, despite its ambitions, had failed to disentangle, that 'the Norman Conquest was the making of the English people'.

Hereward the Wake sometimes seems aberrant beside the two series of lectures, but it grows from the same preoccupation with race and with the early history of England. It is also central to an appreciation of Kingsley's work as an historical novelist, for in it he attempts to examine the concept of a national hero and to relate heroism to national experience. To Kingsley, as to Tennyson, the English were a mixture of Norman and Saxon and Dane; 1066 marked the beginning of the modern era, hence its significance to 1866. The last chapter of the novel effectively rounds off an often ragged narrative by returning to the Fens some eighty years after Hereward's murder, and to the now peaceful Manor of Bourne which had been inherited by Hereward's Anglo-Norman grandchildren. The first paragraph points to the new mood of optimism:

But war and disorder, ruin and death, cannot last for ever. They are by their own nature exceptional and suicidal, and spend themselves with what they feed on. And then the true laws of God's universe, peace and order, usefulness and life, will reassert themselves, as they have been waiting all along to do, hid in God's presence from the strife of men.

But it is men, not God alone, who seem to have been working changes; the draining of the Fens has begun, and the Abbey of Crowland where Hereward and Torfrida are buried has been rebuilt 'in greater glory than ever'. Already 'where there had been lonely meres, foul watercourses, stagnant slime, there were now great dykes, rich and fair corn and grass lands, rows of white cottages'. The landscape, like England itself, has changed into something richer and happier, and the barren or troubled past is forgotten. Hereward the Wake had been interred at Crowland with the epitaph 'Here lies the last of the English'; his grandchildren propose to send to Normandy for 'fair white stone of Caen' to make a new tomb inscribed with the words 'Here lies the last of the old English', and they choose as their own epitaph a third variation, 'Here lies the first of the new English; who by the inspiration of God, began to drain the Fens'. The novel looks to the future not through the vision of its protagonist, but through his progeny which stretches grandly forward to the nineteenth century.

In the Preface which he contributed to *The Saint's Tragedy*, Kingsley's first important literary work, F. D. Maurice outlined its author's dramatic aims. 'A Drama', he wrote, 'should not aim at the inculcation of any definite maxim; the moral of it lies in the action and the character.' Maurice explained further:

It must be drawn out of them by the heart and experience of the reader, not forced upon him by the author. The men and women whom he presents are not to be his spokesmen; they are to utter themselves freely in such language, grave or mirthful, as best expresses what they feel and what they are. The age to which they belong is not to be contemplated as if it were apart from us; neither is it to be measured by our rules; to be held up as a model; to be condemned for its strangeness. The passions which worked in it must be those which are working in ourselves. . . . The unity of the play cannot be conferred upon it by any artificial arrangements; it must depend upon the relation of the different persons and events to the central subject . . . the conscience of the readers must be satisfied . . . that there is an order in the universe, and that the poet has perceived and asserted it.[16]

These stipulations could be applied equally well to Kingsley's work as an historical novelist for they throw light on his ambitions and they present a standard by which he may be measured and found wanting.

8 'Romola's Waking': George Eliot's Historical Novel

Io ritornai dalla santissim' onda,
  rifatto sí, come piante novelle
  rinnovellate di novella fronda,
puro e disposto a salire alle stelle.
                    Dante, *Purgatorio*, Canto XXXIII

No other major Victorian novelist owed so profound and pervasive a debt to Sir Walter Scott as did George Eliot, and few reverenced him as consistently. On New Year's Day 1860, G. H. Lewes presented her with a set of the Waverley novels inscribed on the fly-leaf of the first volume 'To Marian Evans Lewes. The best of Novelists, and Wives, These works of her longest-venerated and best-loved Romancist are given by her grateful Husband.'[1] Towards the end of her life Lewes was to remark in a letter to Alexander Macmillan that Scott was 'to her an almost sacred name'. In the year of *Middlemarch* George Eliot herself described the steady development of her 'peculiar worship' to her own worshipper, Alexander Main:

> I began to read him when I was seven years old, and afterwards when I was grown up and living alone with my Father, I was able to make the evenings cheerful for him . . . by reading aloud to him Scott's novels. No other writer would serve as a substitute for Scott, and my life at that time would have been much more difficult without him. It is a personal grief, a heart-wound to me when I hear a depreciating or slighting word about Scott.[2]

This appreciation of the Waverley novels was not simply an extended adolescent sentiment, it was a vital shaping influence on the nature, form and intent of her own fiction. Scott's spirit can be felt in the manner in which her own first novel opens, as positively 'placed' in its provincial community as are *The Heart of Midlothian*, *The Antiquary* or *Old Mortality*, and in the way in which all of her novels consider the relationship between a particular place and a particular time. The representation of life in the English Midlands in George Eliot's work draws substantially on personal experience, but the evocation of provincial society, through dialect or details of dress and labour, must readily have reminded her first readers of Scott's local colour. Both novelists were fascinated, even preoccupied, by a sense of human community and by the links between the responsive individual and the society around him. In the important early essay on the German realist, Riehl, in which Riehl is praised for his 'conception of European society as incarnate history', she refers in detail to Scott four times, and to Wordsworth (from whom it has been implied she learnt much) only once. If critics of George Eliot tend to see *Middlemarch* as a complex development of patterns established in *Adam Bede* and *The Mill on the Floss*, it is arguable that all three are to an important degree a conscious development from Scott's special understanding of history and society.

When the project for *Romola* was first broached to John Blackwood in 1860, G. H. Lewes was hopeful that George Eliot would 'do something in historical romance rather different in character from what has been done before'.[3] The idea of a Florentine novel appears to have been Lewes's in the first place, but George Eliot 'caught at the idea with enthusiasm', sensing that it was an appropriately ambitious project for a now experienced and established novelist.[4] Given her admiration for Scott, an historical subject was obviously not out of character, merely a departure from the English provincial norm of her completed stories. Her first experiments in fiction had been set back in time from the period of composition, and the distancing had provided a useful critical detachment. The influence of the late eighteenth-century Evangelical movement loosely interrelates the *Scenes of Clerical Life*, and it also provides the opportunity of looking at a recent historical phenomenon in terms of its moral and intellectual impact on fictional characters. In *Adam Bede* Mr Irwine's parish is as yet untroubled by a new earnestness in the Church, despite the evident inroads of Methodism, but there already exists a significant social and religious division between industrial Stonyshire and rural Loamshire. After *Romola*, however, there is a new feeling for history in George Eliot's work, with the life of the fictional community related outwards to political events of more than parochial significance. This relationship, built up by means of careful detailing, and sometimes over-exact reference, is established in

Romola in much the same way as it is in *Felix Holt* and *Middlemarch*, though it strikes most readers as lacking the same immediacy and familiarity.

Like *Daniel Deronda*, the only novel set in the novelist's present, *Romola* is exceptional for its setting and structure, and it can be seen to be strained by its ambition. Both novels broadened the scope of George Eliot's art, requiring a comparable degree of research, invention and firm purpose. Both have been equally disparaged in their time. *Romola* investigates an historical crisis, and it considers its impact on the future through its effect on a select group of historical characters; *Deronda* considers, in its Jewish parts at least, a modern crisis for an historical people, the choice between assimilation and a Zionism which will re-establish roots. The two novels propose a parallel between the progress of the individual towards self-awareness and enlightenment, and the forward movement of the broad mass of humanity in a wider, creative historical process.

The publication of *Romola* at a mid-point in George Eliot's career as a writer has always been taken as indicative of its seminal importance to her later novels, but, as G. H. Lewes pointed out before she had begun work on it, it was also to be unlike the novels which had preceded it. Lewes's real hope was that *Romola* might successfully and intelligently take up the idea of the English historical novel where Scott had left off. In an article in the *Westminster Review* in 1846 he had censured that 'bastard species' of novels, loosely imitated from Scott, and 'crammed for' in history books; there were too many bad novels, he had complained, and most of them were historical, the form 'wherein mediocrity is at its ease'. Lewes continued:

> For the domestic novel a man needs knowledge of character, power of truthful painting, pathos and good sense. For the art-novel he needs imagination, style and a knowledge of art. For the *roman intime* he needs a mastery over mental analysis, passion and lyrical feeling. For the satirical novel he needs wit and knowledge of the world. But for the historical novel, as it is generally written, he needs no style, no imagination, no fancy, no knowledge of the world, no wit, no pathos.[5]

As her first and most immediate critic, Lewes must have been conscious, some fourteen years later, that George Eliot uniquely combined the imaginative resources which might give a new legitimacy to the 'bastard species' he had once so roundly condemned.

Despite a hint of Blackwood's of an 'Italian story' in 1858, the Lewes's appear to have hatched the project for *Romola* in the city in which the story was to be set. They had been moved by Florence; and its 'relation to the history of Modern Art' had aroused in them the kind of keen interest which was shared by many of their educated countrymen. The Victorians, unlike the eighteenth-century Grand-tourists, had rediscovered the Gothic and the early Renaissance, and they were excited by Dante and by the prospect of Italian re-unification. Florence had become for them the most numenous, and the most agreeable, of the sights of the Continent; stimulated, doubtless by the fame of Florence Nightingale and the popularity of Florence Dombey, they even took to naming their daughters after it, while Thomas Adolphus Trollope and the Brownings had made it their home and a frequent source of inspiration. Only Ruskin, of all the notable Victorian Italophiles, was never quite able to overcome his distaste for what the city represented to both the past and the present.

The Lewes's arrived from Rome which, like Dorothea Casaubon, but for different reasons, they had found unsympathetic. The impact of Florence proved to be just as overwhelming, exhausting and dismaying. George Eliot described her mood to John Blackwood:

> As for me, I am thrown into a state of humiliating passivity by the sight of the great things done in the far past — it seems as if life were not long enough to learn, and as if my own activity were so completely dwarfed by comparison, that I should never have courage for more creation of my own. There is only one thing that has an opposite and stimulating effect: it is, the comparative rarity even here of great and truthful art, and the abundance of wretched imitation and falsity. Every hand is wanted in the world that can do a little genuine, sincere work.[6]

The sense of debilitation was soon overcome, but the ambiguity of this first reaction to Florence seems to be directly related to the genesis of the Florentine novel. The humiliating passivity is matched by an evident annoyance at the prevalence of wretched imitation and falsity, and the novel is a response to both. The city was to provide a stimulus not just to Marian Evans Lewes the determined tourist, but to George Eliot the serious and morally committed Victorian artist.

A year after this first visit to Italy she was back in Florence busily foraging for material for her new novel, and able to assert with confidence: 'I will never write anything to which my whole heart, mind and conscience don't consent, so that I may feel that it was something – however small – which wanted to be done in this world, and that I am just the organ for that small bit of work.'[7] *Romola* emerges, therefore, from George Eliot's sense of vocation as a writer, and from a conviction that she was dealing with a vital and relevant subject. Renaissance Italy presented her with contraries and with seemingly irreconcilable glimpses of the worst and the best in human nature, but her artistic detachment springs from a love for the city of Florence as an artifact and a distaste for the baseness of its political history. The Florence of the novel is the Renaissance *polis*, faithfully observed and recorded, but it is also as much a microcosm of the world as Milby, Hayslope, St Ogg's or Raveloe had been in a less spectacular way. Like the fictional English towns, Florence is a specific centre of human activity, though its place and influence in history is greater. In fact, as G. H. Lewes was to point out, probably in order to quieten early misgivings about the novel's scope, most of the scenes and characters in George Eliot's existing books were 'quite as *historical* to her direct personal experience, as the 15th century of Florence', and she already knew 'infinitely more about Savonarola than she knew of Silas'.[8] Though many readers feel that her imaginative invention has been restricted by a need to follow historical sources, one must acknowledge the justice of Lewes's remark in relation to the novelist's own sense of purpose. *Romola* is as much an act of faith in her own art as it is a study of, and a tribute to, the greatest centre of art.

Romola opens with a prelude to which George Eliot gives the appropriately Dantean title of a 'Proem'. Like the much shorter Prelude to *Middlemarch* it establishes ideas and serves to introduce the argument developed in the story as a whole. The Proem gives us the date of new beginnings, the year of the death of Lorenzo de'Medici and of the discovery of America, and we are presented with a vision of Florence, seen panoramically at first, and then, more accessibly, from 'the famous hill of San Miniato'. The first sentence has an upward, consciously epic sweep:

More than three centuries and a half ago, in the mid springtime of 1492, we are sure that the angel of the dawn, as he travelled with broad slow wing from the Levant to the Pillars of Hercules, and from the summits of the Caucasus across all the snowy Alpine ridges to the dark nakedness of the Western isles, saw nearly the same outline of firm land and unstable sea. . . .

Gradually we discern mountains, valleys, forests, fields and cities before we come to earth in the growing light of dawn on the terrace which looks down on Florence. This opening immediately distinguishes *Romola* from its predecessors, for here we are being prepared for something more daring, more self-consciously artful, more universal. Some readers may even have detected reminiscences of Dante and of Shelley's Dantean poem *The Triumph of Life*. Here a panorama of Europe at dawn narrows to a centre in which we are to expect events of international significance, with the turning world held for a space at a single historical moment.

The prospect of the city from the terrace (recommended to Victorian tourists by Murray's hand-book, incidentally) is shared by a Quattrocento ghost, who, we are told, will detect few outward changes in the streets and churches he once knew. Indeed the whole Proem now insists that we should see history in terms of familiar detail, not as a panorama, or as an alien world; readers should see similarities not differences between the human condition then and now. History should be appreciated and understood through approachable, unchanging experience:

The great river-courses which have shaped the lives of men have hardly changed; and those streams, the life-currents that ebb and flow in human hearts, pulsate to the same great needs, the same great loves and terrors. As our thought follows close in the slow wake of the dawn, we are impressed with the broad sameness of the human lot, which never alters in the main headings of its history — hunger and labour, seed-time and harvest, love and death.

Florence represents an unchanging general principle:

. . . an almost unviolated symbol, amidst the flux of human things, to remind us that we still resemble the men of the past more than we differ from them, as the great mechanical principles on which those domes and towers were raised must make a likeness in human building that will be broader and deeper than all possible change.

Like Ruskin, she finds sermons in Italian stones.

The Proem presents a view of history which though it resembles that of Thackeray or Dickens, rejects the 'progressive' idea which one might have expected George Eliot to have taken from contemporary German thought. Her appreciation of Scott and Riehl has perhaps countered any noticeable influence from Hegel, for the Proem is virtually restating the argument she had summarised in the essay of 1856:

> The external conditions which society has inherited from the past are but a manifestation of inherited internal conditions in the human beings who compose it; the internal conditions and external are related to each other as the organism and its medium, and the development can take place only by the gradual consentaneous development of both.[9]

The historical process touches characters in *Romola* precisely as it touches characters in George Eliot's other novels; she is not concerned to show how the past has moulded the present, but that history can be alive to us, and in us, through an awakened awareness of the 'internal conditions' of the men of the past. George Eliot is keenly alert to history and to the idea of spiritual evolution, but her novels take the form of a moral postulation rather than a dialectical argument. More so than most other English historical novels in the nineteenth century *Romola* is a study of character and environment, not an embodied political or sociological thesis. Though we come to understand something of the nature of the political institutions, or of the faith and the art of fifteenth-century Italy through the experience of the novel's characters, we see equally clearly into their private lives and into their essentially unhistoric thoughts, hopes and actions. As in *Middlemarch*, or *War and Peace* for that matter, we are led to understand the complex and incomprehensible movement of history through selected and charged human details. Once we are able to grasp the mechanical principles in individuals, enlarging our sympathy beyond the limits of self, we can begin to perceive the human parts which make a vaster and timeless whole. History is movement, a stream, a flux, and it is glimpsed in the novel at a dawn, but we are to appreciate its meaning only through the passionate intensity of the lives of a small body of Florentines experiencing a crisis which permeates both the internal and external conditions of their existence.

Character, runs the familiar riposte to Novalis, and incidentally to Heraclitus, in *The Mill on the Floss*, is not the whole of our destiny.

Romola is scarcely unique in that it establishes a firm relationship between the external and the internal promptings in the individual, but it does so within an especially significant historical environment. The heroine is not presented as an image of Medicean Florence, but as an ideal and exceptional woman through whom we observe the peculiar stresses of her world. Piero di Cosimo, with his artist's perception, sees her as an Antigone, but she is an Antigone for her own time and in her own way as much as Dorothea Brooke is a Middlemarch St Theresa. The novel is concerned with singular men and women not with norms or symbols; even Tito Melema, the character most susceptible to the corrupting influence of contemporary Florentine *mores*, is an outsider and a foreigner. Tito and Romola come to balance each other, finding divergent paths of exploration and self-expression within the same *ethos*, yet held by and expressive of different aspects of that *ethos*.

George Eliot re-affirmed her belief in the essential links between public and private action in *Romola*'s hybrid and uneven successor, *Felix Holt*, a novel set in a later period of political unrest and reform:

> These social changes in Treby parish are comparatively public matters, and this history is chiefly concerned with the private lot of a few men and women; but there is no private life which has not been determined by a wider public life, from the time when the primeval milkmaid had to wander with the wanderings of her clan, because the cow she milked was one of a herd which had made the pastures bare. Even in that conservatory existence where the fair Camelia is sighed for by the noble young Pineapple, neither of them needing to care about the frost or rain outside, there is a nether apparatus of hot-water pipes liable to cool down on a strike of the gardeners or a scarcity of coal. And the lives we are about to look back upon do not belong to those conservatory species; they are rooted in the common earth, having to endure all the ordinary chances of past and present weather.
>
> (*Felix Holt*, Chapter 3)

Readers and critics who dislike *Romola* tend to class its characters with the fair Camelia and the noble young Pineapple, or they assume that its soil is infertile because it does not have the texture and colour of Loamshire's. Even if we grant that the sameness stressed in the Proem does often seem more akin to the exotic, it is surely evident that in *Romola* George Eliot is studying the effects of a particularly nipping gardeners' strike. Florence and Treby are different spheres, just as Felix Holt's world only barely touches the cosmopolitan one of Daniel Deronda; time, costume, speech, social class and politics divide them one from the other. What George Eliot sets out to demonstrate, however, is that the characters in all three novels are subject both to a formative *ethos*, and perhaps as significantly, to a common humanity. In *Romola* she attempted to consider that humanity beyond the hedges of an Anglo-Saxon garden, and in circumstances which altered the tenor of the whole of Western civilisation.

Despite its ostensibly religious subject – the impact of Savonarola's reforms on Renaissance Florence – *Romola* is a remarkably secular novel. If anything, Savonarola seems to be rather less of a spiritual inspiration to Florence than Edgar Tryan does to Milby, though the effects of his mission, we are led to appreciate, are of a far more resounding historical importance. The political and religious upheavals of the novel are witnessed, however, primarily through their influence on the growing awareness of a small group of Florentines, and, ultimately for the clear-headed heroine, this entails a movement away from the Frate's dogmatic influence. While Tito's actions become increasingly public and political, Romola's are unhistoric in the same way that Dorothea's are in *Middlemarch*, and they have an equal moral and social force. The novel presents only a partial view of Savonarola's mission, but it offers a resolution of it only through the personal and independent quest of the heroine.

We can best appreciate what George Eliot sought to imply in her story by accepting its relation to the history of her own religious opinions. In 1869, six years after the publication of *Romola*, she outlined her view of the future of belief to Harriet Beecher Stowe:

> I believe that religion too has to be modified – 'developed', according to the dominant phrase – and that a religion more perfect than any yet prevalent must express less care for personal consolation, and a more deeply awing sense of responsibility to man, springing from sympathy with that which of all things is most certainly known to us, the difficulty of the human lot. . . . As healthy, sane human beings we must love and hate – love what is good for mankind, hate what is evil for mankind.[10]

This idea of a gradual progress away from an emphasis on the transcendent towards a 'religion of humanity' is a central concern in the novel, even though it entails planting a nineteenth-century seed in a fifteenth-century soul. The human spirit, George Eliot seems to be implying, embraces the same religious urge in all ages, even the urge to find a religion which can dispense with a First Cause. The heroine advances through three stages of faith which resemble those of Western man, though all three, from the semi-pagan to the post-Christian, seem to be equally lacking in a divine dimension. The disquieting element of anachronism in *Romola* lies in this presentation of the Feuerbachian, even Positivist, spiritual journey of a Renaissance woman, and its resolution of her dilemma in a world which appears effectively godless. The effects of Savonarola's crusade are therefore minimised in favour of the evidence that his vision was limited and merely represented a phase in a more general religious evolution.

Savonarola was a familiar enough figure in Protestant hagiography, lauded, from the time of Foxe's *Book of Martyrs* onwards, as a prominent opponent of the aggressive advances of the Papacy. By the mid-nineteenth century his political significance re-emerged in his having a role in the mythology of the *Risorgimento*. *Romola* was directly inspired by Savonarola's Florence, for it was while they were reading about him during their first visit that the Lewes's were struck by the potential and relevance of a novel describing his life and times. In common with most visitors to the city, it was hard for them to escape the reminders of his impact on the culture and history of Florence.[11] Throughout the novel, however, he is seen as a visionary and a teacher but scarcely as a man of deep spirituality and intensity. There is a good deal of evidence to testify to his power over his auditors and his disciples, but we learn little of his inner life, his struggles, or of his unassailable certainties. As a major character in the novel he seems scarcely to exist beyond his public self.

We first become aware of the Frate as a presence at Dino's deathbed; he emerges from the shadows and addresses Romola in a voice which reveals 'a quiet self-possession and assurance of the right, blended with benignity'. He commands her to kneel in submission, and when she does so we know she has felt this 'assurance of the right': 'He was looking at her with mild fixedness while he spoke, and again she felt that subtle mysterious influence of a personality by which it has been given to some rare men to move their fellows.' (Book I Chapter XV) Our reaction to the voice, and to the whole scene in the Convent, is likely to be as confused and ambiguous as Romola's. Savonarola is inevitably associated in our minds with the nervous, prophetic, fanatic Dino, and like Dino he seems remote from the affairs of the sunlit world outside. It is our first experience of Christian Florence and it seems awkwardly alien, both from the indifference of the streets and the dry humanism of Bardo's library. It is a world of silences and shadows. Significantly it is the Frate's voice and not his face, his mannerisms or his mind that we are able to remark, and it is a voice which speaks a harsh and sober mediaeval language. This impression is reinforced when we next see him as he preaches in the Duomo; again the voice is passionate and assured, yet it is somehow disembodied and characterless.

As we would expect of the author of *Janet's Repentance*, George Eliot understands the meaning of evangelical fervour and its likely impact on a nature like Romola's. Throughout the story, however, she exploits the ambiguity in the heroine's relationship with Savonarola. She is repelled by him, but moved; rebellious, but respectful; susceptible to his 'subtle mysterious influence', yet seeking independence. The Frate, as both Romola and George Eliot appreciate, is a rare phenomenon:

> The mysteries of human character have seldom been presented in a way more fitted to check the judgements of facile knowingness than in Girolamo Savonarola; but we can give him a reverence that needs no shutting of the eyes to fact, if we regard his life as a drama in which there were great inward modifications accompanying the outward changes. And up to this period, when his more direct action on political affairs had only just begun, it is probable that his imperious need of ascendancy had burned undiscernably in the strong flame of his zeal for God and man.
>
> (Book 2, Chapter XXV)

The novelist goes on to tell us that she will not 'chalk the dark spots' to render the sacrifice falsely unblemished, yet despite her pretence of historical objectivity, and her honest attempt to present Savonarola warts and all, she never really succeeds in bringing him to life or in giving him the forceful presence of his nearest equivalent in her novels, Klesmer. Much earlier in the novel, when Tito is shown Ghiberti's famous Baptistery doors, he notes the sculpted heads in high relief which 'speak of a human mind within them'; it is a sensation which we can only rarely experience in considering the striking contours of Savonarola's face.

This elusiveness of a central character does not render the entire novel negative, though it does leave large parts of it unsatisfying. This is certainly true of the interviews between the Frate and the heroine, scenes which are crucial to the development of the major theme. The interviews lack the intimacy and immediacy of George Eliot at her most lucid and they compare unfavourably with the scenes which describe the encounters between Janet and Mr Tryan, Gwendolen and Daniel Deronda or even that between Hetty and Dinah Morris. Nevertheless it must be conceded that this stiffness in Savonarola is the direct consequence of George Eliot's decision to give only limited scope to the figure of spiritual authority in *Romola*. The real concern of the novel is to show the growth and development of the heroine's soul and this entails a rejection of the confines of the Frate's faith. Unlike his counterparts in other George Eliot novels, Savonarola and his authority are challenged, and are ultimately superseded by Romola's independent search for the Kingdom. Savonarola does not seem to want to give sympathy, but moral *dicta*; he states precepts founded on a narrow logic and he wants submission not conditioned assent; he loves the sinner out of duty alone, not out of a burning charity. Historically valid as the portrait may be, it fails to give the novel a core of equally vivid characters, for the Frate has neither sufficient mystery nor sufficient blood. Those readers who strain at Dinah Morris are likely to choke on Savonarola.

The final interview between the mentor and his rebellious disciple ends in silence, 'each with an opposite emotion, each with an opposite certitude'. Our sympathies will almost certainly be with Romola and with her impassioned plea for Bernardo, for although Savonarola's countering argument is clear enough, it is cold, legalistic, dispassionate, and framed with a preacher's rhetoric. Once again he places duty above brotherly love. The whole scene is reminiscent of the debate between Isabella and Angelo in *Measure for Measure* on the opposition and balance of justice to mercy. Like Isabella, and of course like Antigone, Romola is engaged in an inner debate brought about by a confusion of public and private obligations, from which she emerges with a new depth and wisdom. The moral victory is Romola's. Savonarola is pained by her dissent, even alert to her reasoning, but he strives to conceal both his irritation and his own inner rebellion against the logic of duty. His feelings are

> nullified by that hard struggle which made half the tragedy of his life – the struggle of a mind possessed by a never-silent hunger after purity and simplicity, yet caught in a tangle of egoistic demands, false ideas, and difficult outward conditions, that made

simplicity impossible. Keenly alive to all the suggestions of Romola's remonstrating words, he was rapidly surveying, as he had done before, the courses of action that were open to him, and their probable results. But it was a question on which arguments could seem decisive only in proportion as they were charged with feeling, and he had received no impulse that could alter his bias.

(Book III, Chapter LIX)

It is a spirited and impressive apologia, but it reveals this conflict within the man for virtually the first time. From this point in the novel, however, he withdraws from the foreground of its action. Savonarola's case, and the cause from which it derives, are judged to be restrictive, and Romola's disillusion with the man and his cause will eventually come to be seen as an act of liberation. We have never really been able to grasp the psychological or religious roots of the Frate's mission, nor the real force of his impact on the faith and culture of the Florentines. A reading of *Romola* will offer few new insights into how he managed to disturb a generation of Florence's greatest artists, from the mature Botticelli to the adolescent Michelangelo. Piero di Cosimo sees Savonarola as trying to 'burn colour out of life', but it is significant that George Eliot chooses as her representative artist one of the few to remain unmoved by the religious revolution blazing around him.

Despite the very real limitation of the depiction of Savonarola's crusade, the evocation of Renaissance Florence can be vibrant and broadly-based, if occasionally arch. The city is divided, caught in a conflict which is as much theological and æsthetic as it is political, and *Romola* brings out much of its variety and its confidence. The story includes sketches of painters, scholars, patricians, soldiers, church-men, tradesmen, peasants, and even itinerant foreigners. In centering her plot on the affairs of a few major characters, however, George Eliot successfully manages to avoid the pitfalls, the confusion, and the general tedium, of a comparable mediaeval historical novel, Bulwer's *The Last of the Barons*. Moreover, unlike a Scott novel set outside Britain, such as *Quentin Durward*, she introduces no Britons to familiarise or interpret the 'foreignness' of Florence to the English-speaking reader. Tito, her outsider, is a Greek, drawn into the city's vortex; Romola, the insider, finds her way to redemption through a very different involvement, but both manage to come into contact with a broad range of representative citizens, fictional as well as historical. Tito, like Bardo, finds Christianity barbarous and antipathetic to the new philosophy; like the young Machiavelli, he adopts a cynic's attitude towards the idealism of the Florentine humanists, and an opportunist's attitude to the mazes of Florentine politics. By way of a contrast, Romola, the heir to her father's neo-Platonism and learning, passes through phases of semi-pagan awakening and Christian responsiveness, to learn a wider freedom in a humanist moral ethic. Husband and wife, therefore, serve to express important aspects of a *Zeitgeist*, and their eventual separation shows something of the inherent divisions in the culture and society of the early Renaissance.

At the opening of Book II of *Romola* we arrive at the year 1494 and are reminded that the Europe that surrounds the central characters is discordant, corrupt, and morally lax, but it is still safe for opportunists:

> Altogether this world, with its partitioned empire and its roomy universal Church, seemed to be a handsome establishment for the few who were lucky or wise enough to reap the advantages of human folly: a world in which lust and obscenity, lying and treachery, oppression and murder, were pleasant, useful, and when properly managed, not dangerous. And as a sort of fringe or adornment to the substantial delights of tyranny, avarice, and lasciviousness, there was the patronage of polite learning and the fine arts, so that flattery could always be had in the choicest Latin to be commanded at that time, and sublime artists were at hand to paint the holy and the unclean with impartial skill. The Church, it was said, had never been so disgraced in its head, had never shown so few signs of renovating, vital belief in its lower members; nevertheless it was much more prosperous than in some past days. The heavens were fair and smiling above; and below there were few signs of earthquake.

As the novel shows, the earthquake prophesied by Savonarola is realised and its detritus begins to block the flow of Florentine civilisation. As many Victorian readers would readily have believed and acknowledged, Florence's, indeed Italy's, magnificence was beginning to decay, to the advantage of the national self-consciousness of Northern Europe, open to the Reformation and to new patterns of government and trade. The picture of Florence in *Romola* parallels the despairing but impassioned image of Venice in Ruskin's work. For both writers a corrupting and corrupted world still produces great art, developed out of a long tradition, but it is quite unable or unwilling to regenerate itself. If the novel shows a society which is effervescent but self-destructive, it places a real hope for the future, not as Kingsley might have done, in the Gothic North, but in an Italian heroine whose path to spiritual enlightenment can stand for that of humanity as a whole.

The tenor of Florentine civilisation is nowhere better caught in the novel than in the tense and moving scene of the supper in the Rucellai Gardens. Here George Eliot brings together at a symposium strands in her historical argument, and aspects of contemporary thinking, and she adds to it the emotions and embarrassments occasioned by the sudden intrusion of Baldassarre. Conversation drifts from food to philosophy, and inevitably to politics. The effete but elegant world of the humanists is posed against the polemics of Savonarola, and then challenged by the look in Baldassarre's 'fierce dark eyes'. His madness interrupts the reasoning and the scheming. The scene narrows first to an observation of Tito's desperate attempt not to give himself away, then to the private agony of Baldassarre, an agony which culminates in his incoherent mumble of 'Lost, lost'. Much as the novel as a whole sees individuals in an environment, this scene moves dramatically from the general to the particular, from the cerebral to the emotional, from the detached to the pathetic. It effectively establishes the painful consequences of the cynical approach to personal relationships which Tito has developed in Florence, and George Eliot uses, as Rucellai does, a symbol of Florentine learning, the edition of Homer, to point Baldassarre's stifled suffering. The supper-party breaks up with Tito temporarily safe from suspicion, but with the striking reminder that he is now as trapped by his environment as he is by 'the terrible usurer Falsehood'.

Rucellai's supper shows how admirably George Eliot interconnects private and public motives in *Romola*. In a roughly similar way, as Barbara Hardy has suggested, she used Florentine art, and especially the work of Piero di Cosimo, structurally and associatively.[12] Piero's masque of Time and Death closes Book I, disturbing the celebration of Tito's marriage to Romola and fulfilling the prophecy of the dying Dino. The triptych of Bacchus and Ariadne, an image of youth and joy for Tito, proves to hold an opposite meaning for Romola once she has been abandoned, like Ariadne by Theseus. When Tito first arrives in Florence, Piero wishes to use him as a model for Sinon in a picture of the betrayal of the Trojans, much as he sees an Oedipus in Bardo and an Antigone in his daughter. Yet more dramatically effective is the sketch Piero takes showing 'Baldassarre, with dark fierceness and a tightening grip of the soiled worn hands on the velvet-clad arm; Tito, with cheeks and lips all bloodless, fascinated by terror.' (Book II, Chapter XXII) Later, in Chapter XXVIII ('The Painted Record'), Romola suddenly recognises the import of the sketch she sees in Piero's studio, and she acknowledges the gulf that now divides her from her husband and his secrets. She cannot bring herself to ask Tito what the picture means, for their trust is shattered: 'There was a terrible flaw in the trust: she was afraid of any hasty movement, as men are who hold something precious and want to believe that it is not broken.' Like Henry James after her, but here with a singular appropriateness to the novel's setting, George Eliot employs the image of a precious object to link Romola's emotion, stirred by a work of art, to the broader implications of the frailty of human relationships. This same frailty conditions most of the social and personal bonds described in the novel, from those of parenthood, adoption and marriage, to those of spiritual and political loyalty. A world which creates and represents perfection, seems to be unable to maintain or even approach it in personal terms.

Tito Melema is the most ambitious and the supremely successful characterisation in the novel. Distinctive and striking though he is, it is important to remember that George Eliot had determined to bring out 'the relation of Florentine political life to the development of [his] nature' and to show his environment as a contributory cause of his depravity.[13] In this sense Tito represents the novelist's idea of the historical conditions of the time more closely than the other characters. Shortly before Baldassarre intrudes into Rucellai's supper she makes a general observation which also relates him to the ramifications of a wider idea in the novel:

> Our lives make a moral tradition for our individual selves, as the life of mankind at large makes a moral tradition for the race; and to have once acted nobly seems a reason why we should always be noble. But Tito was feeling the effect of an opposite tradition: he had won no memories of self-conquest and perfect faithfulness from which he could have a sense of falling.
>
> (Book II, Chapter XXXIX)

The more general first sentence, we sense, touches Romola and through her George Eliot's other heroines, but we already know Tito and Florence well enough to acknowledge the truth of the specific second idea. Tito is malleable and selfish, though he is, like the city, cultivated, learned and attractive. As the novel demonstrates, the two become closely associated, in their successes as much as in culpability; Florence, with its rivalries, factions, backbiting and tradition of perfidy takes Tito up, and it all but lets him succeed.

Tito is not George Eliot's first or only egoist (in *Romola*, at least, he is to some extent paralleled by Savonarola), but he is certainly her most developed and irredeemable.[14] He is self-centred and, like Arthur Donnithorne before him, he shows scant perception of the harm likely to be wrought by his easy nature and his excuses. Tito can be disarming and intelligent, but rarely perceptive; his weak will, his penchant for dishonesty, and his overall lack of a moral tradition lead him to seek advancement, regardless of the likely cost to his personal relationships, in a city which seems to dispense with a need for social and personal commitment. If Romola's progress leads her to altruism, Tito's leads to isolation and cynicism. Godfrey Cass, in the novel's immediate forerunner, *Silas Marner*, might almost be a preliminary sketch for Tito's character, for Godfrey shows a similar combination of moral blindness, duplicity, and terror at discovery. He, too, panics when threatened with the exposure of his past, but once he feels himself safe again it is a simple enough affair to cancel responsibility, and to argue himself out of a need for confession, or repentance:

> As for the child, he would see that it was cared for: he would never forsake it; he would do everything but own it. Perhaps it would be just as happy in life without being owned by its father, seeing that nobody could tell how things would turn out, and that – is there any other reason wanted? – well, then, that the father would be much happier without owning the child.
>
> (*Silas Marner*, Chapter 13)

This brief encapsulation of a mind slipping into the security of excuses is greatly expanded and elaborated in Tito, the deceiving, self-deceived egoist, unable and unwilling to remedy a denial of responsibility, and compounding his guilt in his ignorance of it.

In the opening chapters of *Romola* it is only Piero and Bernardo del Nero who seem to distrust Tito's 'lithe sleekness'; to Romola he is Bacchus dropping 'a wreath of spring' into her 'young but wintry life', and to the excited Bardo he is a fellow scholar and a son restored, though the painfulness implicit in the idea of Tito being a son again escapes the blind old man. In Florence the stranger wins golden opinions; he is comely and young, and his quick wits and his easy smile open doors. When he sells Baldassarre's gems as a first step in establishing himself in the city, however, he finds himself unexpectedly faced with 'the crisis of the first serious struggle his facile, good-humoured nature had known'. Baldassarre's shadow will not leave him and the idea, idly suggested to him, that the five hundred florins obtained for the gems are 'a man's ransom' has to be struggled against by a process of specious, selfish reasoning, Tito's 'first real colloquy with himself'. We are aware of a complex character becoming yet more complex, self-centred but caught in a confusion of impulses and motives. Tito's confusion may be founded on unfamiliar historical circumstances, like the problems of slavery and ransom, but George Eliot renders his internal debate familiar and immediate through a meditative general statement on the consequences of guilt:

> Under every guilty secret there is hidden a brood of guilty wishes, whose unwholesome infecting life is cherished by the darkness. The contaminating effect of deeds often lies less in the commission than in the consequent adjustment of our desires – the enlistment of our self-interest on the side of falsity; as, on the other hand, the purifying influence of public confession springs from the fact, that by it the hope in lies is for ever swept away, and the soul recovers the noble attitude of simplicity.
>
> (Book I, Chapter IX)

The statement is choric and relevant to the development of the novel's major theme of spiritual growth and awareness. Tito slides as his lies redouble on one another and his whole world comes to resemble a series of reflecting, distorting mirrors. He is George Eliot's most subtle and disturbing villain, but because we understand his sin and his dilemma so clearly, we can appreciate why the sinner appears so compelling, even pardonable.

In the opening stages of the novel Tito assumes, like Harold Skimpole, that the world ought to be an agreeable place and that his true place in it is assured by his own agreeableness. If he is supremely selfish, he is motivated by the belief that altruism buys little personal or social satisfaction. Tito has an 'unconquerable aversion to anything unpleasant' and he continually chooses easy ways out of emotional and moral complications; he is a moral coward simply because he is ignorant of the 'moral tradition' of valour. He 'marries' Tessa, for example, unconscious of whether or not his deception might hurt her, but certainly satisfying his own transient need for sexual and emotional comfort. Again we see him buttressing his action with excuses and reasoned compromises, then turning to present pleasure in order to convince himself that the world moves on unchanged by his guilt. George Eliot observes his inner life eaten away by a 'virulent acid' or a 'slow poison', while Tito still seeks a balance:

> He was not out of love with goodness, or prepared to plunge into vice: he was in his fresh youth, with soft pulses for all charm and loveliness; he had still a healthy appetite for ordinary human joys, and the poison could only work by degrees. He had sold himself to evil, but at present life seemed so nearly the same to him that he was not conscious of the bond.
>
> (Book I, Chapter XII)

As far as we can tell, Tito is never really conscious of that bond, though its hold on him, as with Faustus, increases as he finds new anodynes and outlets for his diverse talents. If the world had at first seemed agreeable, Florence teaches him the advantages of a denial of human ties and obligations. By the nineteenth chapter Romola, still in innocence of his deception and separateness, remarks on a change in him to her more suspicious godfather:

> 'You will soon forget that Tito is not a Florentine, godfather,' said Romola. 'See how he is learning everything about Florence!'
> 'It seems to me he is one of the *demoni*, who are of no particular country, child,' said Bernardo, smiling. 'His mind is a little too nimble to be weighted with all the stuff we men carry about in our hearts.'

The contrast between husband and wife is already pointed, as is that between the virtuous and the corrupt politician. Romola's innocence is to suffer with Bernardo's reputation. Tito, who had first awakened new life in his bride, dissolves her trust and her dependence in that other acid of his smiling indifference.

In the two-year gap between the celebration of their marriage at the end of Book I, and the crisis brought about by the sale of Bardo's library in Book II, George Eliot passes over the gradual process of their alienation, substituting the extended scene at the end of which

Romola is forced to admit that Tito's beauty has become loathsome to her. Unlike the Casaubons or the Grandcourts, their relationship does not break down through a strained lack of communication, or mutual resentment, or the irritation of living with each other, but through an incompatability which is evident in their physical separation. Romola is the wronged partner and the blame is Tito's not hers. Those critics who complain of a lack of intimacy in *Romola* do not respond favourably to the fact that George Eliot's historical subject obliges her to pose the private lives of her characters against a particularly varied public life. The division between the husband and the wife arises from Tito's wilful neglect of his bride in favour of an involvement in politics and in the far less straining relationship with the unquestioning Tessa. It is a familiar enough marital pattern of breakdown, ambition and adultery, to the novelist's contemporaries as much as to ours, but it is rendered distinctive in *Romola* by the historical circumstances which intrude into the private lives of the characters. Neither St Ogg's nor Middlemarch are city states of the Italian Renaissance. If we do not see Tito and Romola intimately, it is also because Tito habitually avoids intimacy and the obligations attached to it. He seeks a kind of security in living more on his wits than on his emotions, and his mental agility enables him to avoid an extended contemplation of marriage. The larger, more attractive world beyond the ties of family seems easier to cope with because it does not require ties. Tito treats Romola as he has treated Baldassarre, and he can reject her once she seems to be a threat to his future promotion; Tessa and her children are evidently easier to cope with in that they make fewer demands on his time or his patience.

For a brief period, when Tito feels disturbed by Romola's refusal to acquiesce to his plans, we see him drawn by a residual affection for his adopted father, but still utterly blind to what others might feel:

> Tito longed to have his world once again completely cushioned with goodwill, and longed for it the more eagerly because of what he had just suffered from the collision with Romola. It was not difficult to him to smile pleadingly on those whom he had injured, and to offer to do them much kindness: and no quickness of intellect could tell him exactly the taste of that honey on the lips of the injured.
>
> (Book II, Chapter XXXIV)

Tito, the orphan, rejects the substituted ties of adoption and marriage for he wants happiness and security without attachment or obligation. He sees himself as freer in a public world than he is in a private, domestic one, even though he appears at times to want those private relationships to smooth the tortuous path of his involvement in Florentine politics.

Tito is George Eliot's representation of an aspect of the politics and morality of Renaissance Italy which had fascinated and appalled the dramatists of the early seventeenth century; significantly enough, she too has included Machiavelli and a Machiavel amongst her characters. Tito's attitude to public affairs is as detached, amoral and as cynical as are his feelings for his family; he does harm in both realms without ever being conscious of what he is really doing. He holds no personal malice towards Savonarola, but he is quite prepared to join plots against him, and he seems satisfied by the apparent success of his machinations: 'There was no malignity in Tito Melema's satisfaction: it was the mild self-gratulation of a man who has won a game that has employed hypothetic skill, not a game that has stirred the muscles and heated the blood.' (Book III, Chapter LXV) As the novel demonstrates, however, even Tito cannot escape the consummating Nemesis in which George Eliot faithfully trusted and which she was to reaffirm in the epigraph to *Daniel Deronda*. Tito is pursued, and then destroyed, by the combined fury of a Florentine mob and the waiting, obsessed Baldassarre, but we are also to see that he has been destroying himself without ever allowing himself time to contemplate the idea. His end brings together the elements of his life that he had hoped to sever from each other, and it serves to fulfil the suggestion in all of George Eliot's novels that private, unhistorical acts determine, and are determined by, public ones. Tito is ultimately broken because he had failed to find integrity. Much earlier, in Chapter XI, the novelist had quoted a favourite passage from Æschylus: 'It is good that fear should sit as the guardian of the soul, forcing it into wisdom — good that men should carry a threatening shadow in their hearts under the full sunshine; else how should they learn to revere the right?' George Eliot adds her own meditation: 'That guardianship may become needless; but only when all outward law has become needless — only when duty and love have united in one stream and made a common force.'

In the quotation from *The Eumenides* and in the idea developed from it we have a statement of the central, shaping theme of *Romola*, a criticism of that freedom which is only another form of egotism, and, opposed to it, an emphasis on the restraint which is love. If Tito can be seen to have rejected responsibility, the true union of love and duty is established through the less animated figure of Romola, a heroine who represents the hope for the spiritual and moral development of mankind. Romola is, as her creator readily acknowledged, an ideal, but, like the transfigured Arthur Hallam in *In Memoriam*, she is also the type of humanity reaching out to a heightened awareness and psychic unity. In the closing stages of the novel, the heroine takes on something of the force of a Beatrice, an incarnate *Ewig Weibliche* and a *virgo redemptrix*. The orphans in Florence, the plague-stricken villagers, a chapter title, and one of Leighton's original illustrations, insist that we should see her as the 'Visible Madonna' in contrast to the 'Unseen Madonna', the veiled image carried through the streets. Romola becomes a manifest Virgin Mary, fleshly, loving, and involved in mankind. Through her we glimpse the possibility of religion developed into a new phase, free of dogma, miracles and superstition, but uniting with a new force the vital principles of love and duty.

When *Romola* was first published in 1862–3, the subject of a 'Visible Madonna' had a special currency. In response to the post-revolutionary tide of godlessness and anti-clericalism, the French Church had been actively promoting the cult surrounding the 'manifestations' of the Virgin at Lourdes in 1858. There had been an upsurge in Mariolatry, culminating in the promulgation of the dogma of the Immaculate Conception, and the movement seemed to have been given supernatural approval by the terse words spoken by the apparition to a Basque peasant girl. When Romola is mistaken by the village children for the 'Holy Mother' many original readers must have related the incident to the events at Lourdes some five years earlier. The children report to the priest that the woman they see is 'as tall as cypresses, and had a light about her head, and she looked up at the church'. If George Eliot was indeed thinking of Bernadette's vision she has typically responded by translating a supposedly supernatural occurrence into a natural one. Much as Strauss, Feuerbach and the 'Higher Criticism' had sought to deny the divinity of Jesus, so, in *Romola* we have a humanised, familiarised Virgin Mary. Romola goes about performing acts of charity, tending the sick, feeding the hungry, and succouring the despised, notable amongst them being a persecuted Jewish family. But she acts for altruistic and now un-dogmatic reasons; her duty is to humanity, no longer to Savonarola. Having rejected the narrow path of Church teaching and instruction, she responds freely and willingly to suffering humanity. Her message is unspoken, but its implications are present and Feuerbachian, not doctrinal and transcendent.

Romola is in essence a *Bildungsroman*; it opens with a dawn, and it considers the painful awakening of a woman's consciousness. With Maggie Tulliver and Dorothea Brooke, if less vividly, Romola can be said to reflect her creator's personality and beliefs more closely than do George Eliot's other heroines.[15] Like Maggie, discovering *The Imitation of Christ*, Romola is moved instinctively by a call to duty and selflessness, even though she does not continue to make the same mistakes. Like Dorothea she longs to serve, and at first sees herself as best serving as a scholar's amanuensis; more like her still, she matures through suffering and doubt. Like her creator, whom a phrenologist had described in 1842 as 'of a most affectionate disposition, always requiring someone to lean upon', Romola needs mentors to guide her sense of vocation.[16] A similar dependence on a mentor runs through George Eliot's novels, from *Janet's Repentance* to *Daniel Deronda*, and in the former the 'blessed influence of one true loving human soul on another' is extravagantly rehearsed:

> Not calculable by algebra, not deducible by logic, but mysterious, effectual, mighty as the hidden process by which the tiny seed is quickened, and bursts forth into tall stem and broad leaf, and glowing tasseled flower. Ideas are often poor ghosts; . . . But sometimes they are made flesh; . . . Then their presence is a power, then they shake us like a passion, and we are drawn after them with gentle compulsion, as flame is drawn to flame.
>
> (*Janet's Repentance*, Chapter 19)

Romola's attraction to Savonarola is never blind and unquestioning, but it is nonetheless as deeply felt as Janet's, and for a time, it is as forceful.

> Her trust in Savonarola's nature as greater than her own made a large part of the strength she had found. And the trust was not to be lightly shaken. It is not force of intellect which causes ready repulsion from the aberration and eccentricities of greatness, any more than it is force of vision that causes the eye to explore the warts on a face bright with human expression; it is simply the negation of high sensibilities. Romola was so deeply moved by the grand energies of Savonarola's nature, that she found herself

listening patiently to all dogmas and prophecies, when they came in the vehicle of his ardent faith and believing utterance.

(Book III, Chapter XLIV)

The contrast between these two passages suggests the extent to which George Eliot wishes us to see why Romola will grow to detach herself from Savonarola's influence. The Frate fills the emptiness left by the loss of trust in Tito, but the comfort and the inspiration which he provides give her the strength to continue exploring the depths of her personality, and lead eventually to her discovery of independence.

When we first see her, Romola, a kind of restless Miranda, is reading the story of Tiresias to her father in his secluded library. The broken statues arranged around the room match the two figures and provide a powerful image of the lifelessness of Bardo's philosophy, one that George Eliot perhaps recalled when she gave Dorothea Brooke the impulse to serve a 'John Milton when his blindness had come on'. Tito quickens her, stirring life and opening new prospects of life and love, but her innocence blinds her to his fickleness and duplicity. Savonarola is the third, and supreme guide, and he answers a quite distinct longing for commitment and responsibility; he teaches her the virtue of altruism, and a broader understanding of the relationship between love and duty. The fourth stage in her education needs no mentor, but her independent dedication to the betterment of mankind can be seen to parallel those of Edgar Tryan, Dinah Morris, Felix Holt, Dorothea Brooke and Daniel Deronda. Like them she learns not to lean but to give succour and support. In *Romola* Savonarola is rejected because his disciple grows beyond the limits of his vision, though the coming of Christ's Kingdom on earth is to be realised, we appreciate, only in souls like hers. If Savonarola had prophesied the end of history, with the world anticipating the Second Coming, Romola's final serenity and dedication make for an alternative, forward movement of history, with mankind as a whole growing towards a comparable wisdom and service.

We know from George Eliot's letter to Sara Hennell that Romola's 'Drifting away' and the village with the plague belonged to the earliest conception of the story and were 'by deliberate forecast adopted as romantic and symbolical elements'.[17] Romola's drifting out to sea in an open boat is an attempt at extinction, a desperate act of negation and isolation, but she drifts too on the waters of spiritual emptiness. The symbolic value of rivers and seas had not escaped the

Victorians, and the vague nature of the symbolism was sufficiently diluted to express a whole range of meanings, from the overtly religious to the painfully sceptical. In *The Mill on the Floss*, for instance, water, paradoxically, both gives life and takes it, and throughout the book George Eliot uses the Floss to alert her readers to a unifying, resonant image. We first glimpse the sea-coast in the Proem to *Romola*, where we are reminded of 'the great river courses which have shaped the lives of men' and which are related to the 'life-currents' which ebb and flow in human hearts. Savonarola prophesies a flood of waters representing, like Noah's Flood, the avenging wrath of God, purifying the earth. Though the Florentines, and the Frate himself, seem to believe that the flood is realised in the arrival of the French king's armies, readers surely sense that the prophecy comes to apply too to the heroine's fate. To Romola, abandoned by her husband, 'the wintry days passed . . . as white ships pass one who is standing lonely on the shore – passing in silence and sameness, yet each bearing a hidden burden of coming change'. (Chapter XLIX.) In Chapter LX, immediately before she witnesses Bernardo's execution, it seems to her 'as if she were in the midst of a storm-troubled sea, caring nothing about the storm, caring only to hold out a signal till the eyes that looked for it could seek it no more'. Eight days later this feeling becomes experience, though the signal has been extinguished, when she dreamily pushes her boat out into the Mediterranean near Viareggio.

Romola drifts, therefore, because 'a new rebellion had risen within her, a new despair' and because 'the bonds of all strong affection were snapped'. Her marriage, entered into with joy and expectation, has proved empty and agonising:

> In her marriage, the highest bond of all, she had ceased to see the mystic union which is its own guarantee of indissolubleness, had ceased even to see the obligation of a voluntary pledge: had she not proved that the things to which she had pledged herself were impossible? . . . There is no compensation for the woman who feels that the chief relation of her life has been no more than a mistake. She has lost her crown. The deepest secret of human blessedness has half whispered itself to her, and then for ever passed her by.
>
> (Book III, Chapter LXI)

We are obliged to read through six eventful chapters, describing the fall of Savonarola and the demise of Tito, before Romola awakens in the boat and enters the village by the sea-shore. Her doubt and her restlessness have been mysteriously washed away and the boat now seems like a 'gently lulling cradle of new life'. Free of Florence and the past, for the time being at least, she responds to new duties as the 'Holy Mother, come to take care of the people who have the pestilence'. Her way now is only forwards, and it can broaden out to include Florence again, the martyrdom of the Frate, and the adoption of a new family beyond the confines of marriage.

In the Epilogue, set eleven years after Savonarola's fall, an assured and serene Romola explains what she has come to understand of life, ambition, and the past to Tito's son, Lillo:

It is only a poor sort of happiness that could ever come by caring very much about our own narrow pleasures. We can only have the highest happiness, such as goes along with being a great man, by having wide thoughts, and much feeling for the rest of the world as well as ourselves; and this sort of happiness often brings so much pain with it, that we can only tell it from pain by its being what we would choose before everything else, because our souls see it is good. There are so many things wrong and difficult in the world, that no man can be great – he can hardly keep himself from wickedness – unless he gives up thinking much about pleasure or rewards, and gets strength to endure what is hard and painful.

Romola seems to be contemplating here the lives of the three men who have most influenced her: her father, Tito, and Savonarola, all of whom had sought his own form of greatness. Though all three are long dead, it is still Savonarola's Christian influence which most pervades this Epilogue, just as it clearly continues to shape Romola's teaching. Thus in a real way, George Eliot is relating an historical presence to life which stretches beyond it, considering the 'immortal dead who live again/In minds made better by their presence'. But she is also suggesting that that presence has somehow advanced human experience, allowing Romola, as the ideal, representative figure, to find both her independence and a progress to maturity and selflessness. The past thus impinges vitally and fruitfully on the present, and, rather than confining, it offers freedom.

Romola is a novel about the Renaissance, and it deals with that crucial moment at which a vigorous, revived Christian ethic crossed, and to some extent, married, the new paganism of the humanists.

George Eliot takes this moment and offers an interpretation of it through her heroine's progress to enlightenment. If she tends to see the Renaissance through the eyes of a Victorian sage, it is worthwhile remembering that its spirit and ideas are often in accord with George Eliot's own and that her novel has been often blamed with an excess of philosophy. She may well have come across Pico della Mirandola's *Oration on the Dignity of Man* during her painstaking researches into the background to the story, for the spirit of the Quattrocento thinkers is nowhere better caught. Pico, whose funeral oration was preached by Savonarola, figures in the novel's dialogues, and his account of the words of God to Adam bears directly on its theme of free-will, love and duty:

> Thou constrained by no limits, in accordance with thy own free will, in whose hand We have placed thee, shalt ordain for thyself the limits of thy nature. We have set thee at the World's centre that thou mayest from thence more easily observe whatever is in the world. We have made thee neither of heaven nor of earth, neither mortal nor immortal, so that with freedom of choice and with honour, as though the maker and moulder of thyself, thou mayest fashion thyself in whatever shape thou shalt prefer. Thou shalt have the power to degenerate into the lower forms of life, which are brutish. Thou shalt have the power, out of thy soul's judgement, to be reborn into the higher forms which are divine.[18]

The use of the word divine here refers, in part, to the Renaissance belief that some especially gifted men were inspired by a vision beyond that of the mass of humanity and thereby attained immortality within the pattern of their earthly existence. George Eliot treats an ideal woman in her story, but she renders her ideal human, vulnerable, suffering and growing to maturity. Romola has no apotheosis, and the wisdom she acquires is unexceptional and uncomplicated, but in a real way she stands for man reborn and entire. Men in the Renaissance looked backwards to a Golden Age in order to establish a way forwards; revival was held, paradoxically it seems to us, to be progress, much as it was to the sentimental mediaevalists of the nineteenth century. *Romola*, however, looks back on the Renaissance, not as a Golden Age but as a time of intensified human experience, while its theme looks forward to the ideal spiritual reawakening of man in 'the higher forms which are divine', in terms of a newly expressive faith which no longer requires revelation.

In his biography of his wife, J. W. Cross records that George Eliot regarded *Romola* 'as marking a well-defined transition in her life'; she began it, she said, a young woman and finished it an old one.[19] It is a statement which has been seized upon by those critics who regard *Romola* as uncharacteristic and a failure, and seek to prove it to be so by quoting the many references to the strains and problems its composition entailed. These same critics tend to ignore the note in George Eliot's journal for 1875, also quoted by Cross, in which a similar dejection is recorded in connection with *Daniel Deronda*:

> Each part as I see it before me *im Werden* seems less likely to be anything else than a failure; but I see on looking back . . . that I really was in worse health and suffered equal depression about 'Romola'; and, so far as I have recorded, the same thing seems to be true of 'Middlemarch'.[20]

Though she is simply referring to the emotional states in which she wrote the novels, it is interesting that she links the three together. *Romola* was not just an exhausting experiment, for, when she re-read it in 1877, she was able to write to John Blackwood:

> . . . there is no book of mine about which I more thoroughly feel that I could swear by every sentence as having been written with my best blood, such as it is, and with the most ardent care for veracity of which my nature is capable. It has made me often sob with a sort of painful joy as I read the sentences which had faded from my memory.[21]

Many Victorian readers seem to have assented to the author's judgement on her own work. To the young Henry James, for example, *Romola* was 'the most important of George Eliot's works . . . not the most entertaining nor the most readable, but the one in which the largest things are attempted and grasped'.[22] Lest this should be dismissed as a rash judgement, formed before the publication of *Middlemarch* and *Daniel Deronda*, it should be remembered that in 1885 an older James reaffirmed his opinion that '*Romola* is on the whole the finest thing she wrote', though he is constrained to add that 'its defects are almost on the scale of its beauties'.[23]

It is easy enough to assent to James's view that *Romola* is a deeply flawed novel, but there is good reason to be able to agree with his opinion that the novel's flaws do not diminish its stature, and that it is 'such a failure as only a great talent can produce'. It is certainly one of the major monuments of historical fiction in its period, capturing something vital of the spirit of the past, and expressing that spirit in a fluent, considered and conspicuously nineteenth-century manner. The novel has pleased few readers since the century for which it was written, and this could be seen to be a direct result of the decline in prestige of the historical novel as a form. Critics of the 1920s and 1930s who first revived a serious interest in George Eliot's work did so with little real sympathy for her age, and often in reaction against its values. *Romola* has something of the feel of a great Victorian public building, like G. E. Street's Law Courts in the Strand; it shares with them a majesty, a sobriety, a completeness and a scholarship, but it remains somehow bloodless and unlovable, perhaps, given the nature of its form and function, necessarily unlovable. But the flaws of the novel, like those of the building, are of intention, not of design or execution. Tastes and opinions are refined and re-defined slowly, and it is perhaps only as part of a gradual process that *Romola* will come to be acknowledged as a masterpiece integral to the entire cultural achievement of the nineteenth century.

9 Suffering a Sea-change: Mrs Gaskell's *Sylvia's Lovers*

... We found trouble and heaviness: we were even at death's door.
The waters of the sea had well-nigh covered us: the proud waters had well-nigh gone over our soul.
The sea roared: and the stormy wind lifted up the waves thereof.
We were carried up as it were to heaven, and then down again into the deep: our soul melted within us, because of trouble;
Then cried we unto thee, O Lord: and thou didst deliver us out of our distress.

'A Hymn of Praise and Thanksgiving after a dangerous Tempest'
The Book of Common Prayer

Soon after the publication of *Salammbô* in December 1862, Gustave Flaubert defended his new heroine to the critic Sainte-Beuve; Madame Bovary, he wrote, had been 'rocked by numerous passions': Salammbô, by contrast, remained 'riveted by a fixed idea', she was 'a maniac, a kind of Saint Theresa'. Flaubert added that he was unsure of her reality, 'for no one, ancient or modern, can know the eastern woman, for the reason that it is impossible to associate with her'.[1] Some months earlier, on the other side of the English Channel, George Eliot's *Romola* had begun its serial publication in the *Cornhill Magazine*. Before it had completed its run, late in 1863, the appearance of Mrs Gaskell's fifth novel, *Sylvia's Lovers*, had been greeted with generally unenthusiastic reviews. The contrast between these three important mid-century historical novels is illuminating, not least for what it reveals of three quite disparate approaches to history, and to the treatment of history in fiction.

Salammbô has continued to strike readers of Flaubert much as it struck Sainte-Beuve; it seemed an unlikely successor to the *succès d'estime* (and *de scandale*) of *Madame Bovary*, and its central character was 'strange, remote, savage, thorny, almost inaccessible'. Flaubert had elaborately reconstructed a dead civilisation, content to alienate modern sympathies by disturbing the nineteenth-century reader's expectation of contemporary realism and contemporary values. The reader probably concluded from the novel that he was morally on the better side of a gulf fixed between then and now, and that the world had lost little by the extinction of Punic civilisation. Flaubert had stared intently and *in extenso* at the death agonies of Carthage, much as he had earlier recorded those of a suicide in provincial Normandy. Historical analysis is reduced to a clinical process, with no attempt to conclude with a diagnosis or to presume a prognosis, and Salammbô's *idée fixe*, her monomania, is seen as a product of a culture which is as inaccessible as it was splendid and barbaric.

Romola is based on utterly different historical premisses, far closer to those of *Waverley* than to the scheme of its French contemporary. George Eliot works from the supposition that Quattrocento Florence represents an approachable, understandable, and reasonably familiar world, posing familiar moral problems. Romola, like Dorothea Brooke, is 'a kind of Saint Theresa', but she is free of the mania which so fascinated and repelled Flaubert; she explores a world which is expanding its horizons, and her passions, like her reason, find proper direction in becoming subject to a conditioning maturity. George Eliot indicates that through her heroine we are to grasp an epic historical moral, and we are to understand, through a new and trans-sexualised Romulus, the perennial human quest for spiritual evolution.

Although *Sylvia's Lovers* also tells the story of a woman caught in a confusing and potentially tragic historical environment, it explores neither a monomania nor a quest. Of the three novels it has the least ambitious subject and the smallest range of characters. Sylvia's dilemma might seem commonplace enough beside those of a Carthaginian priestess or a disciple of Savonarola, but Sylvia is a heroine who neither repels as an alien nor provokes disbelief as an ideal. The Monkshaven which contains and limits her tragedy has neither the arcane magnificence and horror of Carthage, nor the portentous significance of Renaissance Florence, but its very ordinariness allows Mrs Gaskell to dispense with the set-piece reconstructions, the vast wardrobes and the street directories which both Flaubert and George Eliot found vital enough to their purpose. The smallness of Sylvia's world is countered by the delicacy, the intensity, and the imaginative power with which Mrs Gaskell observes it. Both *Salammbô* and *Romola* mark new departures and new dimensions in the work of their respective authors, transitions from the affairs of a province to the colourful foreignness of history. *Sylvia's Lovers* remains rooted in a province, described only some 'sixty years since', but it marvellously renews the vigour of the best of Sir Walter Scott's fiction while working out the histories of characters who are distinctively Mrs Gaskell's own.

Like *Madame Bovary* or *The Mill on the Floss*, *Sylvia's Lovers* is especially concerned with the force with which passion can disturb and disrupt the lives of ordinary men and women. If Salammbô's reason appears alien, and Romola's too much a reflexion of that of her reasoning creator, through Sylvia, her family and her lovers, Mrs Gaskell poses an alternative, but perhaps more crucial historical problem, that of the irrational, disordering force of human emotion. The words 'passion', 'passionate', 'passionately' run through the story like a Shakespearian reiteration. Sylvia's and Philip's problem is not that they confuse private and public promptings but that their natural affections lead them away from the possible paths dictated by reason or commonsense. They are not prisoners of fate, of historical necessity, of class, or of economic pressure, but of their complex loving, hating and suffering selves. The novel neither condemns nor bemoans the state of man, it offers a kind of resolution which nevertheless places the characters in an historical perspective, while showing the power of emotion to defy or impede a rigid logic of historical interpretation. It shows us a private dilemma, and it leaves us to draw a conclusion which can relate the individual and his experience to universal experience, and to a wider understanding of man and his past.

Because of this emphasis on passion in the novel, *Sylvia's Lovers* has often been seen as Mrs Gaskell's most 'tragic' work. To the novelist herself, however, it was simply her 'saddest' story, though to Dean Liddell it was 'like a Greek tragedy for power'.[2] The lives of most of the characters are blighted by what happens to them; happiness is transitory, and love brings misunderstanding and pain; careers are marred, families and households broken up, lovers left alone and empty. Above all the relationship between Sylvia and Philip founders on variance, suspicion and deceit; its only moment of serenity comes briefly beside Philip's deathbed. Although the novel does not trace an inexorable drive to destruction, no character manages to achieve the assured worldly contentment which Dickens finally allows to the Darnays, Thackeray to the Esmonds, or George Eliot to her solitary, feminist, Florentine heroine. The Monkshaven of the story, unlike Gray's hamlet, has no even or noiseless tenor. It looks to the sea, the element which determines the lives of its citizens; they, in turn, reflect its restlessness. The novel shows that the passions run deeper than a veneer of responsibility which makes for ordered social life; but if passion can be seen moving men and women in perverse directions, it also shows, with comparable force, that any 'tragedy' is as natural as falling in love and as proper as a sense of natural justice.

Although the story develops unhappily and ends in death and mourning, it does not suggest that history itself is inevitably a tragic process. The war brings maiming and death, it takes sons and lovers away, and it leaves Philip unrecognisably 'faceless', but it can be seen to be no less arbitrary or cruel than the very sea on which Monkshaven's fortunes depend. It is not Fate, or progress, or social disadvantage which ruins lives, but an inner confusion which no power of reasoning untangles. *Sylvia's Lovers* brings together potentially tragic historical circumstance with the constant, potential tragedy of the human condition; the clash produces discord in private lives, not in the heavens, and the blame cannot be apportioned to governments, social conditions, or a malevolent force of destiny. Mrs Gaskell's real strength as a story-teller lies in her ability to convey tiny shifts in emotion and perception, to describe the complexity of human relationships, and to point to the clarity and intensity of ordinary, everyday experience, an experience which can contain both the *coup de foudre* and the petty vexation. Therein also lies her strength as an interpreter of a still, sad human music. Despite its precisely apprehended historical background, *Sylvia's Lovers* is not built around social or political assumptions; it sees individuals in an environment to which they are accustomed and which they generally accept. Characters perceive their world from the limited viewpoint imposed upon them by their environment and they do not enjoy the luxury of a superior or detached historical insight into the relevance of their actions. As a consequence, Sylvia and her lovers seem to be far less victims of historical circumstance than Edward Waverley, Sydney Carton, Henry Esmond or Romola de'Bardi; they have no 'lodestone rock' of ancestry, and they are unable to make the kind of 'political' decision which directly relates them to the decisive issues of their time. Their comparative social obscurity even confines their ability to make grand or traditionally heroic gestures; their geographical remoteness removes them from any internationally significant centre of events. As a rule, they swim unresistingly with the tide of the times in which they live, and if they make real gestures to resist tyranny, the gestures prove to be of greater private than public consequence and go largely unrecorded in history-books, even parish histories. If, like Hardy's Loveday brothers, Philip Hepburn and Charley Kinraid are caught up in a European war, their home-town at least is never threatened with invasion, never receives a visitor as august as Budmouth's, and never produces a hero as celebrated as Captain Hardy. The crucial decisions in *Sylvia's Lovers* are as private as are those of Dickens's, Thackeray's, George Eliot's or Hardy's historical heroes, but Mrs Gaskell's characters have, in their confined world, less of a confusing admixture of the private and the public and only a small element of choice.

This is not to imply that Mrs Gaskell sees history as incidental to her story of humble, provincial men and women, or that she avoids comment on the meaning and relevance of historical experience. In spite of her few chronological slips, her grasp of the essence of the period of the novel's setting is as sure as her understanding of the inner lives of her characters.[3] Nevertheless, we are not shown major political events or social change, but the influence of factors, personal, geographical and elemental, which lie beyond those normally discussed in historical records. Characters are shaped by their total environment, not just by class, or family, or education. Monkshaven itself is isolated, cut off by land and sea from the rest of England; but its provinciality, its seeming inconsequence, and its natural conservatism, are what give it a vitality and relevance to the novelist. In some ways too it is a tiny microcosm of England, dependent on the sea for its trade and prosperity; urban, but still attached to the soil; socially diverse, yet fiercely independent and resentful of interference and change. Land and sea are fruitfully and devastatingly linked throughout the story, standing for opposite forces, both literally and symbolically, and providing the entire framework of Monkshaven's existence.

Sylvia's Lovers considers the relationship between private histories and public history, between tradition and recorded fact, between character and environment. In common with Mrs Gaskell's other novels it evolves, awkwardly for some readers, towards a final moral statement which serves to resolve dilemmas and to relate private circumstances to a received moral idea. It poses the same kind of Christian solution as *Mary Barton* or *Ruth*, and answers social or individual doubt with Christian affirmation. If the end of *Sylvia's Lovers* has been seen as 'tragic', it can also be seen as affirming the spiritual and redemptive significance of repentance, forgiveness and sacrifice. The brief reunion of Sylvia and Philip can be seen to imply hope as much as resignation or despair; it suggests the validity of tears, but they are tears of joy, as well as grief, once passion has been spent. Although history does not emerge as a tragic process, human life is seen as problematic, imperfect and painful, but ultimately it is also hopeful and endurable. The novel looks at the problem of pain not in the context of a *felix culpa*, or of a spectacular divine intervention in history, but in that of human acceptance, maturity and faithful action. No *deus ex machina* imposes judgement or solution, but characters themselves come to acknowledge their failings and go on to seek grace, knowing themselves to be part of a greater but incomprehensible purpose. If we see Philip and Sylvia reconciled only in death, we are also able to see them able, as Mary Barton, Ruth Hilton or Molly Gibson are, to recognise a meaning in the world around them and in the processes of mortality. For George Eliot in *The Mill on the Floss* and for Flaubert in *Madame Bovary*, destructive passion is purged only through the finality of death; in *Sylvia's Lovers* it is resolved, even transfigured. Mrs Gaskell finds no answer to the human condition in the movement of history, she proposes no trust in political progress, in a social dialectic, in evolution, or in a far-off divine event, but in a present, private spiritual assent to God and man. She finds a meaning in the heart's experience of the agonies of the world and in the human capacity for love, for repentance, and sacrifice.

Sylvia's Lovers is nevertheless distinctive among Mrs Gaskell's novels for its historical and geographical setting. It moves away from Mary Barton's Manchester and industry as much as it does from Cranford and the land-locked country town; it draws few distinctions between North and South, and it deals with a landscape which is hard, functional and productive. The novel's second sentence points us to the fact that the story is set back in time by shifting from the present to the past tense; the concluding paragraphs of the final chapter move us forward again into the realm of living memory, with Sylvia, Philip and Hester part of an old woman's reminiscence and a local tradition. But Mrs Gaskell's historical novel is neither aberrant nor experimental; it is the fruit of long meditation and familiarity and it is close in tone and style to her other later fiction. She had evidently considered the possibility of a story set in the past for some years for she mentions an abandoned tale 'the period of which was more than a century ago, and the place the borders of Yorkshire', in the 1848 Preface to *Mary Barton*.[4] In the 1840s, however, the problems of urban Manchester had seemed to be a more fitting subject. The project was revived eleven years later, during a visit to Whitby, and it is perhaps not insignificant that a story dealing with the tensions and divisions of the past should have been begun in the year of *A Tale of Two Cities*.[5]

Dickens had chosen to move his fictional characters from a threatened but relatively peaceful London to revolutionary Paris, and he warns his readers of the private and social consequences of ancient and unremedied wrong. Mrs Gaskell deals instead with a comparatively insignificant town touched indirectly by the wars which follow the Revolution; her characters are seen, however, to be as intimately involved in the events which overtake them as are Dickens's and the press-gang looms as largely and as cruelly as the Committee of Public Safety. But England had produced no Stendhal, and Mrs Gaskell's historical subject was original in that it had been only barely considered by other Victorian novelists, regardless of the steady, peacetime popularity of Nelson and Wellington. Thackeray had touched on Waterloo in *Vanity Fair*, but he had shown comparatively little interest in the accompanying military campaign or in the impact of a European war on domestic affairs; Lever's superficial discussion of army life in his novels was hardly a compensation. Only Captain Marryat's carelessly written, but nonetheless spirited navy stories had popularly captured something of the romance, as well as the horror, of war. If the Englishman's experience of the Napoleonic Wars had not had the epic quality of that of Tolstoi's Russians, as both Mrs Gaskell, and, later, Hardy, were to prove, the press-gang had brought the nastiness of battle into many ordinary households as effectively and oppressively as any foreign invasion.[6]

The appearances of men-o'-war, detailed to empress men, on the East coast of England provide the main historical events of the first part of *Sylvia's Lovers*; in its second part a fresh and consequent military dimension is added in the strange meeting of Philip and Kinraid at the siege of Acre. Despite a few minor inaccuracies, Mrs Gaskell had, as A. W. Ward indicated in his introduction to the Knutsford edition of the novel, a carefully and properly researched background to her story. Although she did not go to the agonising lengths to which George Eliot went for *Romola*, she had at least turned to the sources used for *Adam Bede* or *The Mill on the Floss*. The *Annual Register* provided ample information on the press-gang riot at Whitby in 1793 after which a citizen had been arrested, tried and executed at York for his part in encouraging the rioters.[7] If we except the brief, and somewhat inconsequential, appearance of Sir Sydney Smith at Acre, all of the novel's characters are fictional, and they move in an environment which is imagined by the novelist rather than imaginatively reconstructed from random information. Whitby is metamorphosed into Monkshaven; the old man becomes Robson; Kinraid is introduced into the band of English sailors held in the Temple at Paris; but there is no attempt to interweave real people with fictional ones or to obviously disguise a real place under a false name. In thus centring her tale almost exclusively in a fictional world, and in choosing her characters from humble stations in life, Mrs Gaskell moves her historical novel to an opposite extreme from the heroic mode attempted some twenty years earlier by Bulwer. In doing so she has a freedom, an invention, a clarity and a freshness which had so utterly eluded the author of *Harold*.

The widespread feeling against empressment current in the England of the 1790s pervades the first half of *Sylvia's Lovers*. In Monkshaven the press-gang is especially resented, both as a threat to personal liberty, and an infringement of the town's historic independence. The novelist herself sets the tone in the introductory first chapter, making plain her personal indignation:

Now all this tyranny (for I can use no other word) is marvellous to us; we cannot imagine how it is that a nation submitted to it for so long, even under any warlike enthusiasm, any panic of invasion, any amount of loyal subservience to the governing powers. When we read of the military being called in to assist the civil power in backing up the press-gang, of parties of soldiers patrolling the streets, and sentries with screwed bayonets placed at every door while the press-gang entered and searched each hole and corner of the dwelling; when we hear of churches being surrounded during divine service by troops, while the press-gang stood ready at the door to seize men as they came out from attending public worship, and take these instances as merely types of what was constantly going on in different forms — we do not wonder at Lord Mayors, and other civic authorities in large towns, complaining that a stop was put to business by the danger which the tradesmen and their servants incurred in leaving their houses and going into the streets, infested by press-gangs.

Mrs Gaskell is addressing an audience of 1863, confident of the rightness of its political freedom, and probably as disturbed by this retrospective picture of the press-gang as it would have been by the prospect of military conscription. She renders this 'tyranny' a decisive influence on the events of her novel and points us thereby to its real viciousness. The incidents in the fictional Monkshaven become 'types' of a wider historical distress, but their impact is witnessed through their interference in the lives of a small group of invented characters. The argument about what is happening nationally runs through the opening chapters of the novel, relating Monkshaven directly to the European war.

We see the press-gang at its 'devil's work' and Daniel Robson makes his revulsion plain as his face changes with the 'steady passion of old hatred'. He explains to Philip that he is not opposed to the war as such, especially as it is directed against such natural enemies as the French, but he is set against a tyranny which he finds alien and unconstitutional. His staid, conservative nephew responds with a case for the defence:

> 'I'm for fair play wi' the French as much as any man, as long as we can be sure o' beating them; but, I say, make sure o' that, and then give them ivery advantage. Now I reckon Government is not sure as yet, for i' the papers it said as half the ships i' th' Channel hadn't got their proper complement o' men; and all I say is, let Government judge a bit for us; and, if they say they're hampered for want o'men, why, we must make it up somehow. John and Jeremiah Foster pay in taxes, and Militiaman pays in person; and, if sailors cannot pay in taxes, and will not pay in person, why, they must be made to pay; and that's what th' press-gang is for I reckon. For my part, when I read o' the way those French chaps are going on, I'm thankful to be governed by King George and a British Constitution.'
>
> (Chapter IV)

Philip's voice must have been echoed endlessly, before and since, by honest but narrow men like him. The debate between the two men, both ostensibly patriots, has come to the issue of personal liberty and freedom of choice which dominates the story, but it draws short of an argument on the balance of Liberty to the other Revolutionary ideals of Fraternity and Equality. Robson is nonetheless stung by the suggestion that his hatred of the press-gang is tantamount to treason, and he forcefully insists on his loyalty and his supposed rights as a free-born Englishman:

> 'And when did I say a word again King George and the Constitution? I only ax 'em to govern me as I judge best, and that's what I call representation. When I gived my vote to Measter Cholmley to go up to t' Parliament House, I as good as said, "Now yo' go up theer, sir, and tell 'em what I, Dannel Robson, think right, and what I, Dannel Robson, wish to have done." Else I'd be darned if I'd ha' gi'en my vote to him or any other man.'

Robson's view of the democracy to which he subscribes is biased, hazy, even naive, but it is determined and vigorous; Philip's is, by contrast, undemanding, unquestioning and static. Their debate is about immediate issues, not abstracts, and, as Mrs Gaskell insists, both men have a right to their opinions as responsible citizens. *Sylvia's Lovers* does not deal with kings, or generals or Parliaments, but with the governed. It discusses human responsibility, and where that responsibility touches the relationship between rulers and the ruled it handles the issue as tellingly as Shakespeare does in his History Plays. If the novel, like *Henry V*, does not challenge the *status quo*, it shows accurately and vitally why and what the citizen has a right to challenge, and it upholds the principle of justice as a human reflection of an eternal reality.

The actions of the press-gang in and around Monkshaven fully justify Daniel Robson's passionately rooted hatred of its interference, and he is not alone in seeing it as a challenge both to his private independence and to the maintenance of order and dignity in society. Monkshaven mourns as a community when a sailor is killed resisting empressment, but Mrs Gaskell balances the indignation she clearly shares with her characters against a disinclination to condemn the State, the law, or the officers of the law. It is more than simply an attempt at fair-mindedness on her part, for, as in *Mary Barton* or *North and South*, she seems too ready to accept the basic structure of society to offer any challenge beyond a moral one. [8] She demands a similar acceptance and a similar charity of her central characters, and acknowledges both the strength of a conservative spirit and the real difficulties which beset those who seek a fundamental change in the social order. With Dickens she looks first to a change in heart before she dares to consider the prospect of the coming of the millennium. In *Sylvia's Lovers* she embodies her own fears, and something of her own dilemma, in the divided response of the vicar of Monkshaven to popular dissent from authority. There is sufficient critical detachment for her not to comment on his compromise, and there is a wit and gentleness reminiscent of George Eliot's portraits of clergymen. She presents Dr Wilson as a 'kindly, peaceable old man, hating strife and troubled waters above everything', while offering us an equally telling account of the troubled waters. When Dr Wilson is called upon to preach at the sailor's funeral he finds himself faced with the problem of giving comfort to his bereaved gardener and of interpreting what has happened to the community as a whole. The vicar finally, but nevertheless uneasily, compromises, hastily mumbling a sermon 'which might have done as well for a baby cut off in a convulsion fit as for a strong man shot down with all his eager blood within him, by men as hot-blooded as himself'. In this case there is an inequality in death, and there is a discord between the Laws of Christ and the Laws of Man which Mrs Gaskell sees Wilson as incapable of resolving. The vicar's flock is sent away disappointed, but neither they nor the novelist condemn his weakness. The entire argument of the novel, however, presents a more complex and various approach to his dilemma, and its resolution of the argument in a statement of faith in the Laws of Christ is, in part, a final comment on Dr Wilson's earlier fallibility.

The vicar's inconsistency is reflected, Mrs Gaskell tells us, in that of his flock. She goes on to remind her nineteenth-century readers, and in turn all subsequent readers, that time conditions and distorts judgement. The past, she suggests, will often appear incomprehensible to future generations, and the opinions, hopes and deeds of the men of the past, strange and ill-informed. History, we are told, will judge the dead as odd, hypocritical or confused, but it is a fate that each successive age will face:

> In looking back to the last century, it appears curious to see how little our ancestors had the power of putting two things together, and perceiving either the discord or harmony thus produced. Is it because we are farther off from those times, and have, consequently, a greater range of vision? Will our descendants have a wonder about us, such as we have about the inconsistency of our forefathers, or a surprise at our blindness that we do not perceive that, holding such and such opinions, our course of action must be so and so, or that the logical consequence of particular opinions must be convictions which at present we hold in abhorrence?

She then refers us back to the particular case of Dr Wilson:

> It seems puzzling to look back on men such as our vicar, who
> almost held the doctrine that the King could do no wrong, yet
> were ever ready to talk of the glorious Revolution, and to abuse
> the Stuarts for having entertained the same doctrine, and tried to
> put it into practice. But such discrepancies ran through good men's
> lives in those days. It is well for us that we live at the present time,
> when everybody is logical and consistent.
>
> (Chapter VI)

Her final note of irony is proper warning against the temptation to
impose our own self-righteous preconceptions on the novel, or to
criticise Mrs Gaskell for failing to reach a neat political conclusion
from the evidence she discusses in her work. Her argument here, like
that which opens *A Tale of Two Cities*, suggests that we should
attempt to see our present inconsistencies and supposed certainties
mirrored in the divisions of the past. History presents any novelist
with a puzzle and a maze, and his attempt at unravelling or charting
must emerge from a reasonably detached but nonetheless questionable point of view. As to historical answers or modern redress, Mrs
Gaskell's Tennysonian epigraph implies that they both remain hidden
'behind the veil'.

The idea that our view of history is perpetually conditioned by the
forward movement of time determines both the study of recorded
history in *Sylvia's Lovers* and the examination of the private 'histories'
of the major characters. Private pasts hold and shape characters as
much as do larger 'historical' events, but the ultimate relevance and
meaning of both can be properly perceived only when the veil is
pierced. The burden of past events seems inescapable in the latter part
of Sylvia's love-story. In Chapter XXXIII, for example, Sylvia
returns to Haytersbank in order to collect balm-leaves for her dying
mother; the farm has changed hands once already, but now it is
untenanted, overgrown and melancholy. Like Mrs Robson, it has
lost its purpose in the present:

> Sylvia went slowly past the house, and down the path leading to
> the wild, deserted bit of garden. She saw that the last tenants had
> had a pump sunk for them, and resented the innovation, as though
> the well she was passing could feel the insult. Over it grew two
> hawthorn trees; on the bent trunk of one of them she used to sit,

long ago: the charm of the position being enhanced by the possible danger of falling into the well and being drowned. The rusty, unused chain was wound round the windlass; the bucket was falling to pieces from dryness. A lean cat came from some outhouse, and mewed pitifully with hunger; accompanying Sylvia to the garden, as if glad of some human companionship, yet refusing to allow itself to be touched. Primroses grew in the sheltered places, just as they formerly did, and made the un-cultivated ground seem less deserted than the garden where the last year's weeds were rotting away, and cumbering the ground.

Sylvia forced her way through the berry-bushes to the herb-plot, and plucked the tender leaves she had come to seek; sighing a little all the time. Then she retraced her steps; paused softly before the house-door, and entered the porch and kissed the senseless wood.

Memories, like the lean cat, are haunting but elusive. Haytersbank holds a happier past, but its familiarity has been tempered by time and by the interference of uncaring human hands. It is no longer Sylvia's and the Robson's exclusive domain, in spite of the temporary repossession involved in the act of memory, and implicit in the loving, sorrowing kiss. As Sylvia leaves the farm, however, Mrs Gaskell adds a new dimension and meaning to her experience by making it the occasion of the reappearance of the lost lover; with Charley's unexpected home-coming, imagination becomes a newly disturbed reality. For Sylvia the past has been stirred by the impending death of her mother, by the spring, by the return to Haytersbank, and now by the 'apparition' of one who was thought dead, but it is a jarring and confused experience. For Philip too, Charley is a realisation of an apparition, the unspoken, unshared dread which has haunted his dreams of domestic bliss, but the true meaning of what happens takes far longer to reveal itself.

The power, and conversely, the unreliability, of human memory is recalled at the very end of the novel. For the un-named bathing-woman who addresses the narrator of the story, Sylvia, Philip and Hester are simply a part of local tradition, supplemented by odd personal details. Mrs Gaskell in turn leaves us with the impression that she has reconstructed their story from a vague tradition heard outside the Monkshaven baths, a tradition in which the lovers have been transformed, like the legend of Guy of Warwick which had earlier impressed Philip, by 'popular feeling and ignorance of the real facts'.

A nice distinction, most often attempted by historians, between 'fact' and 'fiction' is now blurred, and the love-story can be seen as part of the still veiled processes of time, and part of the dense, often unrecorded history of Monkshaven, 'a name not unknown in the history of England'. In the end Sylvia and Philip seem one with the 'throneless queen' of whom we heard briefly at the very beginning, but their story has been given a new force, detail and meaning by the novel built around them. In a sense the novelist truly 'makes' history, a more vital history than that recorded by the conventional historian, by shaping it into an historical novel and claiming authority for it.

The introductory first chapter of *Sylvia's Lovers* suggests the extent to which Monkshaven has been moulded by its setting and its past. High on the cliffs stand the ruins of the Abbey which has given the fictional town the first element of its name; its second element, the harbour, has determined both past and present. As we are told in the novel's opening paragraph, the sixty or so years which separate the date of publication from the period in which the story is set have witnessed a doubling in size of the population, and a marked shift in the town's economic function, from a whaling port to a sea-side resort. The passing of time brings inevitable change, economic, social and architectural; the site of the old castle, once co-eval with the Abbey, now contains only the ruins of a later manor-house.[9] In the churchyard where the murdered sailor is buried the past impinges on the present with the force of troubled memory:

St Nicholas had been the parish church ever since Monkshaven was a town, and the large churchyard was rich in the dead. Masters, mariners, shipowners, seamen: it seemed strange how few other trades were represented in that great plain, so full of upright gravestones. Here and there was a memorial stone, placed by some survivor of a large family, most of whom had perished at sea: 'Supposed to have perished in the Greenland seas'; 'Shipwrecked in the Baltic'; 'Drowned off the coast of Iceland'. There was a strange sensation, as if the cold sea-winds must bring with them the dim phantoms of those lost sailors, who had died far from their homes, and from the hallowed ground where their fathers lay.

(Chapter VI)

The parish church, decorated inside like the churchyard with the memorials of mariners, stands above the town, a centre for the community which built it, and suggesting a hallowing of death by water, a meaning in human suffering. Church and churchyard witness to death and to the past, but they also convey the promise of life. For the father of the dead sailor there is at first a pressing doubt — 'How came God to permit such cruel injustice of man? Permitting it, He could not be good. Then what was life, and what was death, but woe and despair?' — but later there is reassurance in 'the beautiful solemn words of the ritual'. Finally, through the repeated whisper 'it is the Lord's doing' he is soothed 'unspeakably'. This scene in St Nicholas' churchyard, placed so prominently near the beginning of the novel, looks forward to its final chapters.

Monkshaven has two communal focuses, its church and its harbour. If the church stands for both life and death, so, in more physical terms, does the sea beyond the harbour mouth. The sea reflects the restlessness in the novel's characters, and it makes and unmakes their destinies. Like Fate it is uncertain, generous, cruel, impersonal and boundless. It moulds Monkshaven's existence, bringing prosperity and death and to the characters a mixture of hope and despair, sorrow and joy. We sense this uncertainty immediately, for when the returning whaler is sighted in the novel's second chapter the news is received with ambivalent emotions:

No one knew what might have happened. The crowd on shore grew silent and solemn before the dread of the possible news of death that might toll in upon their hearts with this up-rushing tide. The whalers went out into the Greenland seas full of strong, hopeful men; but the whalers never returned as they sailed forth. On land there are deaths among two or three hundred men to be mourned over in every half-year's space of time. Whose bones had been left to blacken on the grey and terrible ice-bergs? Who lay still until the sea should give up its dead? Who were those who should come back to Monkshaven never, no, never more?

Death pervades *Sylvia's Lovers* and it is balanced by a hope which is only barely realised and by a love which just manages to transcend pain. The novel places human constants against impermanence, freedom against restraint, law against disorder, justice against cruelty, but it proposes no paradoxes, and offers an essentially private resolution to the public problems it considers. It sees life as a flux, cruel and beautiful by turns, as changeable and various as the sea, but like it an expression of the wonder and mystery of the universe.

The sea determines the life of Monkshaven, the nature of its surrounding countryside, and the character of its inhabitants. The Robsons' farm lies high on the cliffs above the town, protected from the gales 'in the shelter of a very slight green hollow, scarcely scooped out of the pasture field by which it was surrounded'. It is a bleak setting, and the 'long rushing boom of the waves' can always be heard on the rocks below the farm-house, but it is one which seems appropriate for Daniel Robson, who has tried his hand as a sailor, a smuggler and a horse-dealer before turning farmer. He is 'the sort of fellow possessed by a spirit of adventure and love of change, which did him and his family more harm than anybody else'. The remark is prophetic of what is to come, but it also serves to suggest the extent to which character and environment are tied.

Robson is warm-hearted, prickly, opinionated, passionate and foolhardy; his straightforwardness is tempered by recklessness, his endurance by restlessness. It is a character, softened and brightened, whose traits we can observe in Robson's daughter. To Sylvia the same landscape represents freedom and escape. She balances perilously on the trunk of the hawthorn tree hanging over the well, and she takes her knitting to a 'perilous nook' looking out over the North Sea in order to think about Kinraid's travellers' tales. Like her father she is impetuous, a quality which divides her from her mother and the stolid, careful Philip. Much later, when she is married and a mother, she feels a prisoner in Philip's household, forced into an unnatural pattern. She takes solitary walks on the cliff-tops, distinguishing herself from her husband's world and from the 'respectable matrons and town-dwellers' who venture from home only on business: 'She used to take off her hat, and sit there, her hands clasping her knees, the salt air lifting her bright curls, gazing at the distant horizon over the sea, in a sad dreaminess of thought; if she had been asked on what she meditated, she could not have told you.' (Chapter XXX) It is a wild longing akin to Catherine Earnshaw's, but, as we guess, she is also unconsciously yearning for a lost lover whose destiny has been decided by the sea. The suspicion is confirmed in the subsequent chapter as Sylvia continues her rambles, now with her baby:

> She sang to it, she tossed it; it crowed and it laughed back again, till both were weary; and then she would sit down on a broken piece of rock, and fall to gazing on the advancing waves catching the sunlight on their crests, advancing, receding, for ever and for ever, as they had all her life long — as they did when she had walked with

them that once by the side of Kinraid; those cruel waves that, forgetful of the happy lovers' talk by the side of their waters, had carried one away, and drowned him deep till he was dead.

Philip too, deliberately excluded by this craving for solitude from Sylvia's intimacy, guesses the meaning the sea holds for her, but he can never really understand why his wife should wish to escape into wildness. It is only late in the story that he begins to appreciate the power of unrestrained nature and the instinctive sympathy his wife feels for it. He drives himself out onto the moors once his sin has been exposed and has wrecked his marriage, but it is only his final acute suffering and his enforced isolation which brings him to respond to the natural world. If he does not find joy, we at least sense that he has grown closer to the very elements to which Sylvia so readily and freely responds. His hot tears fall into the stream from the bridge upon which his daughter has, unknowingly, offered him food. At the end of his life the waves which have broken his body as he rescued the same child from the sea, continually lap the shore until they at last seem to wash into his consciousness – 'there came a rush and an eddying through his brain – his soul trying her wings for her long flight'. The lovers are at last spiritually one, even though the sea now serves to divide the living from the dead.

The significant use of water throughout *Sylvia's Lovers* links it to such different novels as *Dombey and Son* and *Romola*, but it also partly distinguishes it from Mrs Gaskell's other major novels, with the possible exception of *Ruth*. Although it seems to have been generally assumed that she is a provincial novelist *par excellence*, it should nevertheless be remembered that travel and sea-voyages play a prominent part in much of her fiction. Will Wilson, the sailor in *Mary Barton*, entertains the amateur naturalist, Job Legh, and the heroine herself, with the accounts of his adventures in Africa and the Pacific; in *Cranford* Miss Matty's long-lost brother, 'Aga' Peter, is summoned back from voluntary exile in India, while in *North and South* Margaret Hale's sea-faring brother has to endure enforced exile. Even in the unfinished *Wives and Daughters*, Roger Hamley sets off on a scientific expedition to Africa. Mrs Gaskell herself seems to have been a natural story-teller, drawn in particular, though not necessarily in her novels, to the exotic and to travellers' tales.[10] Although *Sylvia's Lovers* conveys as forceful a picture of provincial life as do the other full-scale stories, we are never allowed to forget that it is set in a working port dependent for its prosperity on a world beyond England, and united by a war at sea to foreign aspirations and struggles.

Charley Kinraid has a larger world to move in than any of the other major characters, even though, as we gradually become aware, he seems to have a narrower sensibility and responsiveness. He enters Monkshaven when the story opens as an outsider with a reputation which precedes him; he is a valued and successful specksioneer, such a one, Molly Corney reckons, 'as niver, niver was, and gets what wage he asks for and a share on every whale he harpoons beside'. He is also thought to be a ladies' man. He arrives as Monkshaven's hero of the hour, the whalers' champion against the assaults of the press-gang from the *Aurora*. To Sylvia he is at first a man of parts, wounded in a just cause as a defender of the right, then later, as her father's honoured guest, he is the supremely imaginative spinner of stories. He comes from a realm beyond her experience, freer, nobler and more admirable than even her father, and somehow larger than life. The aura of romance about Kinraid clearly fascinates her, distinct as it is from Philip's pedestrian interest in security, and her mother's evident interest in Philip. Charley delicately relishes the effect he creates; he exchanges accounts of extravagant adventure with Daniel Robson, but he manages to outdare him in imagination, range and variety, producing tales of a whaler's experience as extraordinary as any in *Moby Dick*. His mind moves from descriptions of the glittering bellies of whales, to tropical islands, from rough seas to 'the fearsome wall of ice' from which 'came leaping flames, all red and yellow wi' heat o' some unearthly kind out o' th' very waters o' the sea; making our eyes dazzle wi' their scarlet blaze, that shot up as high, nay, higher, than th'ice around, yet never so much as a shred on't was melted'. Sylvia listens, 'gazing at Kinraid with fascinated wonder', rapt like Desdemona and, like her, loving the teller for the dangers he had passed. As her father knows from his own experience, it is a sure and tried way of winning a wife in a maritime community, and his wink at the specksioneer confirms the effect he is creating. But Kinraid glances at Sylvia: 'It was no premeditated action; it came as naturally as wakening in the morning when his sleep was ended; but Sylvia . . . coloured so deeply that he looked away until he thought she had recovered her composure, and then he sat gazing at her again.' Charley unexpectedly finds himself as tenderly in love as Sylvia. A real sympathy and likeness draws the two men together, but there is a delicacy in him which Robson lacks.

Despite the local gossips and the imaginings of Bell Robson and

Philip, Charley Kinraid is no mere adventurer. He has a resilience, a spontaneity, a blandness and a simplicity which links him to Mrs Gaskell's other great characters, but though he has a sensitivity which belies his strength, he lacks the emotional steadiness which is marked in a John Thornton or a Roger Hamley. In *Sylvia's Lovers* Philip and Sylvia suffer and learn through their capacity for suffering; Charley is able to shrug suffering off. Like Robson he is variable and restless, but unlike Philip he can readily recognise the force of the passions within him. His way of life and training have given him a distinctive kind of self-control which actively puzzles Sylvia: 'His sailor's life, in bringing him suddenly face to face with unexpected events, had given him something of that self-possession which we consider the attribute of a gentleman.' It is a related practicality which lets Charley marry so soon after discovering what has happened in Monkshaven during his enforced absence, and it is one which again disturbs the trusting, romantic Sylvia. Charley's rise to the rank of an officer and a gentleman is no mere contrivance on the novelist's part, it is the proper consequence of the qualities she has given him. The war helps his rise in worldly fortune, and it takes him out of the limiting social sphere of a single province, but it is not by chance that Mrs Gaskell so often associates 'The Keel Row' with so independent and able a surmounter of difficulties. Like the Northumbrian Johnnie of the song, he seems selected by fortune to be foremost in spite of the fact that

> He has na mair o' learning, than tells his weekly earning;
>   Yet right frae wrang discerning; though brave, nae bruiser he;
> Though he na worth a plack is, his ain coat on his back is,
>   And nane can say that black is, the white o' Johnnie's e'e.

Charley is whistling the song, which we first heard as his ship arrived back in Monkshaven, as he leaves Sylvia before his capture. He whistles it again as he leads his sailors into St Jean d'Acre, quite indifferent to its long history, but determined to save its present from the French. Charley is the kind of self-helper much admired by the Victorians, able to break through class barriers by dint of his native wit, sense of honour, and firm purpose. But Mrs Gaskell does not choose to catalogue his rise in detail, nor does she render him the moral core of her novel and it is the emphases that she does choose which point to the real distinctiveness of her historical novel.

Charley keeps his promise to remain faithful to Sylvia in spite of Philip's desperate conviction that he neither can nor will. His brief return, in a floundering ship which has to be manhandled into harbour, is highly dramatic and it provides the real crisis of the story; but otherwise we sense that the new Lieutenant Kinraid is an intrusion into the book now dominated by the fortunes of Sylvia and Philip. His other, even briefer, appearances at Acre and Portsmouth are of greater interest to the development of his former rival's story than they are to that of the new national hero. When Sylvia is told of his fortuitous marriage to a Bristol heiress, Mrs Gaskell gives her an immediate, unexpected, and challenging insight into the characters of her two lovers:

> The idea was irresistibly forced upon her that Philip would not have acted so; it would have taken long years before he could have been induced to put another on the throne she had once occupied. For the first time in her life, she seemed to recognise the real nature of Philip's love.
>
> (Chapter XXXIX)

This recognition has real force; it is not merely a piercing of Sylvia's blindness, it is an acknowledgement of distinctions within the heart. There are limits to Kinraid's faithfulness in love, just as there are limits to his susceptibility to pain. Once he feels himself to have been betrayed, he responds with positive action, not with brooding melancholia, but to Sylvia his marriage signals a betrayal of her, one which she would not have found in her phlegmatic, but passionately loyal, husband. Kinraid makes his historical mark; Philip and Sylvia appear not to, except as unhappy lovers in a local tradition. But although Lieutenant Kinraid can put pain to one side, he seems to do so at the expense of the kind of insight which is painfully achieved by those he leaves socially and emotionally behind him in Monkshaven.

At an early stage in its composition Mrs Gaskell had considered calling her novel 'The Specksioneer', but she seems to have moved quickly towards the more expressive titles 'Philip's Idol' and the final 'Sylvia's Lovers'.[11] This shift between possible titles suggests a broadening rather than a narrowing of its themes, and a growing acknowledgement that Sylvia and Philip will dominate the story. Through Philip she considers an aspect of the commercial ethic that made England a nation of shopkeepers, and she shows something of an aggressive puritan morality which can distort and stifle passion. In

Philip, honourable, loving, holy inclinations turn sour and selfish; passion betrays reason, and self-interest comes to demand gratification and possession. The whole edifice of what he believes to be happiness collapses on the lie on which he had uneasily constructed it. But the novel does not guide us to condemn either the social or the private sin; it shows Philip as fallible and lacking in self-knowledge, and it follows him through a complex pattern of rediscovery, purgation, penance and ultimate restoration. The final title keeps the idea of love, in its many forms, steadily before us and it comes to embrace the greater love which Philip is able to find. In some ways he is also a full-blooded modern realisation of the shadowy mediaeval figure of Guy of Warwick of whom he reads as a bedesman at the appropriately named St Sepulchre's. Like Guy he comes home as a 'travel-worn hermit', and in his dreams Philip interweaves the legend with his passionate hopes, an as yet incoherent fable with the intimations of a truth he has still to learn for himself.

Philip's idolising love is desperate, but it can also be trusting, long-suffering, elevating. It grows, matures and blossoms with its object, but it blinds the lover to the fact that Sylvia cannot return it. Philip is Kinraid's opposite in most things, not least in the way in which he loves. He is tied to the land and to commerce, while Charley roams free; he reads facts from books, while the specksioneer elaborates stories from his experience. To Sylvia, the distinction between the two men is marked. As he is about to leave for London, on what for him is an adventure and business, she taunts Philip with the comparative inconsequence of his journey: 'Oh that's nought of a going away. . . . Them as goes to t'Greenland seas has to bide away for six months and more.' Understandably, her taunt gives their conversation a new edge, and when they turn, inevitably, to talk of Kinraid there is passion and real bitterness.

In the earlier part of the novel, however, the rivalry between the two suitors can be almost comic, though we know that the comedy barely conceals a genuine enough spite. In one of Mrs Gaskell's finest domestic scenes Philip and Charley are together at Haytersbank; they jockey for privilege, for intimacy, and for sway in the conversation:

Pipes were soon produced. Philip disliked smoking. Possibly Kinraid did so too; but he took a pipe, at any rate, and lighted it, though he hardly used it at all, but kept talking to Farmer Robson on sea affairs. He had the conversation pretty much to himself. Philip sat gloomily by; Sylvia and his aunt were silent; and old

Robson smoked his long, clay pipe, from time to time taking it out of his mouth to spit into the bright copper spittoon, and to shake the white ashes out of the bowl. Before he replaced it, he would give a short laugh of relishing interest in Kinraid's conversation; and now and then he put in a remark. Sylvia perched herself sideways on the end of the dresser, and made pretence to sew; but Philip could see how often she paused in her work to listen.

By-and-by, his aunt spoke to him, and they kept up a little side conversation, more because Bell Robson felt that her nephew, her own flesh and blood, was put out, than for any special interest they either of them felt in what they were saying. Perhaps, also, they neither of them disliked showing that they had no great faith in the stories Kinraid was telling. Mrs Robson, at any rate, knew so little as to be afraid of believing too much.

Philip was sitting on that side of the fire which was nearest to the window and to Sylvia, and opposite to the specksioneer. At length he turned to his cousin and said in a low voice –

'I suppose we can't go on with our spell at geography till that fellow's gone?'

The colour came into Sylvia's cheeks at the words 'that fellow'; but she only replied with a careless air –

'Well, I'm only one as thinks enough is as good as a feast; and I've had enough of geography this one night, thank you kindly all the same.'

Philip took refuge in offended silence. He was maliciously pleased when his aunt made so much noise with her preparation for supper as quite to prevent the sound of the sailor's words from reaching Sylvia's ears.

(Chapter X)

This episode marvellously captures the private, intimate detailing in which Mrs Gaskell so often excels. The Robsons' dimly-lit farm-house is cramped enough to force the lovers into each other's way; Philip uses his advantage as 'family' as far as he can, while Charley plays the fellow sea-man with Daniel and the hero in front of Sylvia. But we guess that the import of the manoeuvres is far from just amusing, and that the rivalry, to a nature such as Philip's, is more than simply a set of surface ploys. The novelist's use of the word 'malicious' for him suggests both the pettiness of the transient emotion, and the very real malice which underlies the interaction between the characters. As the novel makes us aware, by this point in the story he is able to suffer exquisitely, and he is already loving both unwisely *and* too well.

It would be a distortion of so subtle a novel to see Philip purely as the representative of a new, selfish, acquisitive economic order which stands in contrast to the independent skills of a whaling community. Nevertheless, Philip's ambitions are seen to mirror those of an eighteenth-century shop-keeping class steeled against the jibes of Napoleon by a self-sufficient and proud Protestant ethic. Philip starts firmly rooted in a businesslike Quaker ethos, and Mrs Gaskell is quick to notice its spiritual and social shortcomings, but he is able to move, with some alacrity, towards the Church as his fortunes and prospects change for the better. As part-proprietor of a shop, and a newly-married man, he dares to hope for a yet more prosperous future, almost as a compensation for his private spiritual and sexual malaise:

> Henceforward, his ambition was roused — such humble ambition as befitted a shop-keeper in a country town sixty or seventy years ago. To be respected by the men around him had always been an object with him, and was, perhaps, becoming more so than ever now, as a sort of refuge from his deep, sorrowful mortification in other directions. He was greatly pleased at being made a sidesman; and, in preparation for the further honour of being churchwarden, he went regularly twice a day to church on Sundays. There was enough religious feeling in him to make him disguise the worldly reason for such conduct from himself. He believed that he went because he thought it right to attend public worship in the parish church whenever it was offered up; but it may be questioned of him, as of many others, how far he would have been as regular in attendance in a place where he was not known.
>
> (Chapter XXXI)

Philip can be seen, then, as typical of respected, fairly honest tradesmen throughout Britain, but we are to view him predominantly as an individual figure, vexed and troubled by a gnawing lack of satisfaction. His sin, like Mr Bulstrode's, will not lie quiet. If Philip unconsciously confuses religious devotion with a sound business sense, he does so in common with Mrs Gaskell's 'many others'. He also intertwines personal ambition and private passion in his prayers. Much earlier in the novel, in the chapter entitled 'A Difficult Question', he thanks God for the prospect of Kinraid's

departure for Greenland, and again the novelist extends the observation of the Protestant at prayer into a generalisation:

> This night his prayers were more than the mere form they had been
> the night before; they were a vehement expression of gratitude to
> God for having, as it were, interfered on his behalf, to grant him
> the desire of his eyes and the lust of his heart. He was like too many
> of us: he did not place his future life in the hands of God, and only
> ask for grace to do His will in whatever circumstances might arise;
> but he yearned in that terrible way after a blessing which, when
> granted under such circumstances, too often turns out to be
> equivalent to a curse. And that spirit brings with it the natural and
> earthly idea that all events that favour our wishes are the answers to
> our prayer; and so they are in one sense; but they need prayer in a
> deeper and higher spirit to keep us from temptation to evil which
> such events invariably bring with them.
>
> (Chapter XV)

This authorial generalisation is a statement of a central and controlling idea in the novel. Philip's refusal of submission to the will of God
here indicates that for him, as for Jane Eyre, human love can too
forcibly intrude itself between the loving soul and its Creator. Philip
also cannot yet acknowledge that he will only ever receive answers to
prayers that are acceptable to the will of God, a will evident in
historical as much as in personal events. On his deathbed Philip gains a
fuller insight into his past, affirming that he has sinned both against
God and Sylvia seeking to make her his idol, and in serving her with a
desire for worldly goods, for he sees that he had once blindly sought
the aid of a jealous God in worshipping 'idolatrously'.

  This distortion of pure and loving instincts in Philip can also be seen
in the manner in which his love for Sylvia demands a hatred of his
rival. The sight of a piece of the ribbon he had once given her as a
love-token, worn in Kinraid's hat, stirs a final, decisive pang which
twists him into inactivity as Charley is taken by the press-gang: 'He
knew every delicate thread that made up the briar-rose pattern; and a
spasm of hatred towards Kinraid contracted his heart. He had been
almost relenting into pity for the man captured before his eyes; now
he abhorred him.' Private self-justification, signalled by the knowledge of every detail of the ribbon in the sailor's hat, overcomes a
natural demand for public generosity and fellow-feeling. Philip
allows the legal tyranny of the press-gang to express his private,

murderous impulse as a spurned lover. Mrs Gaskell does not condemn him, for we see his sin as neither unique nor damnable; instead she allows him to grow to condemn himself. Philip does not have a simple, fabular moral progress, and there is no easy moral drawn from it. When 'Stephen Freeman' marches off, newly sworn into the marines, the novelist gently reminds us, in the concluding aside of Chapter XXXIV, that our experience, like his, is continuous, and a process of learning and unlearning – 'With a new name, he began a new life. Alas! the old life lives forever!'

Philip must find his own way back. After the great crisis in his life he wanders first into the wilderness, just as Jane Eyre and Romola de' Bardi have to do, and, with them, he finds that sleep ushers in a new reality and a need to go on. To Jeremiah Foster, however, he has been driven forth like Cain, and the analogy seems to have a kind of validity in that we next glimpse Philip in the East, as a soldier in Palestine. He is not an aimless wanderer, for in the Holy Land we see him finding a chance of restitution, risking his own life in order to rescue the wounded Kinraid on the battlefield at Acre. His gesture is as spontaneous and as loving as Prince Andrei's sudden prompting to forgive Anatole Kuragin in the field hospital after Borodino. Philip's confession is far briefer and clumsier, but we know the full weight of meaning in his panted words to Charley – 'I niver thought you'd ha' kept true to her'. There is an added emphasis in his carrying the wounded man in his arms with 'a vehement energy that is more from the force of will than the strength of body'. His action is passionate, 'vehement', but passion has now taken a new, stronger direction, away from self towards a greater love which masters hatred.

Philip's repentance is far from completed by his act of reconciliation with the man he had wronged; he knows that he has still to work the more difficult reconciliation of his love for Sylvia with the wrong he has done her. A pang of sorrowing envy moves him as he witnesses the passionate reunion of his wounded friend Jem with his wife, and through it he learns 'the power of suffering left to him'. Unlike Kinraid he cannot lose the past in the hope of progress away from it. As a bedesman of St Sepulchre's memories haunt him, and he turns over details of words and looks, in order to arrive at the knowledge 'that he was indeed the wretch she had considered him to be'. For Philip, however, this new power of reasoning and of imagining, truly marks a progress, for, by dissecting, he makes a leap into the kind of sympathy he has never before possessed. The novel ends with a final, full and inevitable submission to fate and to the will of God, but it also moves to a reunion which has to endure separation. For both husband and wife there is a need for slow, painful, conscious, progressive movement, a movement which ends with a tenderness and a sympathy which has never before existed in their relationship.

Sylvia's progress is as striking and as self-explanatory as her husband's, but it is also a continuance of the process of maturing, understanding and accepting. The girl we first see, 'much made of . . . by her parents', having her way over the red cloak, moves to an acute awareness of pain and of her susceptibility to suffering. She is first touched by a sense of mortality at the funeral of the sailor killed in the attack on the *Good Fortune*, and nature, time, history and death suddenly loom more hugely than before:

> If she had not been one of those who went to mock, but remained to pray, she had gone to church with the thought of the cloak-that-was-to-be uppermost in her mind, and she had come down the long church stair with life and death suddenly become real to her mind, the enduring sea and hills forming a contrasting background to the vanishing away of man. She was full of solemn wonder as to the abiding-place of the souls of the dead, and a child-like dread lest the number of the elect should be accomplished before she was included therein. How people could ever be merry again after they had been at a funeral, she could not imagine.

We see her developing from this 'childlike' wonder and innocence through painful experience. By the end her awe has a new depth to it, but, if she is wiser, she is also far sadder.

Philip is pleased to note the change in her after Kinraid's sudden disappearance; she is clearly lonely, but she seems more responsive to his advances, and he loves her for it:

> He brought some change into the heavy monotony of her life — monotony so peaceful until she had been stirred by passion out of that content with the small daily events which had become burdensome recurrences. Insensibly to herself, she was becoming dependent on his timid devotion, his constant attention; and he, lover-like, once so attracted, in spite of his judgement, by her liveliness and piquancy, now doted on her languor, and thought her silence more sweet than words.

(Chapter XXIV)

The two, once so starkly unlike, have grown towards each other, though on Sylvia's part this sympathy could hardly be called love. The troubles which gather around her with her father's arrest, trial and execution make her sensible, not of a different kind of affection for Philip, but of an obligation to him, a need to return kindness for kindness. With a lover's blindness he mistakes her new passivity and stillness for the female virtues he ought to seek in the prospective wife of a successful tradesman. His help to the Robsons in their troubles is as real as it is loving, but for Sylvia their benefactor remains, of necessity, a bewildering presence as a lover. She commits herself to him in her loneliness and her confusion, but for her fiancé the anticipated bliss of engagement proves illusory: 'It was not so happy a state of things as Philip had imagined. He had already found that out; although it was not twenty-four hours since Sylvia had promised to be his. He could not have defined why he was dissatisfied. . . . She was quiet and gentle; but no shyer, no brighter, no coyer, no happier, than she had been for months before.' (Chapter XXIX) A little later Philip finds himself longing again for the old 'captious, capricious, wilful, haughty, merry, charming' Sylvia, but he cannot recognise that the circumstances which have served to bring them together are precisely those which have brought about the change in the old Sylvia. If his devotion and his passionate service appear to have achieved their end, they have done so only because something vital in her has vanished with Charley Kinraid and died with Daniel Robson.

Sylvia's reaction to the knowledge that Philip has deceived her shows that something of the old fire can revive. Her mood is impulsive, savage and uncompromising, but it had been glimpsed before in the exchange with Kester after her father's death: 'Them as was friends o' father's I'll love for iver and iver; them as helped for t'hang him' (she shuddered from head to foot – a sharp irrepressible shudder!) 'I'll niver forgive – niver!' (Chapter XXVIII) Both vows have the strength of utter conviction, but, as the last chapters of the novel show, neither can provide her with a steady and fulfilling *modus vivendi*. 'Niver's a long word', Kester had reminded her, and she needs a fuller sense of purpose than hatred and avowals of unforgivingness can give. Though she stoutly and assertively defends her position to Hester and to the Fosters, we sense that she is inwardly drifting and undetermined. Sylvia's quick mind still lacks discipline, just as her heart lacks understanding, and Mrs Gaskell voices the silent aspirations:

If any one would teach her to read! If any one would explain to her the hard words she heard in church or chapel, so that she might find out the meaning of sin and godliness! — words that had only passed over the surface of her mind till now! For her child's sake she would like to do the will of God, if only she knew what that was, and how to be worked out in her daily life.

(Chapter XXXVII)

As Alice Rose recognises, Sylvia needs sufficient humility to match the patience she has already learnt from suffering, but she dare not take the leap. Mrs Gaskell points the difference between the two kinds of unfulfilment in her last chapters, Hester's and Sylvia's, but we realise that Hester's silent devotion has more strength in it than Sylvia's confused inability to admit that she may have been wrong:

'Sylvia, yo' know what has been my trouble and my shame, and I'm sure yo're sorry for me — for I will humble myself to yo', and own that, for many months before yo' were married, I felt my disappointment like a heavy burden laid on me by day and by night; but now I ask yo', if yo've any pity for me for what I went through, or if yo've any love for me because of yo'r dead mother's love for me, or because of any fellowship or daily-breadliness between us two — put the hard thoughts of Philip away from out yo'r heart; he may ha' done yo' wrong, any way yo' think that he has; I niver knew him aught but kind and good; but if he comes back from wheriver in the wide world he's gone to (and there's not a night but I pray God to keep him, and send him safe back), yo' put away the memory of past injury, and forgive it all; and be, what yo' can be, Sylvia, if yo've a mind to, just the kind, good wife he ought to have!'

'I cannot; yo' know nothing about it, Hester.'

'Tell me, then,' pleaded Hester.

'No!' said Sylvia, after a moment's hesitation; 'I'd do a deal for yo', I would, but I daren't forgive Philip, even if I could; I took a great oath again' him. Ay, yo' may look shocked at me; but it's him as yo' ought for to be shocked at, if yo' knew all. I said I'd niver forgive him; I shall keep to my word.'

'I think I'd better pray for his death, then,' said Hester, hopelessly, and almost bitterly, loosing her hold of Sylvia's hands.

'If it weren't for baby theere, I could think as it were my death as 'ud be best. Them as one thinks t' most on forgets one soonest.'

It was Kinraid to whom she was alluding; but Hester did not understand her; and, after standing for a moment in silence, she kissed her, and left her for the night.

(Chapter XXXIX)

It is a slow, scarcely acknowledged, process of growth, but it is a growth away from the death for which Sylvia half longs here, into a fresh confidence in life and in the virtues of living.

Until she comes face to face with her dying husband, Sylvia's spirit remains shrouded, and her life a monotony of unresolved hopes and stifled potential. If she understands, it is secretly and unspokenly. She seems to be waiting for the moment when her heart and her soul can express a single resolved emotion. When that moment comes the knowledge that it is Philip who has saved her daughter from the sea is sudden, almost intuitive:

'Tell me!' said Sylvia faintly, 'is she dead?'
'She's safe now,' said Kester, 'It's not her – it's him as saved her as needs yo', if iver husband needed a wife.'
'He? – who? O Philip! Is it yo' at last?'

(Chapter XLV)

She pauses, 'to gather courage', before she at last goes in to see him. Their reconciliation is heartfelt, purgative, loving and complete, and for Sylvia there is the final, releasing admission of guilt: 'Them were wicked, wicked words as I said; and a wicked vow as I vowed; and Lord God Almighty has ta'en me at my word. I'm sorely punished, Philip; I am indeed.' It is an action which serves to unite the lovers finally and completely, even though the 'ceaseless waves lapping against the shelving shore' outside Widow Dobson's cottage force upon us the knowledge that Philip's death is imminent. Their achieved love, it is implied, must endure separation, and must be seen as a central reality at the core of the painful mystery of life and death. The last interview is passionate, but it is also peaceful, assured and affirmative. It marks both the fulfilment of the potential relationship between Sylvia and Philip, and it is seen as having a place in the natural cycle of things. The lovers have submitted to the will of God, and the wisdom they have acquired contains within it an acceptance of death. For Philip it is a moment of clear vision:

'God pities us as a father pities his poor wandering children; the nearer I come to death, the clearer I see Him. But you and me have done wrong to each other; yet we can see now how we were led to do it; we can pity and forgive one another. I'm getting low and faint, lassie; but thou must remember this: God knows more, and is more forgiving than either you to me, or me to you. I think and do believe as we shall meet together before His face; but then I shall ha' learnt to love thee second to Him; not first, as I have done here upon the earth.'

Human love is mirrored and transfigured in the heavenly, and as for St Augustine or John Donne, earthly love informs and prompts true devotion to a loving Creator and Redeemer. But Mrs Gaskell's God is fatherly and forgiving, never fearful; if He remains the fount of justice and the righter of wrongs, He is also the giver of mercy and liberty. The lovers' reunion, like that of the Prodigal Son with his father, reflects a divine truth. Philip dies in his brief ecstasy, after an almost operatic recitation of confessions and professions of undying love, sure and certain of a shared resurrection. If his is not exactly a *Liebestod*, it is certainly a *Verklärung*.

The last paragraphs of *Sylvia's Lovers* leave the private world of the characters gathered around Philip's deathbed and move us into the more public realm of Monkshaven and its history. The novel comes full circle back to the traditions with which it began. Philip and Sylvia seem doubly released from their present, slipping away from us, not into the oblivion of death, but into a new framework, at once that of eternity and that of the story which has been built around them. In a sense they are free of time. But we are not left at the end, as many bad Victorian novels leave us, with a pious deathbed at the centre of a vision of life, nor are we wrenched away from grief. Mrs Gaskell leaves us with something for tears, but she also presents both the reader and Sylvia with the prospect of life going on, and with a necessary mingling of private histories with public ones, individual experience with shared experience.

The end of *Sylvia's Lovers* is affirmative, but it also suggests the inevitable tension that lies between an affirmative faith and a weight of experience which prompts doubt. It is a tension which we can also find running through the central love-poem of the nineteenth century, Tennyson's *In Memoriam*. Section LVI of the poem provides the novel's motto, and , like it, weighs historical experience, and the fear of meaninglessness, against a trust in progressive development, both in nature and in the individual; it ends with a final assertion of faith:

> 'So careful of the type?' but no.
>   From scarped cliff and quarried stone
>   She cries, 'A thousand types are gone:
> I care for nothing, all shall go.
>
> 'Thou makest thine appeal to me:
>   I bring to life, I bring to death:
>   The spirit does but mean the breath:
> I know no more.' And he, shall he,
>
> Man, her last work, who seem'd so fair,
>   Such splendid purpose in his eyes,
>   Who roll'd the psalm to wintry skies,
> Who built him fanes of fruitless prayer,
>
> Who trusted God was love indeed
>   And love Creation's final law —
>   Tho' Nature, red in tooth and claw
> With ravine, shriek'd against his creed —
>
> Who loved, who suffer'd countless ills,
>   Who battled for the True, the Just,
>   Be blown about the desert dust,
> Or sealed within the iron hills?
>
> No more? A monster then, a dream,
>   A discord. Dragons of the prime,
>   That tare each other in their slime,
> Were mellow music match'd with him.
>
> O life as futile, then, as frail!
>   O for thy voice to soothe and bless!
>   What hope of answer, or redress?
> Behind the veil, behind the veil.[12]

The last phrases quietly provide the answer. *Sylvia's Lovers* too poses this faith against the confusion that the past and the perpetual problem of pain seem to offer. In the novel, as in the poem, the heart is seen, in Pascal's sense, to have its reasons. If passion can disrupt the peace of mind and body, its place in life is acknowledged together with a trust in spiritual development. For Mrs Gaskell's characters the quest for understanding is as painful and demanding as it is for George Eliot's more cerebral heroines; like them they must work towards meaning, and must test knowledge against experience, but for Philip Hepburn an anticipation of resurrection is grounded in the knowledge that he has already experienced regeneration within the pattern of his mortal existence.

Idées fixes or monomanias comparable to those of a Salammbô or a Saint Theresa have no place in Mrs Gaskell's fiction. Obsessions which imprison the self, however altruistically, remain restrictions to the process which most interests her, that of growing, questioning, maturing, feeling, changing, learning and loving. If the faith of *Sylvia's Lovers* proclaims that human life is understood when it is seen within a divine pattern of meaning, and subject to eternal movement, it is because Mrs Gaskell trusts that this is the only valid lesson to be learnt from history, especially a history which is centred around the aspirations of the human heart. The novel does not counsel passivity; it sees love as active and creative, and human relationships as essential to living the full life. Passion needs to find a proper and fulfilling direction, and as all of her novels show, love requires sacrifice and endurance as much as it gives purpose. The egotism of the *idée fixe*, by contrast, only brings isolation. If this was a problem which did not especially concern Flaubert in his *Salammbô* it was one to which he was to come in his *Trois Contes* where love and sacrifice are as central, as personal, even as sad, as they seem in *Sylvia's Lovers*.

10 Marching into the Night: Thomas Hardy's *The Trumpet-Major*

> When I have seen by Time's fell hand defaced
> The rich-proud cost of outworn buried age;
> When sometime lofty towers I see down-razed,
> And brass eternal slave to mortal rage;
> When I have seen the hungry ocean gain
> Advantage on the kingdom of the shore,
> And the firm soil win of the watery main,
> Increasing store with loss and loss with store;
> When I have seen such interchange of state,
> Or state itself confounded to decay;
> Ruin hath taught me thus to ruminate,
> That Time will come and take my love away.
>> This thought is as a death, which cannot choose
>> But weep to have that which it fears to lose.
>
> Shakespeare, Sonnet LXIV

When Jude Fawley is rejected by the authorities of the Christminster colleges to which he has applied after ten years of hard classical labour, he walks abstractly to the centre of the city and stands at the Fourways considering the groups of people who are also standing and waiting:

> It had more history than the oldest college in the city. It was literally teeming, stratified, with the shades of human groups, who had met there for tragedy, comedy, farce; real enactments of the intensest kind. At Fourways men had stood and talked of Napoleon, the loss of America, the execution of King Charles, the burning of the Martyrs, the Crusades, the Norman Conquest, possibly of the arrival of Caesar. Here the two sexes had met for loving, hating, coupling, parting; had waited, had suffered, for each other; had triumphed over each other, cursed each other in jealousy, blessed each other in forgiveness.

He began to see that the town life was a book of humanity infinitely more palpitating, varied and compendious than the gown life. These struggling men and women before him were the reality of Christminster, though they knew little of Christ or Minster. That was one of the humours of things. The floating population of students and teachers, who did know both in a way, were not Christminster in a local sense at all.

(Part II, Chapter vi)

For Jude, the Fourways emerges comfortingly and properly as the real centre of the living, working, continuing Christminster; it is the pivot of the city's real and mostly unrecorded history, and it is the focus and the shared possession of those citizens who are truly Christminster 'in a local sense'.

Thomas Hardy's own local sense of the Wessex of his experience and his imagination is evident in his peculiar alertness to time and place in his fiction, and to the shared history of sites like the Fourways. To Hardy, as much as to George Eliot, society is 'incarnate history', but to Hardy that incarnation was revealed in the continuity of a tight rural community, in seasonal and social patterns, in geography and architecture, and in local traditions and memories. Hardy felt that he belonged to Wessex, tied by his Norman and Saxon blood to a particular English province, and sensitive to both the infinite variety and the consistency of an enclosed provinciality. He opens his strangely elusive third-person autobiography of 1928 with a specific date and a specific place, but before he goes on to claim descent from the grand le Hardys, the less grand Saxon Swetmans, and connections with Nelson's Captain Hardy, he describes the shabby-genteel residents in the cottages next to his birthplace:

The domiciles were quaint, brass-knockered, and green-shuttered then, some with green garden-doors and white balls on the posts, and mainly occupied by lifeholders of substantial footing like the Hardys themselves. In the years of his infancy, or shortly preceding it, the personages tenanting these few houses included two retired military officers, one old navy lieutenant, a small farmer and tranter, a relieving officer and registrar, and an old militiaman, whose wife was the monthly nurse that assisted Thomas Hardy into the world.[1]

Such a community on the edge of Higher Bockhampton was not

shaped only by rural silence and slow time; it was haunted throughout the novelist's boyhood by memories, and especially by the memories of a military and naval presence in the recent past.

Hardy prefaced his only true historical novel, *The Trumpet-Major*, with the observation that 'the present tale is founded more largely on testimony – oral and written – than any other in this series'. It is distinct amongst the Wessex novels not just for its evocation of the past, and of time remembered, but for the clarity of its historical detail and its sense of a community caught up in time. The preface speaks of 'casual relics' of the Napoleonic era familiar enough to a Wessex boy with so developed a local sense – of an outhouse door riddled with bullet holes, of a heap of bricks and clods on a beacon-hill, of worm-eaten shafts and iron heads of pikes, of ridges on the downs thrown up by encampments of soldiers, and of fragments of volunteer uniforms. The very beginning of the novel draws us effectively and immediately into the story, much as Hardy himself must have felt the immediacy of the historical characters he was imagining:

> In the days of high-waisted and muslin-gowned women, when the vast amount of soldiering going on in the country was a cause of much trembling to the sex, there lived in a village near the Wessex coast two ladies of good report, though unfortunately of limited means. The elder was a Mrs. Martha Garland, a landscape-painter's widow, and the other was her only daughter Anne.

The outline is firm and clear, and it already suggests a likely development of the story from a combination of the widow and her daughter and the 'vast amount of soldiering going on'. The details of the women's costume indicate that the novel is set back in time and in the eighteen-hundreds, but the 'trembling' occasioned by the soldiers remains, as yet, usefully ambiguous, neither wholly threatening, nor gently amorous. The Garlands, like the Hardys in the 1840s, are of good report, and they have been given a physical, social, and geographical definition; but unlike them they live in a world in which war is real, in which the uniforms are bright and the pikes sharp.

The first chapter of *The Trumpet-Major* goes on to introduce two convergent aspects of recent historical experience. Hardy is pre-occupied with war, and as the Spirit Sinister later remarks in *The Dynasts*, 'war makes rattling good history', and he is equally fascinated by the effects of the passing of time. The mill in his fictional village of Overcombe, the focus of most of the novel's action, has declined socially from its former function as a manor-house but its flag-stones have nonetheless been 'worn into a gutter by the ebb and flow of feet that had been going on there ever since Tudor times'. The idea of temporal flux is again suggested by the mill-stream which 'steals away, like Time'. At the beginning Anne Garland looks out of her window in the Garlands' domestic half of the Tudor mill, as the heaviness of noon stills and stagnates human activity in the village and in the fields around it, but her private reverie, and that of the whole community, is broken suddenly by the appearance on the slopes of the downs of two mounted troopers whose 'burnished chains, buckles and plates of their trappings shone like looking-glasses'. Like the flash of Lancelot in the Lady of Shalott's mirror, the troopers shatter an insular stillness, riding 'proudly on as if nothing less than crowns and empires ever concerned their magnificent minds'. Overcombe and its inhabitants are shifted into another reality which extends their own; they are brought into the same context as the crowns and empires at stake in the European war and they are made forcibly aware that they too live in a time of 'The Breaking of Nations'. The village has never been outside time or history, but it is now caught up in a new and protracted war, and it is given a fresh historical significance by it.

The two troopers are a prelude to the arrival of a regiment which will disturb the settled provincial rhythms of the village, but the camp on the slopes above Overcombe becomes a new centre of interest for a wide area:

> Though nobody seemed to be looking on but the few at the window and in the village street, there were, as a matter of fact, many eyes converging on that military arrival in its high and conspicuous position, not to mention the glances of birds and other wild creatures. Men in distant gardens, women in orchards and at cottage-doors, shepherds on remote hills, turnip-hoers in blue-green enclosures miles away, captains with spy-glasses out at sea, were regarding the picture keenly. Those three or four thousand men of one machine-like movement, some of them swashbucklers by nature; others, doubtless, of a quiet shop-keeping disposition who had inadvertently got into uniform – all of them had arrived from nobody knew where, and hence were a matter of great curiosity. They seemed to the mere eye to belong to a different order of beings from those who inhabited the valleys below.

Apparently unconscious and careless of what all the world was doing elsewhere, they remained picturesquely engrossed in the business of making themselves a habitation on the isolated spot which they had chosen.

The disturbance is noted by the animals as much as by the human occupants of the surrounding countryside, and is noted too by captains at sea, either French or British, but certainly a brief reminder of the war which has now forced Overcombe into a kind of front-line. Hardy stresses, through reference to the swashbucklers and to those who had 'inadvertently got into uniform' that the army is as much a social and temperamental mix as the village by which it is encamped; indeed, through Miller Loveday's sons, one a sailor, the other the trumpet-major of the novel's title, he reminds us that in an important way the war both disrupts and extends patterns of village kinship and labour. The army contains villagers, just as now the village is obliged to receive the army. When the soldiers first arrive they seem to be a 'different order of beings' going about their separate but intrusive business; as the story develops, however, the village and the regiment interlock and become, temporarily at least, interdependent.

Overcombe is never fought over, abandoned to the enemy, or defended against an invading army, but, as Hardy suggests in his short story *A Tradition of 1804*, an invasion from France seemed to be a real enough threat in the period of the novel's setting. At one point in the story the villagers are readily convinced that the French have landed and prepare to abandon their homes. Nevertheless, violence intrudes in other ways, and, just as in *Sylvia's Lovers*, the press-gang and death in battle can be seen to enlarge a disturbance which already exists within the small community. John Loveday and his Wessex companions are to die on one of the 'bloody battle-fields of Spain', while John's brother, Bob, is pursued by the press-gang; in both cases the military violence hinges on some private motivation, an amatory defeat or an active jealousy. If John dies heroically in some foreign field, Hardy nevertheless reminds us, through old Mr Derriman's death by natural causes, that human mortality is constant in both war and peace. The European war joins Overcombe to the armed forces, to the nation as a whole, and to Europe beyond, through a series of broadening perspectives; though we see national and European affairs from Overcombe's point of view, we see all human affairs subject to the same processes of time and death.

Hardy's sense of the passing of time within an historical perspective gives the relatively simple story of *The Trumpet-Major* its distinctiveness and stature amongst the Wessex novels. He binds the slower time of Overcombe and Budmouth to the epic time-scale of the war abroad, but he shows us kings, statesmen, dying heroes, battles, and invasions almost exclusively as they touch the local problems of Wessex. Bob Loveday helps to carry the dying Nelson from the deck of the *Victory* on which he has been serving, but we see time passing as painfully, if less spectacularly, for Bob's father at home in the mill. The soldiers who camp on the downs are to die, or win victories which will decide the future both for Europe and for Wessex, but we see them held by private matters as lovers, neighbours, companions, and visitors. The army which seemed alien, arriving in 'one machine-like movement', proves to contain individuals with distinct ideas, feelings, hopes and passions, and the novel concentrates on the affairs of a tiny but complex group. Much as *The Dynasts* attempts to persuade us of the vitality and the ultimate smallness of human affairs placed in the huger dimension of time, so the less ambitious novel shows us the microcosm and allows us to draw larger conclusions for the macrocosm.

The Trumpet-Major renders the effects of time familiar much as Thackeray had familiarised history. In the novel's second chapter, for example, Hardy tells us of Miller Loveday's humble ancestors and, in the process, he mocks the aristocratic pretensions of conventional histories and genealogies; Loveday is the present representative of 'an ancient family of corn-grinders whose history is lost in the mists of antiquity', and his ancestral line is 'contemporaneous with that of De Ros, Howard and De La Zouche'. It is perhaps a wry comment on the quarterings essential to the pedigree of an Ainsworth hero, but in *The Trumpet-Major* the Saxon miller's family, and all the families like his, are seen to have contributed as much, if not more, to the fabric of national history as the knights and barons of romance; not only are kind hearts like the Lovedays' more than coronets, but the blood of Norman and yeoman together has made the destinies of England past, present and future. The unwritten history of England is that of the miller's unnamed ancestors, resting in their unvisited tombs; an older Loveday improved the family fortunes and their estate, and indirectly the shared wealth of the nation, by adding a chimney and an extra pair of millstones to his property. Hardy's point is not flippant, for, like the Fourways at Christminster, it is an important key to his understanding of history and how history is made. Loveday is free of an inherited curse, like the one that continues to pursue the fallen D'Urbervilles, and he is free, as his sons are, to make his own significance in the world.

But the novel is more than simply a study of a provincial family in the Wessex of the early eighteen-hundreds, for it considers a small section of the nation engaged in a struggle for survival, a struggle against an external enemy and against the natural forces that determine human destinies. It is built up from familiar objects, and formed around memories and experiences inherited by Hardy himself; the 'oral and written testimony' mentioned in the Preface had been with him from his boyhood up, and he even suggests that the account of the Lovedays' party had come to him through a surviving local tradition. Hardy's own grandfather, like one of his first neighbours at Higher Bockhampton, had been a volunteer at the time of the invasion scare and had later subscribed to the popular periodical *A History of the Wars* which had become the novelist's own favourite childhood reading.[2] According to the account in *The Early Life of Thomas Hardy*, he also vividly recalled his grandmother's anecdotes of the period, and especially her splendidly vague comment one hot, thundery summer – 'It was like this in the French Revolution'. His mother had told him the story of the same grandmother ironing when news came 'that the Queen of France was beheaded'; she had put down her iron, he records, 'and stood still, the event so greatly affecting her mind'.[3] Hardy's attraction to the Revolutionary wars is clear enough in his poems and short stories, but the very proximity of the period to his own lifetime seems to have impressed him far more than any of the novelists who had handled similar historical subjects. His response to the recent past is most clearly reminiscent of Scott's, or of Scott's faithful admirer in the generation before Hardy's, George Eliot.[4]

As the long preoccupation with the idea of *The Dynasts* also suggests, Hardy's fascination with Napoleon and his times was not simply sentimental; it was to prove both lasting and scholarly. On Waterloo Day 1875, for example, he paid a visit to the Chelsea Hospital and talked to survivors of the battle fought sixty years earlier; in the year following, while on his honeymoon in Belgium, he took his new wife to see the actual site of the battle. It is at this period that the notion of a 'Ballad of the Hundred Days', intended to form part of an 'Iliad of Europe from 1789 to 1815', first appears in the novelist's notebooks.[5] By the June of 1877 the idea had begun to form itself into a project for a 'grand drama', or an 'Homeric ballad' with Napoleon as 'a sort of Achilles'. In the same year Hardy had made a note of the features of members of the Bonaparte family at the funeral of Louis Napoleon at Chislehurst.[6] Like Milton, to whose *Paradise Lost* he pointedly refers in the Preface to *The Dynasts*, Hardy's epic was long aspired to and exhaustively worked towards, but his pride in what he regarded as the culminating task of his literary career seems to have led him subsequently to underrate *The Trumpet-Major*.

In this same Preface to *The Dynasts*, Hardy outlines the genesis of his drama and cites as 'accidental' inspirations Weymouth, the open coast-line of Wessex, and the figure of Captain Hardy; the novel is mentioned as though it were merely a *ballon d'essai*, or a prelude which had placed the younger artist in 'the tantalizing position of having touched the fringe of a vast international tragedy without being able, through limits of plan, knowledge and opportunity, to enter further into events'. This tendency to see the novel as comparatively restricted, or thinly thought-out, re-emerges in *The Early Life of Thomas Hardy*, where the process of its composition and publication is passed over with only the barest comment. Strangely, despite the evident unease and even silence of many critics over *The Dynasts*, *The Trumpet-Major* has remained in its shadow. Even beside the other Wessex novels it has been dismissed as slight or uncharacteristic, and its straightforward plot and its sideways glance at political events have been seen as lacking in the tragic intensity of Hardy's best work.[7]

Much of the blame for this comparative neglect must rest with Hardy himself and with his decision to class the novel amongst his 'Romances and Fantasies' rather than with the 'Novels of Character and Environment'. It should be clear enough to any modern reader, however, that *The Trumpet-Major* is a different rather than a lesser achievement than *The Dynasts*, *The Return of the Native* or *Tess of the D'Urbervilles*. It gives us a view of character and environment within an historical framework which is more readily grasped than that of the 'epic drama' on which Hardy hoped that his reputation would be based; like the other Wessex novels, but unlike the epic, its characters are drawn from humble life and they are given a distinctive and crucial historical dimension. In 1884, four years after the publication of the novel, and while he was working on *The Mayor of Casterbridge*, Hardy noted in his journal: 'Is not the present quasi-scientific system of writing history mere charlatanism? Events and tendencies are traced as if they were rivers of voluntary activity, and courses reasoned out from the circumstances in which natures, religions or what-not, have found themselves. But are they not in the main the outcome of *passivity* – acted upon by unconscious propensity?'[8] Hardy again uses the image of a river, or a stream, for time, but he is also extending an idea which had already determined the form and tone of *The Trumpet-Major*; he is proposing a view of history which counters both the English Whig tradition, with its insistence on a notion of beneficial and reasoned progress, and the Carlylean thesis that history is a process forged and moved forward by heroes. Hardy suggests instead that the mass of humanity is passive and incapable of controlling its destinies, despite assertive religious and philosophical claims to the contrary. The 'heroic' figures of his later fiction have nothing of the titanic struggle and the solitary victory envisaged either in an outmoded Romantic ideal or in a new Nietzschean ethic; Tesses and Judes seem to have been born to suffer; given the circumstances which buffet them through life, they passively submit rather than triumph over a groaning creation. Unlike George Eliot, Hardy was not particularly drawn to tracing the progress of the individual towards enlightenment or temporal apotheosis. As *The Dynasts* continually emphasises, man is only rarely able to gain an insight into his historical role and his future destiny, and he is not to be guided by a simplified moral derived from the study of history. In the epic drama, Napoleon is seen to gain and achieve nothing, despite his fond belief, one with which Tolstoi also credits him, that he has mastered Fate; beyond the Emperor, his armies, and his enemies, are forces, part-acknowledged, part-feared, and nearly always wrongly identified as either benevolent or malevolent. The passivity which Hardy stresses in his note emerges both in his historical novel, and as an element in the characters of his late, suffering heroes. Heroism and the idea of heroic advance are, to Hardy, illusions founded on too easy a notion of personal, social, and political history. From the elevated and extended viewpoints of the choric forces in *The Dynasts*, man's struggles are not empty, but man himself has not as yet grasped the meaning of his place in the universe. Hardy sees existing systems of faith and thought as incapable of resisting a radical criticism based on human experience; he proposes instead that the proper duty of mankind is to study itself in particular but limited contexts, contexts which do not require conclusions to be drawn from them. Each spot of time can be observed in its intensity of joy or suffering, and it contributes to a slow and gradual understanding of a wider reality, to the realisation of the universal consciousness.

Hardy's fictional method in *The Trumpet-Major*, despite his distinctive philosophical approach, is close to those of Thackeray and Mrs Gaskell. He had discovered *Vanity Fair* with enthusiasm, and had written to his sister of Thackeray's view of the novel 'as a perfect and truthful representation of actual life'.[9] It was doubtless also appealing to the young agnostic to observe Thackeray's un-Tolstoian lack of an historical moral, and his consideration of war, death and politics outside a neat and determinable historical pattern. Nevertheless, in Hardy's scheme, as in Mrs Gaskell's, there is generally less room for heroes, even questionable ones, than in those of *Vanity Fair* or *Henry Esmond*. Not only does *The Trumpet-Major* move characters down the social scale, from officers and gentlemen to trumpet-majors and yeomen, but it ties them to a private, provincial world and to a particular geographical setting. We see soldiers and sailors in a civilian context, though they serve, are wounded, and die beyond the confines of the village which is the focus of the novel. Captain Hardy is never deheroised, as Thackeray might well have been tempted to show us, but he is seen as a respected son of Wessex who happens to have wider horizons than most of his fellow-countrymen. Both Hardy and Mrs Gaskell concentrate on a province distant from the centre of political power, but Hardy renders his fictional Budmouth – the real Weymouth – significant as the residence of a king on holiday. We see national events through Budmouth's and Overcombe's eyes, but, temporarily, Wessex is the centre of things.

George III comes to the seaside, and it is virtually as a private citizen that he meets Anne Garland by the spring in Budmouth; he is certainly a somewhat ridiculous bather as he surfaces to the strains of 'God save the King' played by his band on the beach. But to Mrs Garland, a glimpse of the royal profile in the dusty travelling coach is a moment of real importance, linking her to her king and to a nation which centres in the same figurehead. Anne's brief encounter with her sovereign carries an equal weight, though it appears to have as small an impact on the development of future events, private and public. Hardy has changed and reduced the emphasis of *The Heart of Midlothian* by bringing king and subject together on the subject's ground, and in the province not the capital. But if war and politics and the pressing duties of monarchy intrude, like the soldiers, into Wessex, their intrusion affects an entire society from top to bottom, and unites them equally in the historical process.

'History', Hardy noted elsewhere in his journal in 1885, 'is rather a stream than a tree. There is nothing organic in its shape, nothing systematic in its development. It flows on like a thunderstorm-rill by a road-side; now a straw turns it this way, now a tiny barrier of sand that. The off hand decision of some commonplace mind high in office at a critical moment influences the course of events for a hundred years.'[10] This image of history as flowing, moving water had also been present in *The Trumpet-Major* as Anne Garland looked up at Gloucester Lodge, the king's house at Budmouth, and felt herself 'close to and looking into the stream of recorded history, within whose banks the littlest things are great, and outside which she and the general bulk of the human race were content to live on as an unreckoned, unheeded superfluity' (Chapter 13). As the novel as a whole shows, Anne's view is too narrow and too self-effacing, for the 'stream of history', as it is recorded in the story, takes in both the affairs of Gloucester Lodge and Overcombe Mill, and it stresses the significance of the latter over the former. Hardy has shifted the emphasis away from the conventional historian's to the experimental historical novelist's. History moves on arbitrarily and unorganically, pulling passive humanity with it, but the 'unreckoned, unheeded superfluity' are as much part of the storm-rill as are the kings, the admirals, the generals, and the commonplace minds in high office.

History is an uncontrolled progress, which can be diverted, as it might seem, and which defies easy interpretation and analysis. Like the storm-rill, history is an expression of the force and indifference of Nature, but Nature, as *The Dynasts* insists, determines both the quality of a harvest and the chance of an invasion fromFrance. Anne is rare amongst the Overcombe villagers in that she attempts to theorise about her world; most of her fellow-villagers, like the citizens of Monkshaven, accept the world as they find it. They are convinced that King George and England are right and that Napoleon and France are wrong, and they seem to seek no further enlightenment; their experience may be harsh, their lives hard, or their horizons narrow, but they seem to understand all they need to know of the forces which have made them and which are moving them passively forwards.

Through *The Trumpet-Major*, and through the rest of his fiction, as he stresses in the General Preface to the Wessex novels, Hardy poses his own, essentially agnostic, view of experience against that of the theologians, the historians, the philosophers, and other novelists, who find history organic, or determined, or malleable. It is also an essentially meliorist view, but one which is argued without George Eliot's confidence in progress. Real achievement for the unadventurous

Miller Loveday and his ancestors consists in adding chimneys and millstones to their inheritance, or simply in conducting their business honestly and profitably. Responsibility for governments, or armies and navies, lies elsewhere, as even George III on holiday in Budmouth, or happily out boating in its bay, seems to hope. Like *Sylvia's Lovers* and *Middlemarch*, Hardy's novel stands at an opposite extreme from those of Ainsworth, whose stories he so much admired as a child, and those of Bulwer-Lytton; we have been moved from the Court, not just to the country, but to a small area of a comparatively remote and inconsequential province. The real strengths of the *The Trumpet-Major* lie in precisely those areas where *The Dynasts* is overstretched and least fluid; the novel does not avoid great matters, but it considers them as they touch a group of humble, fictional characters equally concerned with the common 'unheeded' problems of falling in love, or of enduring time, loss, and death.

Much of the intensity and power of Hardy's vision in the novel derives from the fact that he does not see humanity in a lump, or as an unconscious mass. The picture of society we are given in *The Trumpet-Major* shows us individuals dependent upon each other in a community, and making private and shared history in living out their separate lives. In 'The Dorsetshire Labourer' of 1883, Hardy argued that a true acquaintance with 'Hodge' will make anyone who generalises about rural society aware that his subject has become 'disintegrated into a number of dissimilar fellow-creatures, men of many minds, infinite in difference; some happy, many serene, a few depressed; some clever, even to genius, some stupid, some wanton, some austere; some mutely Miltonic, some Cromwellian; into men who have private views of each other, as he has of his friends; who applaud or condemn each other; amuse or sadden themselves by contemplation of each other's foibles or vices; and each of whom walks in his own way the road to dusty death.'[11] Hardy's novels certainly have their share of mutely Miltonic and Cromwellian villagers, but they tend to be outnumbered by those of their fellows who readily accept or endure their lot. Nevertheless, as his fiction develops, there is a noticeable shift of emphasis in his treatment of the gifted individuals who stand out even in an individualistic community; in the earlier stories a Gabriel Oak and a John Loveday have a steadiness and a steadfastness which balances their innate 'genius'; their later counterparts, the Michael Henchards and the Jude Fawleys, are more open to suffering, or they seem to lack those qualities which might allow them to stand up better to the knocks of the world. It is the idealists, Lawrence's 'aristocrats' and 'pioneers', who die in the wilderness with their ideals unrealised or unrealisable. Society in the earlier stories appears to be more cooperative and harmonious, more able to make room for the expression of individual and social variety.

Disruption in *The Trumpet-Major* comes mostly from the outside. But for the jealousies and complications of the love-making, there are few stirrings of discontent and few inclinations to disturb the universe by declaring independence from the group; the real disturbances are those of the first arrival of the troopers, the coming of the press-gang, the continual rumblings of the European war, and the threat of an invasion from France. As we see it, it is the community as a whole that suffers and endures. There is as little room in the novel as there is in the other Wessex novels for unqualified social, philosophical, political, or historical optimism, but there is at least a sense of shared responsibility and fellow-feeling which continues around and beyond the individual. If life goes on at the end of Hardy's last, tragic novels, it seems to be at the expense of the isolated and dying central characters; Jude Fawley dies obscurely, Michael Henchard alone and self-accused, Tess Durbeyfield publicly but generally unmourned. *The Trumpet-Major* ends suddenly and sadly with the report of John Loveday's death on 'one of the bloody battle-fields of Spain', but we sense that John's death in battle has some national purpose, and that its undoubted sadness is shared by those who live on in Overcombe. John is a victim of war and time, but so, in a less immediate sense, are his family at home, diminished by his death and more aware of the surrounding darkness because he had stepped so 'smartly' into it.

The lives of all the characters in the novel are bound up with the passing of time, a passing measured differently by each. Their present, we are aware, is always becoming their and our history, and their actions part of the history recorded by the novel. In the opening chapter Anne Garland is working fitfully on a hearth-rug when she notices the arrival of the two troopers:

Anne was sitting at the back window of her mother's portion of the house, measuring out lengths of worsted for a fringed rug that she was making, which lay, about three-quarters finished, beside her. The work, though chromatically brilliant, was tedious: a hearth-rug was a thing which nobody worked at from morning to night; it was taken up and put down; it was in the chair, on the floor, across the hand-rail, under the bed, kicked here, kicked there, rolled away in the closet, brought out again, and so on, more capriciously perhaps than any other home-made article. Nobody was expected to finish a rug within a calculable period, and the wools of the beginning became faded and historical before the end was reached.

Hardy's use of the word 'historical' amongst these domestic details is pointed, for the hearth-rug is a symbol of a world indifferently made, and subject to the processes of change, growth and decay; it is to remain imperfect and an unfinished creation to the end. Elsewhere in the story, however, Hardy alerts us, as he does in *Under the Greenwood Tree*, to the passing of time manifested in seasonal and climatic change, though here the seasons are placed within the huger dimension of historical time. It is an effect which is often akin to the references to man dwarfed by the infinity of the stars in *Two on a Tower*, but the story gives us touches of natural detail which perfectly fit into the anthropocentric perspectives of *The Trumpet-Major*. At the beginning of Chapter 23, for example, Hardy passes over a three-month interval with references to the weather, and he suggests how the passage of time can sometimes be welcomed.

> Christmas had passed. Dreary winter with dark evenings had given place to more dreary winter with light evenings. Rapid thaws had ended in rain, rain in wind, wind in dust. Showery days had come – the season of pink dawns and white sunsets; and people hoped that the March weather was over.

As the residents of Overcombe mill wait impatiently for news of Bob Loveday after the battle of Trafalgar, and as John gathers strength to declare his love for Anne in Chapter 37, the 'bluebells and ragged-robins' of the spring of 1806 follow another winter. But Bob still has not returned when, in the following chapter, the year changes again 'from green to gold, and from gold to grey'.

Such references to a natural cycle remind us of the place of change, and death, in the pattern of existence. Life goes on, or it is born again out of decay, but Hardy does not seek to imply, in Bulwer's manner, that history too can be seen as a process which reflects the cycles of the natural world. No old orders are destroyed, and no new ones succeed in their place; instead the process is steady, often imperceptible, and ineluctable. Like Mrs Gaskell, Hardy gives us a love-story, not a revolutionary chronicle, and we see history working in and through humanity 'in a local sense'. His love-story has its complications, its pains, and its disasters, but it is more than simply pastoral, and its interests move outwards from the parochial to the universal; it places love in opposition to time and death much as Shakespeare does in his Sonnets, though in none of his own poems or novels does Hardy proclaim the power of love with Shakespeare's desperate confidence. The story does not end with simple affirmations – Bob merely announces the prospect of his marriage as his stoical brother leaves for the wars, and even Mrs Garland's earlier marriage to Miller Loveday is as much one of mutual convenience as it is based on understanding and real enough affection. The second half of the novel does, nevertheless, centre on the shifting and complex relationship between Anne and her three suitors. Hardy does not arrange his characters as neat couples and he keeps us tense until nearly the end of the story waiting for Anne's decision between the two brothers, a decision which will bind her and which will, unwittingly, send John Loveday to his death.

As we have seen, Anne has only a limited consciousness of history and the meaning of her place in the historical process, but the exhilaration she feels looking up at Gloucester Lodge or after her unexpected interview with the king, suggests an awareness which is not evident in other characters. After she has talked to George III, Hardy notes her special balance of imaginative vision and common sense:

> She had been borne up in this hasty spurt at the end of a weary day by visions of Bob promoted to the rank of admiral, or something equally wonderful, by the King's special command, the chief result of the promotion being, in her arrangement of the piece, that he would stay at home and go to sea no more. But she was not a girl who indulged in extravagant fancies long, and before she reached home she thought that the King had probably forgotten her by that time, and her troubles, and her lover's name.

>   (Chapter 34)

This element of practicality which undermines her fairy-tale dreams gives the end of this chapter a delicate sadness which is to be echoed at the very end of the novel. But Anne's practicality, like her historical sense, has its limits; she is shockable and prim, and she rejects as distasteful other elements of the real world about her. In the delightfully Thackerayan scene at the Lovedays' party in Chapter 4, her sensibilities are easily wounded:

'Your arm hurt too?' cried Anne.

'Knocked to a pummy at the same time as my head,' said Tullidge dispassionately.

'Rattle yer arm, corpel, and show her,' said Cripplestraw.

'Yes, sure,' said the corporal, raising the limb slowly, as if the glory of exhibition had lost some of its novelty, though he was willing to oblige. Twisting it mercilessly about with his right hand he produced a crunching among the bones at every motion, Cripplestraw seeming to derive great satisfaction from the ghastly sound.

'How very shocking!' said Anne, painfully anxious for him to leave off.

Anne shrugs off a practical response here, and with it the reality of war, and Hardy plays her comic embarrassment against the under-lying seriousness.

Like Bathsheba Everdene, Anne combines a certain stiffness with indecision, even capriciousness. It is a trait shared by her rather less acute mother, and we see it early on in the novel when both toy with the social propriety or impropriety of responding to the Lovedays' invitation to the party:

Mrs Garland reflected. 'Well, if you don't want to go, I don't,' she said. 'Perhaps, as you are growing up, it would be better to stay at home this time. Your father was a professional man, certainly.' Having spoken as a mother, she sighed as a woman.

'Why do you sigh, mother?'

'You are so prim and stiff about everything.'

'Very well – we'll go.'

'O no – I am not sure that we ought. I did not promise, and there will be no trouble in keeping away.'

Anne apparently did not feel certain of her own opinion, and, instead of supporting or contradicting, looked thoughtfully down, and abstractly brought her hands together on her bosom, till her fingers met tip to tip.

(Chapter 3)

We later see the same indecision in Anne once she is in love, or playing with love, or making up her mind about loving, and there is a similar inclination to want others to make up her mind for her. Her lovers, like her mother, generally do not help matters; John is reserved and too scrupulous about her feelings; Bob, by contrast, is inattentive and nonchalant; Festus is simply brash. But we know why and how she arrives at her final decision, and we have sufficient understanding of both Anne and her lovers to feel that she has made the wrong one. Anne's heart, like that of so many characters in Hardy's novels, makes mistakes, and the novelist rarely seems to want to affirm a different pattern.

The closing stages of the novel have something of the tension of a Shakespearean comedy, with the two lovers wooing the same woman and the pendulum of affection swinging from one to the other. At one point in his narrative Hardy himself sees the two brothers as stage-managed Dromios 'in seldom being, thanks to Anne's subtle contrivance, both in the same room at the same time', but the manoeuvres are more than just comic and theatrical. Despite the fact that so many of Shakespeare's comedies end with shadows and uncertainties, Hardy makes few gestures to offer a parallel to Shakespeare's compensating idealism; the comedy of *The Trumpet-Major* leads us out of a comic world into one in which love does not triumph, and one in which a lover, perhaps the most truly Shakespearean one, is left, unmatched, to go off to his death. It is not simply a realist's reversal of an earlier literary norm, it is Hardy's comment on what he believes a lover's expectations to be. We see John Loveday's defeat in love becoming one with his last heroic gesture, and he gives up Anne as resignedly and quietly as we expect him to have laid down his life in the Peninsular.

The shared surname of the Loveday brothers is appropriate to them both, but otherwise their natures diverge. They are bright, resilent, resourceful, and practical, but John is the more steadfast and introspective, working in the background and without the assurance to declare his love; Bob attracts attention, but he drifts as casually into decisions as he casually avoids them. It is the extrovert and swashbuckling Bob who is promoted to the rank of lieutenant, while the more plodding 'quiet shopkeeping' John is proud to remain a trumpet-major. John's selflessness in protecting his brother's interests, and the object of them, win Hardy's evident sympathy, but it obliges John to cover his pain from his family and his village:

As he went on, his face put off its complexion of despair for one of serene resolve. For the first time in his dealings with friends he entered upon a course of counterfeiting, set his features to conceal his thought, and instructed his tongue to do likewise. He threw fictiousness into his very gait, even now, when there was nobody to see him, and struck at stems of wild parsley with his regimental switch as he had used to do when soldiering was new to him, and life in general a charming experience.

(Chapter 28)

His dissimulation almost succeeds in deceiving Anne, but she has wit enough to sense the falseness of his cheer; characteristically, however, 'in the blissful circumstances of having Bob at hand again she took optimistic views, and persuaded herself that John would soon begin to see her in the light of a sister'. When, some ten chapters later, the second crisis in the lovers' relationship arises, John once again cannot bring himself fully to undeceive her and he thereby denies himself a last opportunity of declaring his silent love.

The final movement of the novel is away from day and into night. After the news of the great national victory at Trafalgar, and after Bob's selfishly long-delayed return home to Wessex, the story centres again on the private world of the family's reunions and the lovers' disappointments and discoveries. At its very close, however, the persistent theme of war and death re-emerges with a new darkness. John, who has removed himself so as to avoid both his brother and Anne, returns to make his farewells before leaving for the Peninsular to join Sir Arthur Wellesley. He is to be one of the five from Wessex who leave their bones 'to moulder in the land of their campaigns', and he goes off, still disguising his pain and his defeat under a military bravado:

'My dear Anne,' said John, with more gaiety than truthfulness, 'don't let yourself be troubled! What happens is for the best. Soldiers love here to-day and there to-morrow. Who knows that you won't hear of my attentions to some Spanish maid before a month is gone by? 'Tis the way of us, you know; a soldier's heart is not worth a week's purchase – ha, ha! Good-bye, good-bye!'

He leaves learning of his brother's engagement to Anne, and the last sentences of the novel slip away with a vision of the trumpet-major turning out of the wavering candlelight at the door of the mill and into the black night that surrounds them all.

In the Preface added to the novel in 1895, Hardy remarked that 'those who have attempted to construct a coherent narrative of past times from the fragmentary information furnished by survivors, are aware of the difficulty of ascertaining the true sequence of events indiscriminately recalled'. As he goes on to tell us, Hardy had checked the oral testimony against newspaper and magazine accounts of the same events, and he had used the researches of authoritative historians as a further check. He had also filled a notebook between 1878–9 with careful notes of the dates of royal visits to Weymouth, the standing orders of regiments, intrusions of the press-gang along the Wessex coast, and details of uniforms, clothes, furniture and theatres.[12] Thus, though *The Trumpet-Major* may seem artless enough at a first reading, much of its individual success as an historical novel results from an art that conceals art; the story is firmly and minutely based in historical fact, but it is a working-together of the experienced, the recalled, the researched, and the imagined. It orders 'fragmentary information' into a coherent shape as fiction, or, as Hardy aimed to do in *Tess of the D'Urbervilles*, it gives 'artistic shape to a true sequence of things'. The shape and the coherence of *The Trumpet-Major* serve to express a view of history as a 'book of humanity' which is continuous, popular and familiar, and, like the Fourways at Christminster, is 'palpitating, varied and compendious'.

When Michael Henchard meets his wife again at the Roman amphitheatre at Casterbridge, or Tess Durbeyfield is taken lying on the sacrifice stone at Stonehenge, or Jude Fawley senses the life of the Fourways, Hardy uses an historical setting with complex associations to reinforce his picture of man as involved in a lengthy, painful, and largely incomprehensible process of evolution. Unlike many of his early and mid-Victorian predecessors, he was also able to write an historical novel which no longer showed a confident trust in a theory of benevolent human progress, or in a God, transcendent, immanent, or social, drawing creation to its climax. Yet Hardy was perfectly at ease with history, and, as *The Dynasts* suggests, he seems to have shared Carlyle's thrill at the idea of an 'enveloping' history, with its beginnings stretching into 'the remote Time' and emerging 'darkly out of the mysterious Eternity'. He neither felt smug at having escaped from the past, nor sure of having mastered it; his historical novel makes no attempt to interpret history, to examine the motives of a famous man, or to offer a balm for the evident painfulness of existence. Hardy gives us instead, as he said of the full range of the Wessex novels, 'impressions of the moment, and not convictions or arguments'. If we can see Hardy's 'meliorism' moulding his historical novel, and lying behind his suggestion that history is the outcome of

'*passivity* – acted upon by unconscious propensity', it is also succinctly expressed in the short lyric with which he chose to open his
penultimate volume of verse – 'Waiting Both':

> A star looks down at me,
> And says: 'Here I and you
> Stand, each in our degree:
> What do you mean to do, –
>   Mean to do?'
>
> I say: 'For all I know,
> Wait, and let Time go by,
> Till my change come.' – 'Just so,'
> The star says: 'So mean I: –
>   So mean I.'

Notes

CHAPTER I

1 Thomas Carlyle, 'On History Again', *Critical and Miscellaneous Essays* (Centenary Edition), 5 Volumes (London 1899), Vol. III, p. 176. For a further attempt at definitions see the first three chapters of Avron Fleishman's *The English Historical Novel: Walter Scott to Virginia Woolf* (Baltimore 1971). My debt to Professor Fleishman's study will, I hope, emerge as clearly as my occasional dissent from it.

2 G. W. F. Hegel, *Lectures on the Philosophy of History*, translated from the third German edition by J. Sibree (London 1878); Introduction, pp. 57–8.

3 Carlyle, op. cit., pp. 168, 176.

4 T. B. Macaulay, 'Sir James Mackintosh', *Critical and Historical Essays*, 3 Volumes (London 1854), Vol. II, p. 226.

5 Sir Walter Scott, *Waverley; or 'Tis Sixty Years Since* (1814). The Waverley Novels, 25 Volumes (London 1879), Vol. I, p. 399.

6 William Hazlitt, *The Spirit of the Age* (1825). World's Classics Edition (London 1935), p. 86. Heine's introduction to *Don Quixote* is quoted in *Scott: The Critical Heritage*, edited by John O. Hayden (London 1970), p. 305.

7 *Oeuvres Complètes de Honoré de Balzac*, *La Comédie Humaine* (Paris 1931), Vol. I, 'Avant-propos' p. xxviii.

8 Thomas Carlyle, 'Sir Walter Scott', *Critical and Miscellaneous Essays*, Vol. IV, p. 77.

9 T. B. Macaulay, *Critical and Historical Essays*, Vol. I, pp. 113–4. See also Macaulay's important essay 'On History' not republished with the other *Edinburgh Review* Essays.

10 For Scott's debt to the Scottish Enlightenment see Duncan Forbes, 'The Rationalism of Sir Walter Scott', *Cambridge Journal* (October 1953), pp. 20–36.

11 Yale Edition of the Works of Samuel Johnson, Vol. VII, *Johnson on Shakespeare* (New Haven and London 1968), pp. 522–3.

12 Henry James writing in the *North American Review* in 1864. The review is reprinted in *Scott: The Critical Heritage*, pp. 429–31.

13 Georg Lukács, *The Historical Novel*, translated by Hannah and Stanley Mitchell (London 1962), p. 32.

14 Nassau W. Senior's essay is reprinted in *Scott: The Critical Heritage*, pp. 215–6.

15 Twain argued that 'Sir Walter had so large a hand in making Southern character, as it existed before the war, that he is in great measure responsible for the [American Civil] war'. See *Scott: The Critical Heritage*, pp. 537–9. For the Eglinton Tournament see *The Passage of Arms at Eglinton* (London 1839).

16 *Waverley*, p. 400.

17 *Quarterly Review*, Vol. 35 (March 1827), p. 557.
18 *Monthly Chronicle*, Vol. I (1838), pp. 42–4.
19 *Blackwood's Edinburgh Magazine*, Vol. LVIII (September 1845), pp. 341–56.
20 *Westminster Review*, Vol. XLV (1846), p. 35.
21 *Fraser's Magazine*, Vol. 36 (September 1847), pp. 345–51.
22 *Bentley's Miscellany*, Vol. XLVI (1859), p. 44.
23 George Orwell writing in *New Statesman and Nation* (17 August 1940).
24 *Saturday Review*, Vol. XII (12 October 1861), p. 381. The review is possibly the work of the historian E. A. Freeman. See W. R. W. Stephens, *Life and letters of E. A. Freeman*, 2 Vols. (London 1895); Vol. I, p. 257.
25 *Westminster Review*, Vol. LXXVII (1862), pp. 286–7. After his acclaim of Reade's novel the reviewer goes on to dismiss *Great Expectations*: 'We cannot believe, however, that anything but the talisman of Mr. Dickens's name, would induce the general public to buy and read 'Great Expectations'. There is not a character or a passage in these three volumes which can afford enjoyment to anybody twenty years hence.'
26 The essay, included in *Miscellanies* (1886), was first reprinted in the Everyman Edition of the novel in 1906.
27 *The Cloister and the Hearth*. Vol. IX of Ward, Lock and Tyler Edition of Reade's novels (London ND), p. 1.
28 See Albert Morton Turner, *The Making of The Cloister and the Hearth* (Chicago 1938), pp. 5ff. See also Léone Rives, *Charles Reade: sa vie, ses romans* (Toulouse 1940), Chapter 3. For the background to the novel see also Malcolm Elwin, *Charles Reade: A Biography* (London 1931), Chapters VI and VII.
29 Charles Reade, *The Eighth Commandment* (London 1860), p. 190.
30 *Christie Johnstone* (1853), Vol. IV of Ward, Lock and Tyler Edition (London ND), Chapter XVI p. 246.
31 See for example Margaret Oliphant's article on Reade in *Blackwood's Edinburgh Magazine*, Vol. CVI (1869).
32 The letter is quoted in Turner, op. cit., pp. 5–6.
33 *Christie Johnstone*, Chapter IX, pp. 104–6.
34 Amongst the books Reade lists in his letter to Fields are Pugin's *Contrasts* and his *Glossary of Ecclesiastical Ornament and Costume*. Doubtless Pugin would also come under Lord Ipsden's censure.
35 Quoted by David Christie Murray in his *My Contemporaries in Fiction* (London 1897).
36 Samuel Butler, *Erewhon Revisited* (1901); Everyman Edition (London 1932), p. 293.
37 *Ivanhoe* (1819), Vol. IX of 1879 edition of the Waverley novels, p. 16.

CHAPTER 2

All quotations from *The Tower of London* are from the first edition (London 1840).

1 Quoted by Edgar Johnson in his *Sir Walter Scott; The Great Unknown*, 2 Vols. (New York 1970), Vol. II, p. 1000.
2 The Preface to *Rookwood* was added to the 1850 edition.
3 Quoted by Douglas Grant in his edition of Maturin's *Melmoth the Wanderer*

(Oxford English Novels, London 1968); Introduction, p. xi.

4 Ainsworth started his career as a writer at the age of fifteen with plays in the manner of Byron. Transforming his name to 'Aynesworthe' he composed *Giotto, or the Fatal Revenge* and *Don Juan, or Libertine Destroyed.* His early novels, like those of his contemporaries, were adapted for the stage. A dramatic version of *The Tower of London* (combined with sections from Dumas' *Marie Tudor*) was performed at the Adelphi Theatre in November 1840. See S. M. Ellis, *William Harrison Ainsworth and his Friends*, 2 vols. (London 1911), Vol. I, p. 421.

5 See Ellis, op. cit., Vol. I, p. 407. 'The Tower, with its thousand historical associations and tragic reminiscences, presented — no better — immense possibilities.'

6 Anon., *London Interiors, with their Costumes and Ceremonies* (London 1843), p. 57.

7 Ellis, op. cit., p. 325, quotes statistics from the Manchester Public Library in 1909 testifying to the continuing popularity of *The Tower of London, Guy Fawkes, Windsor Castle* and *The Lancashire Witches.* With the exception of *Guy Fawkes,* these novels were still in print in 1977.

8 See Ellis, op. cit., Vol. II, p. 264.

9 See Ellis, op. cit., Vol. II pp. 76, 139, 166 and 172—3.

10 Ed. R. H. Horne, *A New Spirit of the Age*, 2 Vols. (London 1844), Vol. II, pp. 217—18.

CHAPTER 3

Quotations from *Harold* are from the New Knebworth edition (London 1896).

1 Edward Lytton Bulwer, *England and the English*, 2 volumes. Second Edition (London 1833), Volume 2, pp. 105—7.

2 Edward Bulwer-Lytton, *Caxtoniana: A Series of Essays on Life, Literature and Manners*, 2 Volumes (Edinburgh and London 1863), Volume II, p. 154.

3 Ibid., Volume I, p. 151.

4 *Rienzi: The Last of the Roman Tribunes* (1835), The New Knebworth Edition (London 1896), Book VII, Chapter I, p. 384.

5 *Caxtoniana*, Volume II, pp. 300—1.

6 In a 'reverent' aside in *England and the English* (Volume I, p. 277) Bulwer mixes praise of Scott's art with censure of his research: 'The novels of Scott have helped to foster the most erroneous notions of the ignorance of our ancestors — a tolerable antiquarian in ballads, the great author was a most incorrect one in facts.' He returned to the attack later in his career: 'In *Ivanhoe*, for instance, there are many defects in mere antiquarian accuracy. Two or three centuries are massed together in a single year. But the general spirit of the age is made clear to popular apprehension, and stands forth with sufficient fidelity to character and costume for the purpose, not of an antiquarian but a poet.' (*Caxtoniana*, Volume II, p. 297).

7 *Caxtoniana*, Volume I, p. 181.

8 See for example Benjamin Jowett's generous funeral tribute, *Lord Lytton: the Man and the Author: A Discourse delivered in Westminster Abbey* (London 1873).

9 *Caxtoniana*, Volume I, p. 220.

10 Ibid., Volume II, p. 340.

11 The letters are preserved with Bulwer's correspondence in the Hertfordshire County Record Office. That from Macaulay is catalogued (D/EK C4 470); from Palgrave (D/EK C4 144); from Wright (D/EK C2 56).

12 *Harold*, Tennyson's 'tragedy of doom', was published in November 1876 and is addressed to Bulwer's son, recently appointed Viceroy of India, as follows: 'After old-world records — such as the Bayeux tapestry and the Roman de Rou — Edward Freeman's History and your father's historical romance treating of the same times, have been mainly helpful to me in writing this drama. Your father dedicated his "Harold" to my father's brother, allow me to dedicate my "Harold" to yourself.'

13 *Fraser's Magazine*, Volume XXXVIII (October 1848), p. 432. The review is by W. S. Landor. Kingsley's review appeared in *Fraser's Magazine* Volume XLI (January 1850), p. 107. Much of the research for *Harold* was done at Bayon's Manor, Lincolnshire, the house of Tennyson's uncle.

14 *Westminster Review*, Volume LXXXIII (April 1865), pp. 488, 500.

15 *The Last Days of Pompeii* (1834) was translated into Italian in 1836, and into German in 1837. For its early popularity see Michael Sadleir, *Bulwer: A Panorama* (London 1933), p. 366. See also J. A. Sutherland, *Victorian Novelists and Publishers* (London 1976), pp. 56—62. Wagner's *Rienzi* was produced at Dresden in 1842, with a libretto by the composer. Hunt's picture, 'Rienzi vowing to obtain justice for the death of his young brother, slain in a skirmish between the Colonna and the Orsini factions', was exhibited at the Royal Academy in 1849.

16 *The Letters of Matthew Arnold 1848—1888*, collected and arranged by George W. E. Russell (London 1901), Volume II, p. 7.

CHAPTER 4

Quotations from *A Tale of Two Cities* are from George Woodcock's edition in the Penguin English Library series. Those from *Barnaby Rudge* are from G. W. Spence's edition in the same series.

1 Humphry House, *The Dickens World* (London 1941), 1960 edition, p. 34.

2 See for example Chapter V of Steven Marcus's, *Dickens: From Pickwick to Dombey* (London 1971). For a recent restatement of the idea see the article on *Barnaby Rudge* by Paul Stigant and Peter Widdowson in *Literature and History*, No. 2 (October 1975).

3 Orwell's article is reprinted in Charles E. Beckwith (ed.), *Twentieth-Century Interpretations of 'A Tale of Two Cities'* (Englewood Cliffs, N. J., 1972), pp. 96—100.

4 *The French Revolution: A History* (Centenary Edition, 3 Vols. London 1896), Volume III, Book V, Chapter I, p. 203. For Carlyle's influence on Dickens see William Oddie's *Dickens and Carlyle: The Question of Influence* (London 1972).

5 Lukács, Georg, *The Historical Novel*, translated by Hannah and Stanley Mitchell (London 1962), p. 243.

6 John Butt and Kathleen Tillotson suggest in their *Dickens at Work* (London 1957), p. 78, that the storming of the Tolbooth in *The Heart of Midlothian* is the literary inspiration for the central scene, and they further suggest that Madge Wildfire from the same novel and Davie Gellatley from *Waverley* may have

inspired Barnaby. See also Gordon Spence's Introduction to his edition of *Barnaby Rudge* in the Penguin English Library, pp. 18–19.

7 Edgar Johnson, *Charles Dickens: His Tragedy and his Triumph*, 2 Volumes (Boston & Toronto 1952), Vol. I, p. 330. George Gissing, *Critical Studies of the Works of Charles Dickens* (New York 1963), p. 107.

8 Hood's review in the *Athenaeum* (22 January 1842) is reprinted in *Dickens: The Critical Heritage*, edited by Philip Collins (London 1971), p. 103.

9 G. W. Spence, Introduction to Penguin edition of *Barnaby Rudge* (1973), p. 15.

10 For the background to the composition of *Barnaby Rudge* see Butt and Tillotson, op. cit., Chapter IV.

11 Steven Marcus has argued, however, that 'essentially *Barnaby Rudge* contemplates only one kind of personal relationship – that of father and son'. See Marcus, *op. cit.*, Chapter V.

12 Letter to François-Joseph Régnier, 15 October 1859. *The Letters of Charles Dickens*, edited by Walter Dexter, 3 volumes (Nonesuch Edition, London 1938), Vol. III, p. 126.

13 Angus Wilson, *The World of Charles Dickens* (London 1970), p. 261.

14 Letter to John Forster, 25 August 1859. *Letters*, Vol. III, p. 118.

15 It is significant that Dickens cut out almost all reference to the Revolution in his prospective reading, 'The Bastille Prisoner', choosing instead to stress the father/daughter relationship. See Michael Slater, 'The Bastille Prisoner: A Reading Dickens never gave', *Études Anglaises*, T. XXIII, No. 2 (1970), p. 191.

16 John Gross, 'A Tale of Two Cities' in John Gross and Gabriel Pearson (eds.), *Dickens and the Twentieth Century* (London 1962), pp. 191–2.

17 Though the future prophesied for the Darnays is quiet, Carton also foresees that the child named after him will become 'foremost of just judges and honoured men', thus introducing a concept of human justice largely absent from the novel.

18 Taylor Stoehr, *Dickens: The Dreamer's Stance* (Ithaca: Cornell University Press 1965), p. 60.

19 This article is accredited to Forster by Philip Collins in *Dickens: The Critical Heritage*, pp. 424–6.

CHAPTER 5

All quotations from *Henry Esmond* are taken from the Penguin English Library edition edited by John Sutherland and Michael Greenfield (1970). Quotations from *The Virginians* are from the Centenary Biographical Edition (1911).

1 William Burges writing in the *British Architect* in 1875. Quoted by Elizabeth Aslin in her *The Aesthetic Movement* (London 1969), p. 45.

2 *The English Humourists of the Eighteenth Century*: A Series of Lectures delivered in England, Scotland, and the United States of America (1853), 1858 Edition, pp. 113–4. Given Thackeray's remark, Avrom Fleishman's argument that the novelist tended 'to see history as affording the moralist food for thought' and that 'the prevailing tone of *Esmond* . . . is one of nostalgia strongly tinged by disgust' strikes me as misguided. (See *The English Historical Novel*: Walter Scott to Virginia Woolf. Baltimore and London, 1971. pp. 129, 136).

3 Georg Lukács, *Historical Novel*, translated from the German by Hannah and Stanley Mitchell (London 1962), p. 203.

4 Gordon N. Ray, *Thackeray: The Uses of Adversity* (London 1955), p. 19.

5 John Lothrop Motley quoted by Ray in *Thackeray: The Uses of Adversity*, p. 20.

6 Anthony Trollope, *Thackeray* (London 1879), p. 26.

7 As John Forster suggested in his review of *Esmond* in the *Examiner* (13 November 1852), Thackeray may well have been influenced in his decision to publish the novel in mock antique format by the two volumes of *The Diary of Lady Willoughby* (1844, 1848), by Hannah Mary Rathbone, purporting to be the memoirs of a lady of the time of Charles I. The first volume was the first book to be wholly printed in revived Caslon type.

   There had been fresh interest in reprinting important seventeenth-century books in appropriate type-faces in the 1830s and 1840s, most notably by the scholarly publisher William Pickering.

8 For an account of the composition of *Esmond* see J. A. Sutherland, *Thackeray at Work* (London 1974), Chapter 3, 'Henry Esmond: The Virtues of Carelessness'. See also Chapter 4 of Sutherland's *Victorian Novelists and Publishers* (London 1976).

9 6 November 1852. Reprinted in *Thackeray: The Critical Heritage*, edited by Geoffrey Tillotson and Donald Hawes (London 1968), p. 139.

10 G. H. Lewes in the *Leader* 6 November 1852, and John Forster in the *Examiner* 13 November 1852. Both reviews are reprinted in *The Critical Heritage* volume, p. 138 and p. 150.

11 *Letters and Private Papers of William Makepeace Thackeray*, edited by G. N. Ray, 4 Volumes (London 1945–6), Vol. II, pp. 807, 811, 815; Vol. III, p. 15.

12 For Thackeray's confusion, and the virtues of his 'carelessness' see Sutherland's *Thackeray at Work*, Chapter 3.

13 Gordon N. Ray, *Thackeray: The Age of Wisdom* (London 1958), p. 373.

14 *Letters*, Volume III, p. 253.

CHAPTER 6

All quotations from *Hypatia* are taken from Volume IV of the Macmillan edition of *The Works of Charles Kingsley* (London 1887). Quotations from *Fabiola* are taken from the 1860 edition in the Popular Catholic Library Series, those from *Callista* are from the 1873 edition (London, Burns, Oates & Co., Basil Montagu Pickering).

1 J. H. Newman, 'The State of the Religious Parties', *The British Critic*, XXV, April 1839. Reprinted in *Essays, Critical and Historical* (London 1872), Vol. I, p. 268.

2 John Keble in a review of Lockhart's *Life of Scott* in *The British Critic*, XXIV, 1838. Reprinted in *Occasional Papers and Reviews* (Oxford & London 1877), pp. 1–80.

3 *The Library of the Fathers* was begun in 1836 under the editorship of Pusey, Keble and Newman.

4 J. H. Newman, *Sermons Preached before the University of Oxford* (Oxford 1918), Sermon VII (27 May 1832), p. 126.

5 *British Quarterly Review*, Vol. XVIII (August 1853). Bishop Phillpotts, a High

Churchman of the old school, had become notorious in 1847–8 as a result of his battle with the Rev. G. C. Gorham, whom Phillpotts had refused to institute into a living in his diocese because of Gorham's dissent from the doctrine of Baptismal Regeneration. The reviewer refers to the Bishop as 'that ecclesiastical mud-volcano, which, always growling and simmering, may explode in an instant with such terrific force its bespattering baptism of abuse'.

In his study of the literary influence of the Oxford Movement, *Faith and Revolt* (London 1970), Raymond Chapman assumes that Cyril 'is almost certainly based on Wiseman', but he gives no evidence for his assumption.

6 *Charles Kingsley: His Letters and Memories of his Life*, edited by his wife (Macmillan Edition, London 1894), Vol. I, p. 292.

7 Charles Kingsley to his publisher, Parker, in 1852, quoted by R. B. Martin in his *The Dust of Combat: A Life of Charles Kingsley* (London 1959), p. 147.

8 Edward Gibbon, *The History of The Decline and Fall of The Roman Empire*, XI vols. (London 1827). Vol. VIII, Chapter XLVII, pp. 20–21.

9 It is possible that Kingsley saw resemblances between the slums of Alexandria and those of the London he had described in *Alton Locke*; the social horrors of the earlier novel are now threatening to affect the spiritual world and create new foes. There was already an inclination amongst Anglo-Catholics to work in slum parishes, especially so after Dr Pusey himself had financed the building of St Saviour's Church in Leeds, consecrated in 1845. Irish immigration also made the slums of the industrial cities centres of missionary activity by Roman Catholics.

10 See Fanny Kingsley's *Charles Kingsley: His Letters and Memories of his Life*, Vol. II, pp. 158–9.

11 Quoted by D'Arcy Power in his entry on Wiseman in the *Dictionary of National Biography*, Vol. XXI.

12 *Dublin Review*, Vol. 40, June 1856, pp. 425–6.

13 See Wilfred Ward, *The Life and Times of Cardinal Wiseman* (London 1897), Vol. II, p. 100. Wiseman is using the Douay Bible's spelling of the king known to users of the Authorised Version as Ahasuerus.

14 See Ward, op. cit., Vol. I, pp. 34–6. While he was a schoolboy Wiseman had cooperated with a friend on a novel called *Fabius*.

15 For the relationship between *Callista* and the Catholic Popular Library see the note by Charlotte E. Crawford in *Modern Language Review*, Vol. XLV (1950), p. 219.

16 Quoted by Geoffrey Faber in his *Oxford Apostles: A Character Study of the Oxford Movement* (Pelican Edition, London 1954), p. 270.

17 J. H. Newman, *Apologia Pro Vita Sua: Being a History of His Religious Opinions*, edited, with an introduction, by Martin J. Svaglic (Oxford 1967), pp. 109–111.

18 *The Christian Remembrancer*, Vol. XXXIII, January 1857, p. 135.

19 *The Decline and Fall of the Roman Empire* (London 1827), Vol. II, Chapter XVI, p. 362.

20 *Apologia Pro Vita Sua*, Part I, 'Mr. Kingsley's Method of Disputation' (Svaglic edition), p. 396. For Newman on the rights of conscience see also his later *A Letter Addressed to His Grace the Duke of Norfolk on the Occasion of Mr. Gladstone's Recent Expostulation* (1874).

CHAPTER 7

Quotations from *Hereward the Wake* are taken from Volume XI of the Works of Charles Kingsley (Macmillan, London 1884).

1 *Blackwood's Edinburgh Magazine*, Vol. LXXVII (June 1855), p. 625.
2 Frederic Harrison, 'Charles Kingsley's place in Literature', *The Forum* (July 1895), p. 560.
3 Henry James in a review of *Charles Kingsley: His Letters and Memories of his Life* in *The Nation* (January 25 1877). Reprinted in *Literary Reviews and Essays by Henry James*, edited by Albert Madell (New York 1957), pp. 301–2.
4 Edward Augustus Freeman (1832–1892) published his *History of the Norman Conquest* in five volumes between 1867 and 1879. His interest in the subject was first evident in his Oxford Prize Essay of 1846.
5 Kingsley refers to Bulwer's *Harold: The Last of the Saxon Kings* in Chapters XVII and XVIII of *Hereward the Wake*.
6 *The Gospel of the Pentateuch* (Macmillan Edition, London 1885), p. 259. According to the Oxford English Dictionary the term 'muscular Christianity' was first used by T. C. Sandars in a review of Kingsley's *Two Years Ago* in the *Saturday Review* (21 February 1852).
7 Quoted by Guy Kendal in *Charles Kingsley and his Ideas* (London 1947), pp. 160–1. See also Fanny Kingsley's *Charles Kingsley: His Letters and Memories of his Life* (Macmillan Edition, London 1894), Volume II, p. 344.
8 Fanny Kingsley, op. cit., Volume II, p. 298.
9 Ibid., Vol. I, p. 341.
10 *The Roman and the Teuton: A Series of Lectures delivered before the University of Cambridge* (Cambridge and London 1864), 'The Limits of Exact Science as Applied to History', p. xii.
11 Ibid., p. xiv
12 Ibid., 'The Forest Children', pp. 6–7.
13 Ibid., 'The Strategy of Providence', pp. 339–340.
14 *Westminster Review*, Volume XIX (April 1861), p. 305.
15 *Historical Lectures and Essays* (Macmillan Edition, London 1880), 'The First Discovery of America', p. 246.
16 *The Saint's Tragedy*; or The True Story of Saint Elizabeth of Hungary, Landgravine of Thuringia, Saint of the Romish Calendar (London 1848), Preface, pp. i–ii.

CHAPTER 8

All quotations from *Romola* are from Blackwood's Cabinet Edition (2 vols. 1878). Quotations from George Eliot's other novels are also from the Cabinet Edition. I have also consulted the edition of *Romola* prepared by Dr Guido Biagi (two volumes, London 1907).

1 See G. S. Haight *George Eliot: A Biography* (Oxford 1968), p. 319.
2 *The George Eliot Letters*, ed. by G. S. Haight (London 1954–6), 7 Vols., VII 65; V 175.

3 Haight, III, 339.
4 Ibid., III, 295, 300.
5 G. H. Lewes, *Westminster Review*, XLV, March 1846, p. 34ff. Lewes is reviewing Thornton Leigh Hunt's *The Foster Brother* and *Whitehall*, by the author of *Whitefriars*.
6 Haight, III, 294.
7 Ibid., III, 417.
8 Ibid., III, 420.
9 'The Natural History of German Life' (July 1856). Reprinted in *Essays of George Eliot*, ed. by Thomas Penney (London 1963), p. 287.
10 Haight, V, 31. J. B. Bullen has argued that *Romola* is a 'Positivist Allegory' (R.E.S. 26, No. 104, 1975). His argument is persuasive, but in emphasising the Comtist element in George Eliot's thought he plays down the more likely influence of Feuerbach. See also Bernard J. Paris, 'George Eliot's Religion of Humanity' (E.L.H., 29, No. 4, 1962).
11 In her discussion of *Romola* (*Victorian Studies* Vol. VI, No. 1, Sept. 1962), Carole Robinson has argued that 'although Savonarola is George Eliot's only possible "hero", her attitude toward his party is ambivalent'. This may be so, but I dispute the contention that George Eliot's 'treatment of Florentine Politics reflects Victorian political apprehensions', and particularly her earlier assertion that 'the historical apparatus over which George Eliot labored with so Victorian an assiduity may probably be ignored for all but its Victorian connotations'.
12 See Barbara Hardy, *The Novels of George Eliot* (London 1959), 1973 edn., pp. 170–6.
13 Haight, IV, 97.
14 For George Eliot's egoists see Barbara Hardy, op. cit., Chapter 4.
15 Interestingly enough in his illustrations to the novel Leighton seems to have given Romola more than a hint of George Eliot's own profile.
16 See G. S. Haight, *George Eliot: A Biography*, p. 51.
17 Haight, IV, 104.
18 See *The Renaissance Philosophy of Man*, ed. by Ernst Cassirer, Paul Oskar Kristeller, John Herman Randall Jr. (University of Chicago Press 1948), p. 225.
19 J. W. Cross, *George Eliot's Life as Related in her Letters and Journals* (3 vols. Edinburgh and London 1885), Vol. II, p. 352.
20 *Ibid.*, Vol. III, p. 270.
21 Haight, VI, 335–6.
22 Henry James, *Atlantic Monthly* (October 1866). Reprinted in *A Century of George Eliot Criticism*, ed. by G. S. Haight (London 1966), p. 52.
23 In his review of Cross's *Life*, *Atlantic Monthly* (May 1885). Reprinted in *George Eliot: The Critical Heritage*, ed. by David Carroll (London 1971), p. 500.

CHAPTER 9

All quotations from *Sylvia's Lovers* are taken from the Knutsford edition of Mrs Gaskell's novels, London 1906.

1 See *Oeuvres Complètes de Gustave Flaubert: Correspondance* (Nouvelle Edition Augmentée) 5. Série (1862–1868) (Paris 1936), p. 58. The correspondence is

reprinted in English as an appendix to the Everyman translation of *Salammbô* (London 1931).

2 A. W. Ward quotes both writers in his Introduction to *Sylvia's Lovers* in the Knutsford Edition (1906) pp. xii, xxvi. The 'tragic' aspects of the novel have been recently stressed by W. A. Craik in her *Elizabeth Gaskell and the English Provincial Novel* (London 1975), Chapter 4.

3 For Mrs Gaskell's chronological slips and other factual errors see Graham Handley's note in *Notes and Queries* (August 1965), pp. 302–3.

4 *Mary Barton: A Tale of Manchester Life* (1848), The Knutsford Edition, Preface, p. lxxiii.

5 For a wide-ranging, clumsy, but very literal study of the relationship between Whitby and the Monkshaven of the story see Mrs Ellis H. Chadwick's well illustrated *Mrs Gaskell: Haunts, Homes and Stories* (London 1910), Chapter XVIII. The novelist does not mention *A Tale of Two Cities* in her letters, but we can safely assume that she knew of it.

6 The dramatic effect of introducing the press-gang into a story had, of course, been found by Crabbe in his 'Ruth', one of the *Tales of the Hall* (1819). Its influence on Mrs Gaskell is considered by A. W. Ward in his Introduction to the novel.

7 For the sources of *Sylvia's Lovers* see Ward's Introduction to The Knutsford Edition, pp. xxii–xxvii.

8 For a consideration of the idea that 'it is not . . . wholly surprising that the author of *Sylvia's Lovers* is also the author of *Cranford*' see Terry Eagleton's perceptive and provocative article in *Essays in Criticism*, Vol. XXVI (January 1976), No. I.

9 The importance of the history of a particular place, and the relationship between character and environment, is also stressed in the opening chapter of Mrs Gaskell's *Life of Charlotte Brontë* (1857).

10 For evidence of Mrs Gaskell's interest in anecdote and story-telling see for example Lady Ritchie's *Blackstick Papers* (London 1908), XI, 'Mrs Gaskell'. Her interest in local tradition is also clear from her letter to Mary Howitt of August 1838. See *The Letters of Mrs Gaskell*, edited by J. A. V. Chapple and Arthur Pollard (Manchester 1966), Letter 12, p. 28.

11 See *The Letters of Mrs Gaskell*, pp. 595, 667, 678.

12 The use of the last three lines of these lyrics as the novel's epigraph is believed to have been suggested by Mrs Gaskell's daughter, Meta. See John Geoffrey Sharp's *Mrs Gaskell's Observation and Invention*: A study of her Non-Biographical Works (Linden Press, Fontwell, Sussex, 1970), p. 405, note 168.

It is perhaps interesting to note that in The Knutsford Edition the word 'thy' is capitalised. This does not occur in editions issued in Mrs Gaskell's lifetime.

CHAPTER 10

All quotations from *The Trumpet-Major* are taken from the New Wessex edition (London 1974).

1 Florence Emily Hardy, *The Early Life of Thomas Hardy 1840–1891* (London 1928), p. 3.

2 Ibid., p. 21.

3 Ibid., p. 282.
4 The short stories concerned with the period of the Revolution and the Napoleonic Wars are *A Committee Man of the Terror*, *The Grave by the Handpost*, *The Melancholy Hussar*, and *A Tradition of Eighteen Hundred and Four*. The poems, written between 1870 and 1897 and published in *Wessex Poems* are 'The Sergeant's Song', 'Valenciennes', 'The Alarm', 'Leipzig' and 'San Sebastian'.
5 *The Early Life of Thomas Hardy*, p. 140.
6 Ibid., p. 168.
7 Irving Howe, for example, considers *The Trumpet-Major* to be 'the one among [Hardy's] books that is most clearly intended as an entertainment' (*Thomas Hardy*, London 1968, p. 41). Timothy O'Sullivan in his *Thomas Hardy: An Illustrated Biography* (London 1975), remarks 'Hardy was far too conscious of the shadow of Thackeray's *Vanity Fair* to say all that he wanted to say about the Napoleonic era in a novel, and let it rest as a good read'. Merryn Williams, in her *A Preface to Thomas Hardy* (London 1976), p. 29, finds the novel 'pleasant and entertaining' but 'very slight' compared to its predecessor *The Return of the Native*.
8 *The Early Life of Thomas Hardy*, pp. 219–20.
9 Ibid., p. 53.
10 Ibid., p. 225.
11 Thomas Hardy, 'The Dorsetshire Labourer' (*Longman's Magazine*, July 1883). Reprinted in *Thomas Hardy's Personal Writings*, edited by Harold Orel (London 1967), pp. 170–1.
12 For the notebook see Emma Clifford, 'The Trumpet-Major Notebook and *The Dynasts*', *Review of English Studies*, Vol. VIII, no. 30, 1957, p. 149ff.

Index